Happy 40th Birthday

hope this gives you inspiration
on your journey.

All our love,
Tom, Jilly, Charlie + Seb
xxxx

Salmon Poetry Ltd. is based in County Clare, Ireland, half a mile north of the world-famous Cliffs of Moher. Salmon was established in 1981 with the publication of *The Salmon*, a journal of poetry and prose, as an alternative voice in Irish literature. Since then Salmon has become one of the most important publishers in the Irish literary world. By specializing in the promotion of new & established Irish poets, and developing a large list of international poets, Salmon has enriched Irish literary publishing. 2007 marks Salmon's 26th year of literary publishing.

Salmon has continually taken risks; publishing unknown writers since its very first days with *The Salmon Journal* and with its first books by Eva Bourke and Rita Ann Higgins. Many of these 'unknowns' are now firmly established with their own contribution to Irish literature. The challenge for Salmon has always been how to walk the tightrope between innovation and convention. The conventional approach is what makes art comfortable for people, accepted and necessary, but creative expression is not always so.

In recent years we have developed a cross-cultural and international literary dialogue for which Salmon has been acclaimed... "broadening the parameter of Irish literature by opening up to other cultures and by urging new perspectives on established traditions. That enviable balance of focus and ranginess is a rare and instructive achievement" ('Opening up to Other Cultures' *Poetry Ireland Review* 54, Kathleen McCracken.

The Salmon catalogue includes initial works by now-established Irish poets Rita Ann Higgins, Moya Cannon, Mary O'Donnell, Eamonn Wall, Mary O'Malley, Eva Bourke, Janice Fitzpatrick-Simmons, Joan McBreen, Patrick Chapman, and Mark Granier. We have published a range of international poets including Adrienne Rich, Marvin Bell, Richard Tillinghast, Carol Ann Duffy, R.T. Smith, Linda McCarriston, Ron Houchin, and Ben Howard.

SALMON

A Journey in Poetry

1981-2007

salmonpoetry

Published in 2007 by
Salmon Poetry Ltd.,
Cliffs of Moher, County Clare, Ireland

ISBN 1-903392-57-8 (paperback)
ISBN 978-1-903392-66-9 (hardback)

Edited by Jessie Lendennie
Cover artwork by Maunagh Kelly
Cover design & typesetting by Siobhán Hutson

Salmon Poetry gratefully acknowledges the financial assistance of The Arts Council/An Chomhairle Ealaíon and Clare County Council/Comhairle Contae an Chláir towards the publication of this book.

Salmon Poetry, Knockeven, Cliffs of Moher, County Clare, Ireland
Email: info@salmonpoetry.com | Tel/Fax: +353-(0)65-7081941
Editor: Jessie Lendennie | Production/ Design: Siobhán Hutson
www.salmonpoetry.com

for

Angela, Anne, Eithne, James, Michael, Nadya, Robin, Ted

CONTENTS

Introduction

I am writing this from a hilltop in northwest County Clare on a cold late August morning just before dawn. In a little while I'll see daylight over Lahinch and Liscannor Bay down the valley, three miles away.

If someone had told me when I was a melancholy, poetry-addicted adolescent that I would eventually grow up to have a life filled with space, books, writers and poetry, I could not have imagined it. Yet here I am, in one of the world's famous beauty spots surrounded by books and totally immersed in poetry.

This volume comes out of that immersion. These are poets and poems I love; poets who are friends and colleagues; poets I respect and admire. People of vision.

This volume needs no long introduction; there's been a lot written about Salmon, and there will be much more. I just want to send this book off to you, with deep gratitude for these poets and their poetry.

*

The organization of the volume is simple: two poems from the poet's Salmon collection (or collections) and one uncollected poem. In some cases it wasn't possible to have an uncollected poem, so another poem from their Salmon collection was included. Also, as you'll see from the bibliography, a few of the poets we published are not represented by poems. Various reasons for this, but mostly copyright restrictions, as in the case, alas, of Adrienne Rich.

My thanks and love to the people who have been crucial to Salmon's development and continuance: Siobhán Hutson, typesetter, designer, webmaster, and extraordinary workmate; Tim Jeanotte, my son, who steps in to help when we need him (Siobhán and Tim's baby girl, Eve Catherine, may well inherit the Salmon empire!). And Michael Allen, who was there with me in the beginning.

Jessie Lendennie
August 2007

NADYA AISENBERG

Constantly Describing Itself

The red Virginia soil colours the rain
puddles red so they can't reflect the sky.
Everything that lives strives for color,
Goethe said. Not true. I strive for no-color,
no-sound, whatever can take me unto itself
in the singular steps of withdrawal,
erasure a kind of absolution
from the mind's thin repetitions.

There is too much blankness in the world
to be charged to inscribe, yet no one
waits for words, not the upturned faces
with open mouths, words are not their manna.
They wait to be claimed by some spirit
of devotion, to be rid of the self,
as waves and clouds appear
and disappear, never the same one twice.

from Measures (2001)

The Day The Horizon Disappeared

Cast out, flung to the furthest rim of neediness,
then caught there in the branches of the danger tree,
where meaning dwells, out of reach, attached
on its green stem at the very edge of dreaming,
a sign repeating itself through branches
surging in air. Wind surrounds and blows through us.
And whose hand is tearing strips from the sky,
And whose hand will seed wild grasses
on the worn nap of the threadbare world?

from Measures (2001)

Excerpt from Measures

i.

Let us forsake footnotes
and the compilation of bibliographies
Let us abandon forever
the temptation to make much of little
to scratch our initials in the dust
Let us remember stars evolve and have life histories,
death throes
and the sun our brightest star and sometime god
consumes itself at its innermost core

Let us recall of creation
there is no vestige of beginning
no adumbration of the end
By which sense can we know time, its deep interior,
our five senses cannot reach?
We measure by invisible intervals
the obedient twice-daily tides
uncountable layers of prehistory
gods creating and destroying
on the Wheel of Time.
Mountains thrust up and erode,
seas cover all.
Sands inter Pharaonic monuments
of immortality.

Let us wonder where we stand—
a many-islanded universe
every nebulous star appearing
as the firmament of some other world
universe without center, without edge
Where will the arrow of Amytas fall?
Let us recall Pascal's alarm
at the eternal silence of infinite space

All ponderable things seek to lay
their heaviness down

Newton affirming that gravity belongs to God
Let us remember that 'atom' means 'uncuttable'
and feel chagrin
Everything in a state of becoming
world of potentiality
where electrons strike scintillas of light
waves spread out and interlace

Our lives like virtual particles
may spend one brief ecstatic moment
before we die, but
even an unhappy life may be enough.

from Measures (2001)

NUALA ARCHER

A Breaking, A Bread-Coloured Light

Then Anne who is also
Ruth, & Nuala who
is also Miriam, came to me
as I lay curled in the ear
of a seashell. And Anne,
also Ruth, unlaced
my shoes & let them slip
to the sand of the black sea-
bed. She cradled &
kissed each step of my tired
feet while Nuala,
also Miriam, tenderly ran
her fingers through my hair
like a lover
calming my roots, combing
my broken ends.

       And to their
coming I called back: "You
are my two girls. My always-
&-for-never two girls. Ruth
also Miriam. And Nuala, also
Anne." And they lifted me up
then to the high boats
of their silence, their
beautiful bodies, & in
the boats of their bones, into
the breaking, bread-coloured
light, we set sail, we broke
free, we gave thanks.

from From A Mobile Home (1995)

The Lost Glove Is Happy

Is it in the terminal I left
the brown, rabbit-fur-lined gloves
made in Taiwan? Gloves
I've worn in Ireland.
Gloves that kept my fingers
warm walking the bitter cold
coastline of Bull Island
with Howth and her necklace
of lights in the background.
Gloves lost now between Stillwater,
Oklahoma and Lubbock, Texas
on the way to see my mother.

Come, she said, I'm in
the midst of desolation. Come.
Take Southwest Airlines, past
Love Field. I'll be waiting
for you. I'll be waiting.

And in the mall, when I got
to Lubbock, arrived to embrace
my mother in desolation, she had
me strip, try on outfit
after outfit—sweaters, trousers,
skirts, shirts, shorts, slips
and blouses—to see like
Mary, Mary, quite contrary,
how does your garden, my garden,
grow? She in her mid-fifties
and I at the cliff-edge of
twenty-nine. My mother had me
fly to Lubbock and on the way
I lost my rabbit-
fur-lined gloves. When I got
there, when I arrived, when
I reached desolation, my mother
alone, in the middle of crazy
cottonfields, my mother in

desolation, I reached her,
I travelled to her,
to desolation, and in desolation
we were as lost as any
two mismatched gloves and
for a few moments we relaxed, lost
and strangely happy,
in the Lubbock Mall, without
labels stripped to our bones.

from The Hour of Pan/Amá (1992)

Risk

this mid-October evening,
this room's open-ended mess,
today's last salmon & citrus clouds shuffling,

breathing,
precarious
as this mid-October evening's

spider spinning
filaments, fractals—by the sliding glass
door—into salmon & citrus clouds shuffling

seven womens' lives, dealing
them death by breast cancer, vitalness
in a grass menagerie on this mid-October evening

like none other, like every other birthing-
Call it being.   Call it chaos, consummation sweet Ness
curling into clouds shuffling

Away from known weather.   This-*whatever!*-is worth our lingering
k   i   s   s
brimming over this mid-October evening
with its salmon-citrus-periwinkle-umber shufflings

LELAND BARDWELL

Moments

for Edward McLachlan

No moon slides over Harcourt Terrace.
The canal is black. The barracks
crouches on her left.
She sees the child. He holds his coat
across his chest. On his hands,
old socks blunt his fingers.
The handle of his fishing net
has snapped.

Sleep escapes the old woman
on her angry couch. Such images
assault, torment and tease
the sense of her.
Time rolls back on its silent wheels,
empties itself into moments.

How many guilts can one human endure.
One human in all the world, alone
one man or woman holding moments
of a child running, holding shut his coat
with socks on his hands.

Mad Mrs Sweeney

For one whole year
I've watched Mad Sweeney
above in his branch.

He has forgotten how to fly
and stares down at me.
Occasionally he spits.

Today I plucked up courage
to address him.

Mad Sweeney, I said,
I am madly in love with you.

If you'd just bend down that wing
and give me a hike

I'd be up and away,
space shuttle to the moon.

He fluffs his plumage
in that acid way he has

strops his beak
on an outgoing twig.

Well at least shake down a feather
and I'll culture it
with a ball of seaweed

and when it has grown full size
I'll fly to the top of your tree

and be mad Mrs Sweeney
gone in the head but heart whole.

Nothing Else

for Nicholas McLachlan

Cloonagh, below the sweep
of Ardtrasna, a pocket unfilled
where the hill rises. Trá Bhán
the beach where the barge buckled
in '95 and bothered us
with possibilities. Trá Bhán
no longer white but sheeted over
with shloch and erannach and rock
limestone steps to the blow-hole
under the alt, is the end of the road
and nothing else.

Above this crescent
I share my house with time
and nothing else
gaze at the pictures of my children
who have treated me well
for my imagination
but pass me by as the wind passes the house
and takes its sigh with it.

all from The White Beach: New & Selected Poems 1960 - 1998 (1998)

MARCK L. BEGGS

Kilty Sue

Instincts jammed by lack of sheep
in this region, she attends to babies, ducklings—
anything small and in need of care.
A border collie whose eyes, opposite
shades of brown, offer the look
of a slightly retarded devil-dog. And,
if you must know, she bites people:
my brother, presumably, because he was mean
to me at a younger age; the UPS man
because he carried a package too quickly towards
my pregnant sister; my mother-in-law, I suppose,
to keep in shape. And various relatives
and strangers—Kilty Sue reminds them
of the precise location of the Achilles' tendon.
Mind you, she never actually rips it out,
but merely offers a sharp touch. Like a pin-prick,
only deeper, her bites spring out
from a sudden vortex of silence. When Kilty Sue howls—
in a voice high and piercing as a drunken soprano,
and you wish your ears would just drop off and die—
you are safe. She is protecting you.

from Libido Café (2004)

Fire

A hundred acres of dry forest
begins to flap its smoky wings
against the sky, surrounding our home.
And for three days the world

becomes a hot, gray cloud.
Our neighbours have called, complained
of smoke and the black edge
scarring their boundaries.

In *Njal's Saga*, neighbours
hammered each other
into the nearest grave,
as one rash decision

swelled into a decade
of intimate revenge: an alternate
clan-member, each year, paid
with his life for that original error.

Our own neighbours complain again
when we cross their land
to replant the trees. They don't ask
if we're okay, if our house

survived. They don't ask if we're alive.
We must be careful, mother.
Whom you bow to each Sunday
would not, necessarily, spare us

from a drunk, neighbouring, land-owner
with a shot-gun,
would not even load his gun with blanks
to save your spirit

from its brief splatter of departure.
Thor sat still as the Buddha
throughout the old feuds, even when Njal
gathered his family into bed,

so that they might enter
that final moment together in a house
feeding a flue of flame up
into the dark, gray Nordic clouds.

But even if we died together—
your body and father's burned to ash
along with mine—think of it: your souls
evaporating towards Heaven. And,

my own soul, plowed into the garden.

from Libido Café (2004)

Canadian Sonnet

Now she has flown north to the white blanket
of her youth, the fields spread out like a quilt
over a past archived in permafrost:
the story of a girl, the sudden tilt

from a bench as her lungs shut out the air
and collapsed like broken wings in her chest.
Not even the chords from her repertoire
could fasten her hands, folding in like nests.

Yet you breathe still today. The noisy geese
from your homeland land in my pond, their wings
jubilant as they crash into water,
in time to fleece corn from mallards, to sing

vulgar arias in honks of cold air.
Would that one were you flown home to my care.

MICHAEL S. BEGNAL

Burned Hut

(An Spidéal, Cois Fharraige)

(waiting for the Galway bus)

Glass of the window
swims as you look
toward the Both Loiscthe bridge,
the language commandos
strike away English
on the Conamara road signs—
all the rivers
will bear their true names
in the dark of evening

all the villagers
will know
of what they speak
under the red rain
of their endless servitude,

and the waves lap
at the rock

Ancestor Worship

Not like the bones of parents
carried out in procession
from their dark vaginal tombs
among the rocks,
mummified skin stretched
and tanned in mockery of death

it's not like the imagined
rituals of an old old age
before iron or bronze,
the metal of our mythology,
though the faces look the same
in the rain

but the warm blood
that flows through to this age,
dangerous and violent in veins,
hanging heavy like burlap sheets
on a dewy day

the right hook of history,
the slow motion arc of the punch,
the strange figure
on a modern city street
who burrows into your eye
and says, "Who're you?"

It's like when Lennon laid
his *New York* album on you,
and appeared in pictures
in his new image—
Revolutionary,
sudden Irishman,
Manhattanite,

gritty…

like LeRoi Jones's move to Harlem,
broke with his white friends,
changed his name:

> ancestor worship
> is the only religion
> truly compatible
> with the fact
> of evolution

There's No Present

There's no present
just a continual becoming
past

(hot sun on the Paddy's Day parade,
S.F. '94, bo-ing out, ass on the kerb,
collection for the cause,
free newspapers)

now,
oh now is gone,
then, in front of an electric fire
I'm slanging it all over the place,
cash rules everything 'round
while the twilight flows
in from the Border

and girls with red faces
    sit in the diffused light
        of steamy air that
            was

all from Ancestor Worship (2007)

MARVIN BELL

Theory of Relativity (Political)

When I was young, dreaming of luminescent escapades set against the light of a great pearl hung in a sky that would otherwise be black, as if it were the one thing certain to survive the overwhelming forces of the tide of an invisible sea, I once thought of becoming a policeman but gave it up and became something else. Then one day the sea rose up and heaved itself from the sky, collapsing in exhaustion on the earth where it lay trying to catch its breath. From this I learned that the fiercest incandescence can be swallowed by accident if an open maw goes by, swimming or flying. From the cultivated moon we must shift our attention to a speck of sand hung in an eye from which tears have fallen onto the earth and lie sighing. If we are going to be the world's policemen, we had better train for microcosms and the faces of wristwatches, for the damage one does in a small area just by turning around can cause tremors that travel by root and branch and spread like cracks in the crust of the desert. I and my countrymen, being patriotic, listen for organic pressures building under the surface, and in any event one does not want to play God when God plays God.

from Wednesday: Selected Poems 1966 – 1997 (1998)

Treetops

My father moves through the South hunting duck.
It is warm, he has appeared
like a ship, surfacing, where he floats, face up,
through the ducklands. Over the tops
of trees, duck will come, and he strains
not to miss seeing the first of each flock,
although it will be impossible to shoot one
from such an angle, face up like that
in a floating coffin where the lid obstructs
half a whole view, if he has a gun.
Afterlives are full of such hardships.

One meets, for example, in one's sinlessness,
high water and our faithlessness,
so the dead wonder if they are imagined
but they are not quite.

How could they know we know
when the earth shifts deceptively
to set forth ancestors to such pursuits?
My father will be asking, Is this fitting?
And I think so—I, who, with the others,
coming on the afterlife after the fact
in a dream, in a probable volume, in a
probable volume of dreams, think so.

from Wednesday: Selected Poems 1966 - 1997 (1998)

"Why Do You Stay Up So Late?"

Late at night, I no longer speak for effect.
I speak the truth without the niceties.
I am hundreds of years old but do not know how many hundreds.
The person I was does not know me.
The young poets, with their reenactments of the senses, are asleep.
I am myself asleep at the outer reaches.
I have lain down in the snow without stepping outside.
I am frozen on the white page.
Then it happens, a spark somewhere, a light through the ice.
The snow melts, there appear fields threaded with grain.
The blue moon blue sky returns, that heralded night.
How earthly the convenience of time.
I am possible.
I have in me the last unanswered question.
Yes, there are walls, and water stains on the ceiling.
Yes, there is energy running through the wires.
And yes, I grow colder as I write of the sun rising.
This is not the story, the skin paling and a body folded over a table.
If I die here they will say I died writing.
Never mind the long day that now shrinks backward.
I crumple the light and toss it into the wastebasket.
I pull down the moon and place it in a drawer.
A bitter wind of new winter drags the dew eastward.
I dig in my heels.

from Mars Being Red (Copper Canyon Press, 2007)

EVA BOURKE

The Lamentations of Annie

I put up my claim
outside the bakery in High Street.
Here I tap the copper mine
in passing ladies' pockets.
My working hours are well over forty,
yet I have no beggars' union
to contend my rights.
Should I picket my employer man,
my Joseph in black and red checked cap?
I am Madonna of the cardboard box,
of the broken back at 35.

Cross my palm with silver,
mistress of the bungalow,
always in a hurry from shop to shop
while your husband
is scraping the pavement with nervous shoes.
I'll say ten Hail Marys for you.
Your life rises and swells,
a well-baked loaf,
mine is a piece of stale bread
crunching between my teeth.

I was mothered by misery.
Misery is my legacy
to my thirteen children.
Stuffed away they are in a plastic tent,
a rubbish bag by the roadside,
their bowels coughing up blood
and slime.
Their year is one hard season
of winter nights.
Earth turned her cold back
on them, moon her dark side.

The others don't like my smell.
I am an onion to bring tears
to their eyes.
Below my seven layers
of charitable rags
my heart murmurs and screams,
turning my lips blue:
Why do their doctors not heal us,
their builders not house us,
their teachers not teach us?

Their god is good.
A milkwhite dove.
Mine is a dark and vicious bird.
He took my youngest child on the market place
and flung it under the wheels of a truck
that knocked me down
with an angry red face.
Waking up in hospital
I saw the Bleeding Heart by my bedside
bending over me.
I turned away.
That day the Pope danced his holy dance
in a carpeted park,
spreading his arms wide.
Not wide enough for me,
not wide enough for my child.

from Gonella (1985)

Voltaire's Monkeys

How tiresome this business of love
and its pitiful claim
on the entire world's attention!

Pat loves Edel

We who have our eyes everywhere
see with distaste
how love spreads nightly
on walls and fences like weeds.

Martina loves Paul

It would be laughable
in the face of our moral authority

Philemon loves Baucis

if we hadn't failed in controlling
a single butterfly's lust,

Dante loves Beatrice

unfortunately the fishes and crabs
on the bottom of rivers and seas
are way out of earshot

Mary loves Joseph

and the trees tend to have
such a forceful leaning towards each other.
See how shamelessly they caress every breeze
with thousands of fingers!

David loves Jonathan

Even the crows sit very close together
on the budding branches

we can only guess
what they are up to up there

Romeo loves Juliet

and the proximity of stone to stone
is more than we can bear.

What else can we do but turn our backs
on all those disgusting signs
of the magnetism of the flesh

and like Voltaire
hold four monkeys in captivity
and mistreat them daily
with sermons and speeches.

from Litany for the Pig (1989)

The Walk-In Heart

In the Trans-Alpine struggling uphill to Brennero
our compartment door kept sliding open
and shut again with a small click:
the day outside had trained its wide-angle lens on us.

A snow-covered book lay open beyond the windows
into which conifers printed their names, a cuneiform text
as far as the timber line. From three chimneys
smoke rose into the sky, scrolled as the hems
of saintly garments—a threefold assumption.

In the strip show of mirrors above our seats
peaks swung round and orbited away from us,
viaducts receded on stilts,
lakes lay still under the greenish sheen of marble.

I was neither here nor there, felt as though
a strange language was drifting through me. Each word
weighed less than a breath. The engine pounded
and pounded as it climbed higher as though aspiring
to gain on some unquestionable transcendence.

It was as set in its purpose as the heart
in a Chicago museum inside which
I had stood and listened a long time ago.

At the last stop before dark
border guards verified us. The night rose slowly
like water. We speeded downhill
past platforms with unspellable names. Towns
spread their brocaded ribbons across the plain
glimmered and dissolved in a bowl
full of blackness.

RAY BRADBURY

With Love

For Leonard Bradbury

My father ties, I do not tie, my tie.
On some night long ago, in June
I tried to try
My first tie snarled upon my vest,
My hands all thumbs,
And presto-chango,
Something Awful This Way Comes.
My father quietly came by
And studied me and stood behind.
"Be blind," he said.
"Stay off of mirrors.
Let your fingers
Learn to do."
His lesson lingers. What he said was true.
Eyes shut,
With him to help me over-up, around and under-out
Somehow a knot miraculous came about.
"There's nothing to it," said my Dad.
"Now, son, you do it. No; eyes shut."
And with one last dear blind perceiving
He taught my crippled fingers
Arts of weaving. Then, turned away.
Well, to this day, how dare I boast,
I cannot do it.
I call that long-gone sweet-tobacco-smelling ghost
To help me through it.
He helps me yet;
Upon my neck, his breath, the scent of his last cigarette.
There is no death, for yestereve
His phantom fingers came and helped me tuck and weave.
If this is true (it is!) he'll never die.
My father ties, I do not tie, my tie.

from I Live by the Invisible (2002)

They Have Not Seen The Stars

They have not seen the stars,
Not one, not one
Of all the creatures on this world
In all the ages since the sands first touched the wind
Not one, not one,
No beast of all the beasts has stood
On meadowland or plain or hill
And known the thrill of looking at those fires;
Our soul admires what they, oh, they, have never known.
Five billion years have flown in turnings of the spheres
But not once in all those years
Has lion, dog, or bird that sweeps the air
Looked there, oh, look. Looked there, ah God, the stars;
Oh, look, look there!
It is as if all time had never been,
Or universe or sun or moon or simple morning light.
Their tragedy was mute and blind, and so remains. Our sight?
Yes, ours? To know now what we are.
But think of it, then choose—now, which?
Born to raw Earth, inhabiting a scene
And all of it, no sooner viewed, erased, gone blind
As if these miracles had never been.
Vast circlings of sounding light, of fire and frost,
And all so quickly seen then quickly lost?
Or us, in fragile flesh, with God's new eyes
That lift and comprehend and search the skies?
We watch the seasons drifting in the lunar tide
And know the years, remembering what's died.

Oh, yes, perhaps some birds some nights
Have felt Orion rise and turned their flights
and turned southward
Because star-charts were printed in their sweet genetic dreams—
Or so it seems.
But see? But really see and know?
And, knowing, want to touch those fires
To grow until the mighty brow of man Lamarckiar-tall
Knocks earthquakes, striking moon,

Then Mars, then Saturn's rings;
And, growing, hope to show
All other beasts just how
To fly with dreams instead of ancient wings.
So, think on this: we're first! the only ones
Whom God has honored with his rise of suns.
For us as gifts Aldebaran, Centauri, homestead Mars.
Wake up, God says. Look there. Go fetch.
The stars. Oh, Lord, much thanks. The stars!

from I Live by the Invisible (2002)

Old man, is the young man in?

Old man, is the young man in?
Under the skin, yes, under the skin.
Old man, in what neighborhood,
In the blood, fool, there in the blood.
And what does he dream, old one, what does he dream,
Women like strawberries, women like cream.
And if he speaks for you, what does he say,
Loving till midnight, then dawn, then day.
I hear the young humming, and what does he hum,
Life is worth living and women its sum.
Old man, what's he seeking, and where does he seek,
The way to tomorrow, the sill of next week.
So you're not dead and buried, old man in the clay,
Not as long as the young one basks here one more day.
Does the young man not worry, locked here in your skin,
He turns in my sleep, doesn't like staying in.
So the two of you wander, seeming one, but your face
Shows the youth that you keep in a well-lighted place.
So the jailed and the jailor, shadow twins, go to sleep,
Just at dawn, you've forgotten, that you're old,
You seem fair. And the ghost of you, ancient,
Is discarded flesh there, and the flesh that you're wearing
Is a young suit you'll keep.
Then you wake and turn over.
Old man, why do you weep?

RORY BRENNAN

The Paper Kisses

A secret invasion of cherubs was what it was like,
This littering of the house with impressions of lips,
Immaculately printed, love's own personal calling cards,
Ghost-mouths whispering inaudible promises,
Ripe beauty hinted in their Cupid's bows.

Pink, mauve, rosé, ochre, vermillion, deep red,
Their shades could match some prism of the moods
Fired by first love's blinkering firework display.
The paper kisses were so perfect as to seem great art,
Fugitive sketches from a Primavera folio.

But they were planted on old bills, junk mail, torn envelopes,
Flyleaves of paperbacks, runic scraps of their father's foolscap,
Mingling with last demands, free offers, blurbs and poems,
Gracing the quotidian with their luscious blooms,
Reminding us we are insubstantial and forgotten without love.

Mostly they were to be found near mirrors and telephones
Where hectic lipstickings took place before the dash
To disco, rave, club, bar. Only these last minute dabbings
Were the departure signals of our lovely daughters.
May those who kiss their lips earn their warm hearts.

from The Old in Rapallo (1996)

The Shellybanks

for Ulick O'Connor

Long distance trucks have shaken the genteel terraces
For far too long, lugging their deep-frozen innards
Towards Hamburg or Milan past neat bow windows
Where brass telescopes once traced the horizon's
Receding hairline for a tuft of sail. On past
The smart new housing for the unemployed the diesels
Churn and hiss, trailing a dragon tang out to
The crane-forested docks and the ferry's leviathan jaw.

Needing a shield of silence I stride the beach,
Its lined brow gathered at the crowsfeet of pools,
And make for a fringe of tide, the limbs of the bay
Braced to bear the shifting ballast of the city.
Steps squelch in the coiled moulds of worms
I once mined for bait when what preoccupied
Was more innocuous. Far back a heap of bikes
Memorials boyhood like a maritime mark.

Reclaimed land—the very metaphor of memory.
Once all this was something, somewhere else.
The chemical mix of a million households
Is alive to its trove of trinkets and tokens—
Loveletter, prayerbook, photograph, toy, doll, sketch—
Interred like a ring for luck, a key for a prisoner.
What spells ferment under this skim of earth?
The unsettled ground refuses to rest in peace.

I catch myself glancing round yet again at the town
That exerts some tidal pull on the sargasso weed
That tangles the heart's arteries—or draws it on the rocks.
What stirs in the dark folds of the cauldron of currents?
Love and delight are swept in and out on the ribbed sand
And love's truces are sanctioned in the clasp of hills,
From the slumbering shoulder of Howth to the blunt nipple
Of the Martello Tower on the fallen breast of Dalkey Island.

I need no wind at my back to hurry me on,
On towards the spur of beach and the granite ashlars
Of the breakwater, its slabs locking like giant vertebrae,
An uprisen Cyclopean road faring out to the lighthouse.
Here are the Shellybanks and here there are still shells—
Fans, blades, scallops, razors—flecked and spilt
Like sodden confetti in an apse of sand,
Under the scrollwork and tracery of the sky.

Out on the seawall there are gusts and cuffs,
Two centuries of the waves' swell have curved its spine.
On one side the surface is all shot silk,
The other a rag rug. Nightfall footpads the pier.
Here is the aloneness before homecomings,
Moments when the self is braced once more
For the brunt of love and its broken turnings.
The lighthouse wraps its scarf around the shore.

from The Old in Rapallo (1996)

58

Equality is not Defeat

In the bloodspray of a mist
Edward Carson shakes his fist,
Stormont looming to his rear
From the blueprint of Albert Speer.
In 1913 in the Lock Out
Larkin climbs on a box to shout.
Both men are ripping out a page
From history's rulebook in their rage,
Carson (Freud is not in sight)
Holds his inch and holds it tight
While Big Jim Larkin in despair
Flings both arms into the air
Like a Goya figure at the firing squad.
Rome and Ulster invoke God
As police baton charge the underfed
And the Somme engulfs a million dead.
So these declamatory statues stand
Berating an ill-divided land.
Now that sacred inch is yielded up
And all can share a bite and sup
Carson glares down the long drive
Appalled at those he sees arrive
While Larkin still implores a street:
Equality is not defeat.

HEATHER BRETT

One Indian Summer

for Philip

September;
little breeze to fan the leaves
of trees
just enough
to dry the lines of clothes.
The kids could play without their coats
and shapes had shadows we'd forgotten;
A respite,
a last late harbour
for the migrating summer,
a wild tumble of golden-flecked colours
and the day as long as a winter's night.

from Abigail Brown (1991)

Sleeping Partners

I slept with an eagle
he was all talons
and cracked whispers
I had a long way to fall

I slept with a snake
but his scales were razors
and he never closed his eyes.
I had to use camouflage.

I slept with a red deer
he was all velvet and bone,
my wounds all under the skin,
O Sweet Jesus Pain

I slept with a shark
his teeth weren't the problem
but his eyes were death pebbles
and he kept staring

I slept with a rat,
he was fond of sharing me
my shame he distributed freely
I had no place to hide

Now, I sleep with spirits
my bed never so full,
phantoms play on the ceiling,
my bed is warm with skins.

from Abigail Brown (1991)

Prayer for the untouched

This is not the place of passion.
Everything crumbles and the air
stinks of naphthalene and mildew;
Why we persist in preserving the dead
is beyond me.

Long ago these walls breathed fire,
the air soaked with purple incense and laughter
and I was young
and touch a pyromaniac's dream—
I was that ready

something gold once spilled here
this is hallowed ground, every caress
a blessing, splintering age old invocations
to the earth, to lust.
I can taste the flesh.

Bite then, on memories and spit the sawdust
out. Everything's dust and dry and bone
yellow with age. I hide in the dead tissue.
Once or twice a breath wafts through.
It smells of want.

PATRICIA BURKE BROGAN

Exiles

They remember mountain shapes,
bony masses hulking
from black-umber bogs.
They remember lilac shadows
moving across bulked rock.

Crushed between skyscrapers,
baked in underground carriages,
deafened in discos,
they remember sky-lakes
rough with tears.
They remember
peppery incense
of saffron furze.

Viridian thorns wrap
granite and limestone,
where haloes wild with colour
dissolve over Maam valley.

Fossiled and transformed
in the ring-round of life,
ancestors' clay,
their own clay calls to them.

from Above the Waves Calligraphy (1994)

Sanctuaries

A June sun offsets
sanctuary-window purples,
saffrons, vermilions
on crypt-grey limestone
in the Cathedral
of Tuaim Dha Ghualain.
Dramatic in crimson robes,
the mitred Archbishop
anoints row after row
of young foreheads.
Round scent of oil on skin.
Our shining whiteness
in stony distances.

Kneeling next to me,
Eileen O'Brien picks scarlet varnish
from her fingernails.
In answer to His Grace,
'Say the Apostles' Creed, my child!',
she stumbles and forgets
the drilled profession of Faith.
Veils flutter over satin dresses,
while the choir chants
'Veni, Creator Spiritus.'

But the secretary forgets
to register my name.
Shedding veil and dress
in the afternoon,
from the river bank
I dive into watery greenness.
I swim without fear
through an emerald tunnel.
With pilgrim heron and kingfisher
with pike and salmon,
I carve watery images.
Miracles of water anoint my body.

A strong and perfect Christian,
my fingers break through watercress.
Chant of the river throbs in my ears.
Taste of viridian, incense of
meadowsweet stretching my senses,
I glory in my limbs.
Joy undiminished,
my body is no prison
to contain my spirit.

I swim and swim
with minnows and dearogs,
with brown trout and otters
through cloisters of malachite.
Candelabra of wild iris light the banks.
Waterlilies float with me,
as I salute the clouds.

I write my name in water.

from Above the Waves Calligraphy (1994)

Décollage

I.

From darkness
I drag black refuse bags,
unwind fastenings,
pull out shredded crimsons,
tumble scraps of siennas, burnt umbers
with starched whites and torn ultramarines.

The ghost of Petrushka pirouettes on CD,
criss-crosses, turns head-over-heels,
weaves polytonals for Stravinsky,
as I arrange and seal netted colours,
build slabs of ochre,
mix textures coarse and delicate
with ragged memories, forgotten loves.

II.

For these anniversaries
I scrape and slice colours,
slit and gouge surfaces,
dig out haunted potato fields
stained by another Holocaust.

From that child of Hiroshima
I tear off multiple images.
Shadows remain
and I begin again.

from Décollage (forthcoming)

SIMMONS B. BUNTIN

Hiking the Summit

Thirteen miles have passed beneath
these broken boots, though I
have been lost since the first step.
I cannot see snow-crowned
peaks or a canyon gone crazy
upon itself, but only my breath, thick
as frost on the evening ridge. As
the trail grows twisted, I lose level
ground and fall into a rushing spring,
the water drowning my call
with the taste of panic,
sweetness. I work the current
like a cutter through ice, reach
the bank to dream of sleep,
and fall upon the hardened earth.
As the moon slides across the frozen
sky, distant wolves hurl their calls
against my camp. Waking, I spur
simmering coals and return
the howls, watching as my fire
grows. When the flames
form a ladder, a straight line
of smoke opens the night.
I climb in, and the trail is gone.

from Riverfall (2005)

Great White Heron

She is a ghost of her former bluegray
self, cautiously feeling
her way through mangrove
roots twisted upon themselves
like watersnakes held motionless in the wood.
I want to say she is a pale
Cleopatra, but then she calls—
scroawk scroawk—and one cry
reminds me she is queen only of marsh.

§

The cut of her eyes
is sharp as her tawny beak, quick
as the speared mullet she brings up
gasping through blood-red gills.
In one swift movement the fish
is flipped and swallowed headfirst—
to the surprise
of a thieving tropicbird
rising abruptly
before facing that spear.

§

When the heat of late summer stales,
she slips deeper into the shade
of a bald cypress stand and stares me
into submission.
And I step toward her,
lifting my reed-thin legs
through the braided roots.
Now I am spreading my dusty wings, coming
upon her as she raises that sharpened spear.
We twist our smooth necks
like branches beneath the waterline.
We move, eyes motionless
to the slow rhythm of rising waves.
And we dance, wings extended
to the reckless wind...

§

Waking, the great white heron
spreads her elegant wings
across the bay—
in the low cry that stills the air,
we vanish.

from Riverfall (2005)

Her Mission of Light

Seven months after the death of my mother,
the pregnant C-130s circling the air base

remind me how, when she was nine,
the Swedish girl they called *matchstick legs*

(who could sprint the sandy length
of seaside lane in record time) first heard

and then saw the Nazi bombers
in their razor-tight formations scraping

the low chin of the horizon, en route
to Norway and dark England beyond.

She too passed like a recondite
mission, whispering from 17,000 feet,

a near-anonymous entry into the endless log
of the world's migrations. Sixty-one years

later, I take the vacant road past
the base's back gate, along the brilliantly

destructive rows of F-4s and A-10s,
with their own secret missions to

Vietnam and Bosnia and Iraq, places
she could have lived in her 1950s

migration to America—places like the vast
and abundant plains of Rhodesia or

the rich golden avenues of Naples and Rome.
The street here is not glowing, nor

full of life. But it leads to the blue
hills beyond the river, and from there

the pink cliffs of the Santa Catalinas—
and sometimes, as now, the light off a curving

wing catches and holds the mountains and clouds
and, higher still, a vapor trail to the heavens.

First published in The Manhattan Review

SAM BURNSIDE

From Grainan of Aileach to Derry—21 December

Like champagne, not long opened, the bound stars
stir behind furred ice. Storms are fermenting
up in the artic. There's a rawness now
in the air, and word of sleet and snowstorms
pervades the streets. On ranked Christmas trees
lights flash and are gone and in those many
little interludes hope flickers: or say, rather,
that fear is bestirred; and then the lights rekindle.
At its furthest limit the winter sun
Stiffens into stillness. Time hesitates.
Silence wraps itself about the rage and roar
of all those last minute gettings and baggings;
all breathing ceases in this dark confrontation
of all the earth's bright days and all dark nights.

from Walking the Marches (1990)

In and Out of Derry

The Donegal mountains, sit out there
blue, blunt heaps of lignite, sad hinterland
to a burning city; and the heavy stone walls
and houses, shops and factories, fronts erased,
sag into the bog-ground while light title-deeds
change hands in the mute communion of commerce.
The city's odd shop-keepers, sour and mean enough,
clang their rat-trap tills and keep the doors guarded:
for there are those who disregard limb and life,
who blast and bomb with red-eyed, mad-dog malice;
then again there are those who disregard even that,
who live only for profit and tomorrow's gain.
If things were different there'd be no buts but
life goes on, has, and somehow always will,
despite the bombs and assassinations;
we remain successful in ignoring these things
and carry on forming—from the old twin cultures—
some new kind of human resistance and bloody-minded calmness.
In a hundred years it will warrant a paragraph
in a history book; the common people they'll call us
(our fathers, they will note, paid a shilling for a rat
and ate quartered dogs to live) and they'll not know
or not reckon the itch of fear in pubs, in shops,
the daily bumping over ramps, the body-searches,
the tension of fire-sirens singing in darkness.

from Walking the Marches (1990)

The Salt Box

(For Anne)

We were just chatting—
you know, the way people do—
when I asked,
where's home?
Well, she replied,
I love Quigley's Point
that's the place I always return to—
the hills behind, the water in front,
the road running between
taking us away
bringing us back
back
to the house
to our house
to our home
to memories
to presences
my father and his father—
all those generations
tending to it.
But, I feel at home in other places:
places like Hampstead Heath;
I love, best of all, that place
(it's in a painting by Constable),
Hampstead Heath, and a house called
The Salt Box, with Branch Hill Pond
beyond, a shimmer, rising off it
like you'd find on the Foyle
when seen from our door-step
early on a cool May morning.
Yes.
These are the places:
places, people,
homes of the heart, really—
Branch Hill Pond
and the Foyle
The Salt Box

and Quigley's Point
and most of all
all those men and women
who make them real
who give them life.

CATHERINE BYRON

My Father's Son

Travelling east from Death Valley

I heard the voices of the women scolding:
— Other men's sons, he works with other men's sons—
Down in the Nissen hut he pulsed a stripped
frog's heart with rhythmic shocks. Its sinews flexed
and other men's sons stood round admiring him:
        — O herr professor—

I hear my mother's wail of proud reproach:
— Other men's sons, he teaches other men's sons—
Stonily staring at the Chevrolet's
soft furnishing, I refuse to be led out
to examine Utah's strata in the flesh.
        No no, professor.

        I am journeying east from possibilities
        from doing what other men's sons have done
        with another's father.
                                Alone I anatomize bikes
        spanner works into parts, power into idleness.
        Stranded in Utah, I watch as the gold men drink
        a whole month's pannings in a greasy glass.

I hear the voice of my father, weary now:
— Other men's sons, I have raised up other men's sons—
I will not mount that charger now or ever
nor travel westward, pricking through tumbleweed
to your laboratory filled with the art of blood,
        father professor.

from The Getting of Vellum (2000)

By the Calf Bay at Lumb Bank

It was the woman of the house
who reared the calves.
Did she keep them in this crypt
to have them handy?
Not as handy as the hens
but close enough.
And where were the cows
who'd dropped them only
a week, two weeks before—
before their calves were kept
apart, before the woman
trained them to the bucket,
her hand in the warm milk
making finger teats to wean them?
A cow is a fierce mother,
dangerous as a bull
in the hours and days after
she has dropped her calf,
nuzzled it onto its knees,
and licked its coat
to whorl and peak
clean of the birth waters.
Were the calves' mothers taken
over the Colden Water
along Gamaliel Gate
to the high pastures—
or were they here, in earshot,
in House Meadow, that falls
to the alder and beech of the brink,
and the Water that runs always?

from The Getting of Vellum (2000)

In Praise of Burglars

He gave me your oval mirror
the very day you died.
I took it to my house.
I turned it to the wall.

Next he gave me your
Victorian jewelry box.
Empty. I checked, relieved.
Never been one for stones.

Before your 'month's mind'
my house was broken, entered.
They cherry-picked that silver
repoussé jewelry box

and shook it free, as they ran,
of insignificant chaff:
a charity pin, a kirby
grip, and on the sill

the tiny drop-shaped crystal
a child gave you once
to hang where the sun could catch it.
This stone I have kept

hung in the re-glazed window
on its silver thread.

LOUISE C. CALLAGHAN

Moving Out

An armful of novels
  her favourites
a bundle of frayed-lip
  envelopes
   photos
the ravelled clothes
  the ones she likes the best
slivers of pale underwear
  spread all over
 her bedroom floor
      a couple
of her softest teddybears.
What a hoarder!
She claims each
  is treasured
  for a childhood
    forgotten
(fractured
   by separation).
We watched a video:
  Women on the Verge
of a Nervous Breakdown.
Unreal, she says
  to pack
   everything
into one suitcase.
   Midnight
staring into the dark,
  beyond it
 I start to write:
my daughter is moving out

and this   is what   it's like.

from The Puzzle-Heart (1999)

Excerpt from 'Remember the Birds'

The little tray

In my hall, the walnut console
holds Father's wood-crafted tray,
the flute-lip tidy for assorted keys, letters,
household bills, a bottle of *Rescue*.

That he made it himself never
struck me so much as the motto,
the words he'd chosen to groove
into the surface: *Remember the Birds*

as if there were nothing more
meaningful he could think of;
his dead-pan sense of the absurd.
Remember the Birds: no

philosophy, no moral. I let
my lofty expectations go,
I'll use the little tray for crumbs,
to carry and to scatter them.

from Remember the Birds (2005)

Grandma's Summer Cottage

No niin, hey-hey/ So long, bye-bye

perfect
At the summer cottage we raised
mosquito nets over each narrow bed,
as a bride hangs her wedding dress.
The air, sweet as birds' milk.
We woke, one, then the other,
with lake-water lapping
at the wood slats, birdsong,
a flickering light in the window,
to see where we had slept.
Under branches of giant antlers
that are mounted on the wall
and the silent cuckoo-clock.

pluperfect
Everything on the wall is either old
or discarded, a series of still-lives:
a glossy head-bone of an antlered moose,
bark-licking tongue, lake-eyes long gone,
the clock that has been prompted to start
time again—its laquered bird inside
jacks out the hours and half hours—

one pine cone on the weight-chains
droops deeper the later it gets.
The sun never sets this side of mid-night,
it's dusk till dawn. A hunter's horn,
strap-hung on the uprise-antennae
and a man's green hunting jacket.
A poster of burnished autumn fruits.

present
You tied a switch of birch branches
to take with us to the cottage.
Each evening in the steam-house cabin
we use it to whip arms and legs,
our buttocks to our blood's content,

the leaves release a pungent scent.
Ahead of me I see you flit
between the trees like a naiad,
then being swallowed by the lake.
On nights like these we eat lightly,
massage each other's feet,
lie awake through the watchful hours.

imperfect
Prepared once more
for the ceremony of sleep,
I notice the night inside
is darker than the night outside,
your breath-light snores,
the lake-sibilance
against the shore,
where rounded rocks earlier
seemed like seal visitors.
Your poor Grandma
is trapped indoors
in her city cot.
The flight of stairs
prevent her coming down.
Death will take her soon
and bring you back to Kuhmo.
Out now on the verandah
the lake is blueberry.
In this tenseless hour, the sun,
lighting towers of cloud.

future
When I was leaving, Grandma invited me
back again: *You must stay*, she said
with Tuula, out at the summer cottage.
She held my hands, aged with rust stains,
her own hands locked and twisted.
Eyes that had witnessed the Winter War.
But I will not be here then, she said, *next year.*
You translate all this for her from Finnish.

SEAMUS CASHMAN

Excerpt from Secrets: Thirteen Poems 2005-2006

XIII That morning will come

When the morning comes will it lie so distant, cold and hidden—
    like your eye to mine?
When the song is sung will it wait a call to stall the bone,
    marrow-full and sweet?

We have felt the night march on, ravishing the crevices of history,
    and tempting our resolve.
We hold our borderlands through taint and taunt of dark and day.

You and I could share a bed of sandy clay and red porous rock;
and though the wall is high the coin that spins will fall.

Let morning's melody rephrase the stormy beats, our tune become
    the athanor of dark
for when a die is cast between our distances, its roll will call the
    world to tilt
toward flags unfurled.

We know that dawn has gleaned its shine and that day waiting its
    share is near.
Here is a time to play beyond the shadows we have tented in the hills.

There is a gentleness in no, in words unsaid, in looks unseen.
There is the ochre brilliance of a rising sun, and when we kiss again
a second birth at dawn …

That morning will come.

Saroya

At Clonmeton with the Fingal Sunday Walking Group

Listen—and wonder. Is it a murmur
of the wind, this nemeton she holds,
this nest of pulses flowing from her dance?
'Saroya,' soft-calls a mother's voice.
She light-foot skips across the stile
ahead of the crowd onto this grave-stoned ground.

Her dark eyes and sallow skin centre our attention
as Paddy Boyle spikes names and places for us;
words ripen into prayer within his oval tellings;
familiar berries long fermented
fill history's apertures with passion.

We wonder about holy places
as the little girl steps on the slim surround
of a Clonmeton horseman buried where we congregate.
She is touching stones and finger-tracing symbols
to make her story.

'Clon-ne-me-ton,' he measures out today's draught
in the margins of a mound below the hillock
where hidden waters nourished meadow grass.
The sheltering oaks are gone;
a rubble pile now taunts buried bones.

'Nemeton,' he explains, as if in echo to her name.
'Drú-nemeton. A site near Ankora in Turkey.
—a holy well; a muslim grove ... a nemeton.'
His fierce look lingers druid-like, and his words cling
as lichen to the churchyard stones.

We listen under the grey stone arbour for our here and there,
as midstream, an abandoned church embeds
between sky and sacred ground pulses granulled
as the whorls spun by the echoing hills at morning.

In the sunlight lithe and lovely as the little girl
a thousand shadows flickering whisper: 'Nemeton.'

Yew Tree

I have been a bad messenger
these past days, rainy, sunny, grey.
The clouds are never set on pause,
they seep, and drift away. The sun
bids strongly still.
October underway pretends;
autumn edges trees and hedges,
hill and field, with pigmentation,
lore and leaf.

Children now too old to summon home
take grinds, go 'out', ignore, advise,
grow up like seasons do; cloud-like, mature
through thundery shadow shapes. Endure.

Mother earth,
when were we seeded? Yew. Tell me.
In a time of plenty? Blossom drop.
Was I seeded then? You tell me
that sapling planted on your breast,
that for us marks your time, marked me,
and leached you into some forever.
Here I am tasting berry flesh.

Leaf and bark and root now ghost
the chapel bell nearby, rebuilt
to power our centuries. Their lives as mine
were hardened by the glint of day.

We reap to sow; for who would live this long
to mould with your magnificence our flow?
Yew, live night as day, knight of clay!
The waterlogged decay that seeps
in hole and bole encircled rhyme
absorbs your hand that buries down
into its own sour to root and grow more—
re-seeding pride, re-birthing you.

all from That Morning Will Come: New & Selected Poems (2007)

85

DAVID CAVANAGH

Montreal Blues

I come from disappointed people.
Mowers of late autumn lawns,

pushed-mowed and cross-cut into squares,
the cut grass caught in a canvas hook-on

emptied over and over into battered trash cans.
I come from ironers of underwear,

a people who stretched wool socks by the dozen
on wooden frames hung from basement pipes,

a father who spent forty-two years
hating a job to feed us, which he did;

his first job tearing used carbons all night
1934 long to reinsert into blank order pads

for use by busy sellers all the bright next day;
his last job filling blank order pads 1976

with thousand-dollar sales and taking crap
because he couldn't learn French in a city

full of chic he could no longer understand,
though he was proud of this Montroyal,

showed visitors its sights and history
like a parent holding out photos of a child

who somehow has outgrown and now ignores him.

from The Middleman (2003)

It's So Much Like Missiles

One day you hear they've been fired—
the missiles I mean—you imagine them
curving like so many Golden Gates
between a hundred cities, serene vapour trails
with some message you cannot imagine,
and don't have to, for you know
you have one half of one hour.

And everything's suddenly simple,
like the time you heard your father had died,
long-distance the phone clicking
softly as a heart while you felt everything
freeze in your tiny kitchen, altered,
and impossibly unchanged.

And the funny thing is not that they've gone
up—the missiles I mean—but that they remind
you of something you didn't do, some words
you didn't say, just didn't take the trouble
to say, like the time you were leaving town,
and a friend, and you never told her how much
she meant to you, and you never saw her again.

Now missiles are flying, and it's just
like when your father died, and the visit
you'd put off became a dream-train you lived
on nightly, dark train pounding on smoothest
rails of guilt, and never ever arriving.

The thing about what's unsaid is
you can never take it back.
If you had made that final visit
you'd have fought with him, most probably,
over Trudeau, or disarmament, something
not too close. And it would have been
furious and futile till it hit you
that this time he was dying,
and you'd have stopped, and so would he,

both of you sheepish, feeling
each other sheepish, awkwardness
your last strange sharing.

But the thing about not visiting, not
loving enough to say or fight or apologize
or see something new between you—
the thing about not saying is

it's so much like those missiles
up there, on the way, on the final way,
so undone, so unsaid, and so impossible
to take back.

from The Middleman (2003)

Waitress I Never Knew

Harelipped you were beautiful,
    loon-lonely eyes and lithe
shape split by the veering, renegade
    lip. Asymmetrical, utterly

stirring. After the surgery I wasn't
    even sure it was you, so nearly
regular your mouth, just a hint
    of up-pull, so flashing

your look. You seemed younger, less
    sad, less sure, too, as if you
had become your own little sister.
    How I wanted that wildly rising

line still to be there. I had no right.
    I know your life is better now,
hear it in the loose swing of your chatter.
    But your glance—more flit

than flash. Something has been smoothed
    away I loved. At least one self
wrenched from bed by thugs you never
    knew, hustled off, never seen

again. Now it is left to find out
    what was lost in that line
you were born with, what became
    of the disappeared, what grace

resides in that thin river you
    no longer have to cross,
and where it may be found again,
    and why I worry so.

First published in The Malahat Review

JERAH CHADWICK

Absence Wild

Not silence but quiet
without calm,
falling snow like static
the hills blur into.

All colours in this absence
of colour, this confusion
of sight turned back
on itself: whiteout, white noise.

Listen, the snow
speaks for itself
and says nothing, deafening
as avalanche.

Sounding the stillness,
my words, some sense of a trail
in the storm's stalled light.

The vastness in me
returned by this place.

from Story Hunger (1999)

Drifters

in memory of Mary Tall Mountain

Among her people she tells me
since ancient times, hunters
on spring ice, shifting
leads, one false step, almost
inaudible fracturing, then
the gurgling drum of cracks and scramble
for solidity. We knew them

by their animal eyes
and appetites, those who survived
by chipping ice and chewing
clothes' leather
even after weeks of drifting.

You could not get near
and if you trapped and dragged them home
you'd have to tie them
to the roof posts.
They would wail and waste away.

We learned to leave
cooked food and clothes
outside our village
to avert our eyes
and show no fear, coaxing
each one to speech and recognition.

Now, bed, booze, powder,
pills, black outs
of broken faith with the body.
'Look, the lamps are lit,
come warm yourself.'
We call them also

Those Who Have Been Taken Over by the Sea

from Story Hunger (1999)

Cormorant Killer

I want to believe the old stories
that you will come back
as what you have wasted: aurora
of black swan neck, seaworthy wings
bearing you to/from your chicks
in the rock, along the cliff

faced yawn of some beach
where a middle-aged man waits
out his free time, whiskey
in one hand, already drunk
with the gun in his other.

Shoot one and its mate
will soon come searching
he brags at work of the weekend
trips, blasting the same
empty bottle he keeps becoming

as shards of your feathers fall
and you fly again, snake raven
for fish or with gullet full.
May it always be nesting season.

PATRICK CHAPMAN

Break Up

In Marie Laveau's, a witch has made a spell
With alligator tooth and powdered snail shell:

You will leave me for a woman you can love.

Later, in a Mississippi market
—Arcade cornucopia of flower, anther, stamen, shoot—
We pass a cardboard sign above a still-unpurchased cot:

'Pregnant, or just thinking about it?'

I distract you with enamel earrings (blue):
I, not you, will leave and when I do,
I'll sleep with any gin-dead stranger who
Will have me and my crazy love for you.

from The New Pornography (1996)

Easter Comet

In New York you had contracted poison ivy.
Undeterred, you wandered Broadway in a night dress.

This image of you, fearless of the muggers, jugglers, yuppie scumbags,
Comes to me tonight as I stare, standing on my front step,
Up at Hale-Bopp in the northern sky:

A portent of the plague in other ages, but in this,
An imperfection in the firmament,
Across from what is now a bloated moon
That runs fat rays into the clouds
And seems to call: 'My jaundiced skin!'
As though the sky has run off with some luminous new stranger.

Those clouds will drift and scatter over your side of the city
Till some hour of the morning when the sky begins to lighten. Now
The tide is rolling out. The sea goes on into the dark
Beyond lighthouses.

from Breaking Hearts and Traffic Lights (2007)

Eidolon

Years go by and all your loves devolve into a composite,
Passing on time's travelator, gliding to a terminal,
Never to be seen again, and you watch from Security,
Frisked as though this stood for sex, this stood for *intimate*.

Ghosts—and you are ignorant of exorcism rites.
Whenever you're entangled in some temporary angel
Comes the shadow of another love: a flicker of a dimple
Or the first arrested syllable of laughter soft as promises.

You meet her in Departures after half a decade lost
And it's no longer her but her extrapolated. Someone
Calls her over—time to make the plane—and flings
A prophylactic glance at you, you melancholy revenant.

from Breaking Hearts and Traffic Lights (2007)

MARY COLL

A question of time

I need no commonplace reminders
of the passage of time,
all that stuff about spring brushing hesitantly
against the tips of trees,
and tentative stretches of light
tugging greedily at the darkness,
I know well the time that brought you to me,
for the first time,
and seemed to lie before us
indolent and infinite
until those long empty stretches of time
that took you away again.
Through it all, your comings and your goings
were the cadence of my life
during each moment we stole
and strung together to make
a time we called our own.
Time and again,
on a day like this,
these are the times I will remember.

from All Things Considered (2002)

Postcards

Sometimes I get postcards from another life,
the one in which I speak three languages
and travel alone through South America,
the one in which I throw on any old thing
with a scarf that's just perfect,
picked up at a flea market outside Zagreb,
the life in which you sit all night watching me sleep,
make me coffee when I wake,
feed me breakfast, insisting I lie in the sunlight
that falls in from a window overlooking the old square,
and kiss the inside of my wrist, and then my feet,
swearing you'll never let me leave, never,
and I send them back every time,
not known at this address.

from All Things Considered (2002)

Just Deserts

In the café around the corner from where Marie Antoinette
    lost her head,
You also lose yours over a cake.
At home, you inform me, we could have three for the price of
    a slice here.
But we are not at home now, my dear,
We are in Paris,
At least one of us is,
And besides, who needs three cakes anyway.
You flick through the guidebook, eager to narrate us on
    our way again,
Determined not to miss a trick,
But then you do.
At the next table the man in the pale grey suit
With the mauve silk tie, lifts a forkful of impeccable pastry
    towards the
Lips of a girl half his age,
His hand perfectly poised before them,
And they open to him, for the umpteenth time that day,
While he smiles the smile of one who knows the real pleasure
Of having his cake, and eating it.

ROZ COWMAN

The Goose Herd

The first angels must have been
like this, intolerant, haughty,
slightly clumsy, their wings
more beautiful than themselves,

and not respectful to the godhead
but watching, chins lifted,
hearing false notes with
spiritual ears.

There would have been no mutiny,
but a remembering of wild
blood at the equinox,
a stir of stony wings

against dark cloud, taking
the last light with them,
leaving the godhead resentful
because it missed their noisy blasphemies,

cursing them, and naming as Hell
their destiny ... a wild, lonely place
of sudden laughs, wailings, grey
down clouding the sight like ash.

from The Goose Herd (1989)

Peanuts

The way it was, for us children
during the forties
in those narrow market towns,
cow-spattered curtain-twitching
tinker-crazed on fair-days,
and we picking our way through forests
of drunken giants' legs ...

things should have turned out better
for Charlie Brown and Snoopy
roller-skating top-spinning
in backyard prairies of bungalows
down the broad sidewalks of America,
and all the giants invisible,
at work behind the scenes.

from The Goose Herd (1989)

The Robber Bride

I am'nt always my real self
with you, but I had a great
time with you last night, and you
not even here.

I was boiling the jam
all evening, and the heat,
and the street children at their game
of being me—
the hotel's daughter—
'tis as good as Queenie Carrigaline
to hear them.

Then it was eleven, and everyone gone—
so, a nice hot bath—'twas like blood
from the jam stains.
I wished we could meet
only when I'd be clean.
But sure that was only a dream
my love.

Then in my room I was lonely
but I said I'd just rehearse
for you. So I pictured you there
and wore the silk pyjamas I told you of
in the pink and mauve
and then the plain pink silk
and then the nightie. I asked you
how you like them, and you liked
the nightie best of all.
I gave you a hug,
and felt you'd want to hug me
with an etcetera.

It was almost as good as
if you were there—
the hotel empty and the night
hot and red with the smell of jam

the whole top floor to myself
and I running from room
to room, from mirror to mirror,
and the pink and the mauve
and the silk.

(Published in *Poetry Ireland Review* as 'August 1922', and in *Dancing with Kitty Strobling*, Antoinette Quin, editor, as 'Robber Bride'.

VICKI CROWLEY

Song of an Exile

Paint me a picture
Let it be blue:
The sea where I once swam
Had boats with painted eyes
That watched as phosphorescence
Studded my hair and fingertips
With diamonds.

Or let it be gold
Radiant as the sun
That bleached old ochre walls
Where lizards preyed
And sharp shadows tossed
Our laughter down narrow streets.

Red is recalled
In a blur of birth,
The flash of gills
In laden nets
Or defiant hibiscus blooming
In unending drought
Where each tuft of grass
Makes an oasis
In a sea of dust.

In dark reflection
I see the mirrored hue
Of a lover's hair,
Rusty black gowns
That sway to litanies
In baroque halls.

The sudden night
Exploding in a thousand lights
As church bells ring
When infants sleep
Until that magic time
When black is streaked
By dawn
And crickets sing in harmony.

from Oasis in a Sea of Dust (1992)

The Sky Road

She combed her thinning hair,
Dull, no longer bright,
Then slowly walked the broken path
Where cobwebs trapped and held
The dying summer light.
Beside the house that lay
Tossed upon the endless road
Like a single whitewashed stone,
She seems to wait,
Lonely figure, ringless hands
Upon the peeling gate.
Her evening apron
Is her Jason's shield,
Protective powers in its print.
She is silent in her solitude;
(It is the insane who talk alone.)
So when some passing stranger
Stops to ask the way,
She delights in the tone
Of her own voice
Savouring the syllables
Like some longed-for sweets.
Cherishing the luxury
She is so generous to share,
She unwittingly reveals
Her secret fantasy
'This road?' she replies,
'Ah yes, this road,
This road can take you anywhere.'

from Oasis in a Sea of Dust (1992)

The Needlewoman

When I was four and Malta was at war,
My mother made me a silk dress
From father's honeymoon pyjamas.
'Don't tell anyone from where it came',
She said, but in my innocence,
Of course I did.

I remember the quilt she sewed
For my convent-school bed.
Homesick, I would touch
Each square, each jig-saw part
That made our past.
I could evoke the smell of coffee
That my father brewed with his
Obligatory pinch of salt
From the patch of kitchen curtain,
Or hear the lapping waves
Of the turquoise sea rising
From a strip of beach dress
Until, wrapped in its comfort
I fell asleep and dreamt of home.

The needles in her now still hands
Are of another kind that bring
A sleep that feels no pain.
Through my vigil I think of all the
Gowns that she had made for me,
Each one emerging from the night;
The Schiapparelli pink sack,
The Sputnik creation with its balloon hem,
The fish tail and the one sleeved velvet,
In endless procession of her artistry.

Then, as dawn breaks,
Her skin turns to alabaster
And with the coming of the light,
I realise that she has stitched
Our very souls together
In a tapestry of living memories.

THEODORE DEPPE

For Caitlin, Setting Off to See
the World Without Her Coat

Let the heart go, then. Let the heart
seek its landscapes, knowing
nothing but its own desire. No, not even
knowing that, no plans except to fill herself
with as much world as possible—Bulgaria,
because of a Gypsy wedding dance heard years ago,
and Wessex, maybe, "to visit Thomas Hardy."
No forwarding address: when did the heart
ever leave one?

Oh, Thomas Hardy, her red toothbrush
is gone from the mug by the sink
and it's strange and almost funny
the story she told about your cat.
She said the vicar's compromise allotted
your body to Westminster, to satisfy the nation,
while your heart was to be tucked in
beneath the green yew tree
surrounded by moorland you loved.

Strange about the cat.
After the country doctor's bonesaw cracked
the sternum's parapet,
after he snipped a gate into
the pericardium, then reached
into the smooth cave of the thorax
and severed the heart—
like a trussed chicken, but smaller, like
the body of a thrush—

after he lifted the glistening thing into the light
he covered it (even in January
there are flies) carefully
with a tea cozy.
And when they had taken away the body?
And when the heart sat in state, waiting
for the little coffin to be made
and the hayride across the heath
to the village churchyard?

Then the double-pawed calico,
the author's favourite cat,
smelled out the choice meat
and dragged it from the table,
cameling its back at the parlourmaid's approach,
refusing to release the heart,
gripping tightly as the maid seized the broom
and shrieked—oh daughter, how is it done,
how do I let the heart go?

from Cape Clear: New & Selected Poems (2002)

Thousand Mile Journal

Peter cooks an apple pancake for my birthday
and I stay in bed late, reading journals
from the walk I made around Ireland
a quarter-century ago. For six months,
everything I needed fit in a rucksack.
I know at last, I wrote, *and forever,*
my home is the road. How romantic,
how nineteen, and how unsettling
to read those words in this house I love
and almost own. The spiral notebook leads me back

to a small port, four homes perched
above miniature cliffs, the delicious smell of peat
rising as I descend. It's not on my map
(Melville says true places never are.)
Late sun at the boat slip and an old man
patching his bike tyre with the same tar
he uses for his curragh. Two pages later
I'm in a hostel in Dunquin, writing about
my childhood hero, Gene Conley,
the 6'8" Red Sox pitcher who found his life too small.

Stuck on the team bus in heavy traffic,
he stepped down into a crowd
and set off midseason for Bethlehem.
As a boy, I listened to radio reports of his vanishing
and didn't know if this was comic or serious.
Forty-five now, grateful for a day off work
in which I'll hike with my wife in the Holyoke hills.
It's possible, I wrote, *just to keep walking.*
I copy the words into this year's journal.
A man might set off, anytime, for the Holy Land.

from Cape Clear: New & Selected Poems (2002)

The Singing

That morning, two nuthatches sauntered head-first down the pine
to a place where it was written in the wind *Yes, they like it,*

and for that moment it was the house of the world,
the green bough where they chatted and strolled upside-down.

Then, our daughter called from Greece,
giving her first and last name as if to make sure

we knew who she was. Her four-thousand-miles-away voice
pleaded for help as a man hammered on heavy glass

and we thought we'd have to listen to each scream of her rape,
or murder. No. Neighbours intervened. We stayed on the phone

until a woman told us, *Stop worry. Please, stop worry.*
Alone again in our living room my wife said she felt *weak*

from the inside out, and I asked if she'd heard
something like a girl chanting the whole time. *There was this*

singing on the line, I said, but my wife hadn't heard it
and answered, *Do I have to start worrying about you now?*

I've never mentioned it again, it must have been some part of myself,
some knowledge that we can't, finally, keep each other safe.

Our daughter changed her ticket, crossed the night, and came home,
though what home is keeps changing since that call.

There is a map and a clock and a humming in the room,
there is coffee, or champagne and kofta curry,

there is a family, or at least the hope that someone might, if not
rescue us, hear us. There is this chatting together

as we amble about upside-down and try to get used
to the perspective. And there is this shared time,

which is the green bough, for which I am grateful.

MARY DORCEY

The Breath of History

I am not an ordinary woman.
I wake in the morning.
I have food to eat.
No one has come in the night
to steal my child, my lover.
I am not an ordinary woman.

A plum tree
blossoms outside my window,
the roses are heavy with dew.
A blackbird sits on a branch
and sings out her heart.
I am not an ordinary woman.

I live where I want.
I sleep when I'm tired.
I write the words I think.
I can watch the sky
and hear the sea.
I am not an ordinary woman,
No one has offered me life
in exchange for another's.

No one has beaten me until I falldown.
No one has burnt my skin
nor poisoned my lungs.
I am not an ordinary woman.
I know where my friends live.
I have books to read,
I was taught to read.
I have clean water to drink.
I know where my lover sleeps;
she lies beside me,
I hear her breathing.
My life is not commonplace.

At night the air
is as sweet as honeysuckle
that grows along the river bank.
The curlew cries
from the marshes
far out,

high and plaintive.
I am no ordinary woman.
Everything I touch and see
is astonishing and rare—
privileged.
Come celebrate each
privileged, exceptional thing:
water, food, sleep—
the absence of pain—
a night without fear—
a morning without
the return of the torturer.

A child safe,
a mother,
a lover, a sister.
Chosen work.
Our lives are not commonplace—
any of us who read this.

But who knows—
tomorrow or the day after ...
I feel all about me
the breath of history—
pitiless
and ordinary.

from The River That Carries Me (1995)

These Days of Languor

These days of languor—
loosed of everything
but pleasure
and time.

Enthral to sense,
we put on clothes
only at late evening.
One moment

leading to the next
and back again.
At last,
light fading

on the balcony,
we spread a cloth
and eat—
oysters,

avocado,
new strawberries.
In candle flame, as
you lift your glass

I see love's stain—
wine red
under your
fingernails.

from Like Joy In Season, Like Sorrow (2001)

The Finest Gossamer

Perhaps the heart is constant, after all.
Perhaps it makes no difference who we love,
what voice lures us, what name we call?

It's always the same love, is it not? Drawn
from the one spring, coursing the same track?
It's always the same thirst we slake, the same

Image in the pool; the same blood dimmed gaze.
Perhaps it makes no difference who we lust for.
Isn't it always the same veil we cast over each

New form, the finest gossamer illusion can buy,
spun from the sheerest silks, of faith, hope and deceit.
Perhaps it makes no matter what voice lures us. It's

Always our own ears we stop, the same sirenian
song. The same wine on the tongue, the same salt
in the wound. If the heart is constant in the least

Is it to the elemental, the universal theme?
Is it only in particulars that love alters?
The setting and the costumes? A particular sky,

A particular bridge, oleander by an open gate,
a particular white linen coverlet? The language
and the houses, the weather and the streets;

Surface things, easily exchanged, forgotten.
Shed like leaves or skin, like memory itself,
and the imprint of touch, of sight. Breath

On glass, a particular face. Yes, perhaps even at
last, this too will be shed—that bridge, that night,
that scented gate, the scarred river, that turning

Back, once, twice. Even at last, this too, will
fade. Shed like time itself—like the memory
of her face. Like the memory of that lie.

CAROL ANN DUFFY

Mrs. Aesop

By Christ, he could bore for Purgatory. He was small,
didn't prepossess. So he tried to impress. Dead men,
Mrs Aesop, he'd say, tell no tales. Well, let me tell you now
that the bird in his hand shat on his sleeve,
never mind the two worth less in the bush. Tedious.

Going out was worst. He'd stand at our gate, look, then leap;
scour the hedgerows for a shy mouse, the fields
for a sly fox, the sky for one particular swallow that
couldn't make a summer. The jackdaw, according to him,
envied the eagle. Donkeys would, on the whole, prefer to be lions.

On one appalling evening stroll, we passed an old hare
snoozing in a ditch—he stopped and made a note—
and then, about a mile further on, a tortoise, somebody's pet,
creeping, slow as marriage, up the road. Slow
but certain, Mrs Aesop, wins the race. Asshole.

What race? What sour grapes? What silk purse,
sow's ear, dog in a manger, what big fish? Some days,
I could barely keep awake as the story droned on
towards the moral of itself. Action, Mrs. A., speaks louder
than words. And that's another thing, the sex

was diabolical. I gave him a fable one night
about a little cock that wouldn't crow, a razor-sharp axe
with a heart blacker than the pot that called the kettle.
I'll cut off your tail, all right, I said, to save my face.
That shut him up. I laughed last, longest.

from The Salmon Carol Ann Duffy: Poems Selected and New 1985-1999 (2000).

Pilate's Wife

Firstly, his hands—a woman's. Softer than mine,
with pearly nails, like shells from Galilee.
Indolent hands. Camp hands that clapped for grapes.
Their pale, mothy touch made me flinch. Pontius.

I longed for Rome, home, someone else. When the Nazarene
entered Jerusalem, my maid and I crept out,
bored stiff, disguised, and joined the frenzied crowd.
I tripped, clutched the bridle of an ass, looked up

and there he was. His face. Ugly. Talented.
He looked at me. I mean, he looked at me. My God.
His eyes were eyes to die for. Then he was gone,
his rough men shouldering a pathway to the gates.

The night before his trial, I dreamt of him.
His brown hands touched me. Then it hurt.
Then blood. I saw that each tough palm was skewered
by a nail. I woke up, sweating, sexual, terrified.

Leave Him Alone. I sent a warning note, then quickly dressed.
When I arrived, the Nazarene was crowned with thorns.
The crowd was baying for Barabas. Pilate saw me,
looked away, then carefully turned up his sleeves

and slowly washed his useless, perfumed hands.
They seized the prophet then and dragged him out,
up to the Place of Skulls. My maid knows all the rest.
Was he God? Of course not. Pilate believed he was.

from The Salmon Carol Ann Duffy: Poems Selected and New 1985-1999 (2000).

Scheherazade

Dumb was as good as dead;
better to utter.
Inside a bottle, a genie.
Abracadabra.
Words were a silver thread
stitching the night.
The first story I said
led to the light.

Fact was in black and white;
fiction was colour.
Inside a dragon, a jewel.
Abracadabra.
A magic carpet took flight,
bearing a girl.
The hand of a Queen shut tight
over a pearl.

Imagination was world;
clever to chatter.
Inside a she-mule, a princess.
Abracadabra.
A golden sword was hurled
into a cloud.
A dead woman unfurled
out of a shroud.

A fable spoken aloud
kindled another.
Inside a virgin, a lover.
Abracadabra.
Forty thieves in a crowd,
bearded and bold.
A lamp rubbed by a lad
turning to gold.

2.

Talking lips don't grow cold;
babble and jabber.
Inside a turkey, a fortune.
Abracadabra.
What was lost was held
inside a tale.
The tall stories I told
utterly real.

Inside a marriage, a gaol;
better to vanish.
Inside a mirror, an ogre;
better to banish.
A thousand and one tales;
weeping and laughter.
Only the silent fail.
Abracadabra.

MICHAEL EGAN

Letter to My Daughter

Elusive as North Atlantic winds
and as wilful, you foraged the water's edge,
a landbird at sea along the shoreline,
a barometer Gretel in wax and wane

with the sun. Mornings you scoured the dunes,
clearing nests in the thistles, curling
in some sandman's morning-after rest,
in lumbering sleep, uneasy as surf;

and nights, floating free, you circled
the boardwalk comedy, the bible-thumpers
and bikers, or met with friends, and talked
until talk was a trouble, too,

and moved on, free of grounding, as if
the flesh had gradually melted to spirit
under the hands grappling your wrists,
the nameless untyings of your swimsuit,

the sprite in her own Tempest, in hand
to hand combat with nothingness.
If air is all we are, its lulls
are deaths. The spirit knows itself,

and self-contained, may flash with a fire
that sets us free, from net and tether,
the alarm slumbering mornings, the fondlings
we cling to, and finally, even from death.

Send me news of the sea. Know that
I'll hold you always, in the air of blood
crackling between us always, the remembered
voltage of touching the flesh of my flesh.

from We Came Out Again to See the Stars (1986)

119

We Came Out Again to See the Stars

When I was born that stormy night
in April, racing the turn of day,
the growth of spring, the first, chaste
bloodshed of the war, I hurried so
I seemed to burn the bridges of her womb;

then, they say, I paused halfway-born
as in reflection, and drenched with pain
and tugging at the cord, I kissed
the flames of maidenhair around my neck.
Tonight, half a lifetime later, restless,

I share my birthday with a dappled foal,
dropped to a chilly field; with friends
waiting inside, laughing at the dark—
with that death-haunted man, Henry Vaughan.
And though the days accrete at glacial speed,

I know that once each year unknown
to me—as a poem says—I keep holy
the anniversary of my death, the day my heart
rebels, taxed beyond its will, or cells vexed
too long grow teeth and devour their brothers.

I think of all the poems I failed
to write, or wrote in vain. Their breath,
that first so richly swelled my lungs,
grew thin and stale in working the words,
or spent itself in drink or songless work.

As surely as if I'd burned them, the books
crackling into ash, the words to cinders,
they are gone, those poems, into the deep
and dazzling dark where God lives.
Tonight, as every night for months, I watched

my daughter await her first menses,
her tide-turn from schoolgirl into woman.
We danced a few moments before her bedtime,
and as we spun, a feather of ashen
hair brushed my cheek, and she was gone.

At times I feel I'm deep inside her,
crawling between the layers of her womb
to lie with her, with a father's need
to deflower his first daughter, with fear
for the dark woman growing as she grows.

The house sings with the reedy voice
of my few friends, and bottles ring
the table. I go inside to learn
my hardest lesson: compassion for others;
for others, too, light and darkness are as one.

The sky tonight is low and soft
beneath the dark underbelly of the Ram,
and there is music in its silence. We dance,
my love and I, I stroke her hair,
and we come out again to see the stars.

from We Came Out Again to See the Stars (1986)

Excerpt from Leviathan

Scientists say some form of forms
or basic pattern, some shrewish link
with hot, nocturnal blood, nimble
grasping hands and thought-sized brains—
father of man, weasel, and bat,
and cousin to apes—was the whale's Adam,
knowing, like man, his nature was one
of movement, its essence flexions of change,
and always that and only that,
that rest, stillness or stasis, is death.
Nuzzling for grubs in marshy bottoms,
hungry as always, his brightening wit
shot shyly outwards, seawards, scouring
the ocean's rich crustaceous life.
When seagoing reptiles disappeared,
landlocked in Scottish lakes, or numbed
and fixed in ice for lurid movies,
the knot of warm fur put out to sea,
through dim shallows, brackish, bitter,
then darkness sweet as salt, and walked
the ocean floor with staring fish.
For aeons the water worked its changes:
the arms flattened into flippers,
trim for the crawl, the breast- and backstroke;
the hindlegs tailed off into flukes;
and buoyant, light in the lifting brine,
free of gravity's earthward drag
in part, its plodding physics, the limit
it sets to heft on spindly legs,
the bones bulked up like seagoing timbers,
and the body grew. Drawn by the waters,
expanding like some universe
of cells, the flesh massed in new
configurations, constellations
annealed by water: The Yawl, The Frigate,
with sides solid as bulkheads, The Ark
the size of fifteen pairs of elephants—
such bulk, such massed fatty flesh

storing more life-heat, more fuel oil,
like a tanker shuttling the Persian Gulf,
or whaler headed home to Nantucket,
awash with sperm oil, followed by gulls.
And other changes a sea life required:
whole families lost their bite—the teeth
replaced by plates for filtering krill;
others grew horns or humps, or blunt
or beaked or bottle noses, or lofty
thoughtful brows and magnificent heads;
all learned the water's long patience,
its final kindness, and, come of age,
altered their bearings with their features,
gentle, reflective, self-contained.

Amused, the wry eyes seem to hold
some secret, learned from the sea, some sense
of heaven's silence beyond our own,
conceived in larger brains than ours,
in the guts of thought more deeply primal,
of what waits beyond the Primum Mobile,
humming unheard in time and space—
or, as they dive to thousands of feet,
what moves the waves within each atom
of Being, whispering, melodic
to a pure unconsciousness of joy.
Basking on summer days, when the water
bends like grass before the wind,
or sheltering under disheveled seas,
the blue delirium of storms,
they are at one with their world and at home.
Prowling the ocean floor, with senses
and frightening powers we cannot grasp,
instincts, astonished intimations,
the only witness to its seasons,
perhaps they glimpse—perhaps become—
the play of evolution's play,
creation for joy and joy alone.

MÍCHEÁL FANNING

Rún
for Tom Walsh

Friends join me
in my west coast retreat.
Lights from the villages
candle our walk,

beacon from the ports
of Tralee, Fenit
Ballyheigue to Maharees,
Castle and Derrymore.

I have overheard the fishermen collogue
as they shoot lobster pots, miles from Muchaloch;
other times, haul nets from pelagic,
summer waters, ten knots from here.

I am the demure fisherman,
born of the sea ;
Survivor of a green ship
I am loveless and disaffected.

I quit all that I have known.
I'll map
across the cerulean sea
for five and twenty years.

When confidence is conferred,
I shall gybe from any world port,
to concourse with you, friends,
on our social shores.

from Verbum et Verbum (1997)

Pád's Crib

for my brothers and sisters

Pádraig constructed the pyramidal
crib with alder twigs

to capture lusty, speckled
thrushes in the snow.

The six timid children
from ten down waited

behind the screen curtain
in the holly adorned kitchen.

The eldest, Pád, yanked the twine
to incarcerate the captive.

We settled for a blackbird
Anno Nivis Magnae:

The Year of the High Snows
and Blissful Blanket Blizzards.

The Culpable Captors
liberated her, whom they feared.

She flew off amongst
The Snow Sky Pines.

from Verbum et Verbum (1997)

Abigail & David

Abigail bowed to David
and threw herself on the ground
at David's feet.

I bring you two hundred loaves of bread,
five roasted sheep, ten stone of roasted grain,
a hundred bunches of grapes,

two hundred cakes of dried figs
and two leather bags full of wine
to give to your men. Eat, drink and be merry.

David, appointed
through Samuel
after the fall of tall and moody Saul,

you stand on the boundaries of the spirit-dream world
betwixt our fathers, our mothers
and on the boundaries of sanity and compassion.

And yours like ours is not a life of peace
as you hide from danger after danger, year after year.
Take cover, lie low and go to ground.

Mary Garvey, Bríd Pat Moriarty, John Martin and
Séamus Kennedy—dip the sheep and milk the cows.
Pádraig Ó Siochrú, round Coláiste Íde walk the hound.

The Assyrians replenish their stables
with a hundred horses a day in their cosmic fight with evil.
Empires loot, grow in leaps and bounds.

from Homage (2006)

GABRIEL FITZMAURICE

Sonnet to Brenda

I won't compare you to a summer's day,
The beaches all deserted in the rain—
Some way, this, to spend a holiday
(You're sorry now you didn't book for Spain).
No! The weather can't be trusted in these parts—
It's fickle as a false love's said to be;
I could get sentimental about hearts
But that's not my style. Poetry,
The only thing that's constant in my life,
The only thing I know that still is true
As my love remains for you, dear wife—
This, then, is what I'll compare to you.
The iambic heart that pulses in these lines
Measures out my love. And it still rhymes.

Knockanure Church

A place of worship, simple and austere;
Sixties architecture past its date.
I wonder what it is that draws me here
To a building local people seem to hate.
The church of their affection, knocked, made way
For the "garage on the hill" in its design –
Bare brick, flat roof, no steeple, here I pray.
The spirit of this building's kin to mine.

My God's a God who strips me in this place—
No cover here, the lines are stark and spare;
Through the years, I've grown into this space
Where work of human hands raised art to prayer,
The same the builders raised up once at Chartres
But plainer here, an answer to my heart.

The Solitary Digger

after Paul Henry

Not a spire in sight but thatch and hay.
She pauses from her digging. All alone
She digs out good potatoes from the·clay.
She'll fear no winter when the work is done.
The crop is good. She pauses for a rest—
No famine now will skeleton the land;
A simple faith submits that God knows best—
There are things she knows she needn't understand.
Just a simple peasant standing with her spade,
Knowing through her hands the fertile earth
In a landscape with not a tree for shade—
This land is hers by labour and by birth.
She pauses from her digging; there is time
To compose oneself where heaven and nature rhyme.

in memoriam Sister Anna Danaher

All from Twenty One Sonnets (2007)

MÉLANIE FRANCÈS

V. Night Walk

I walked outside and I had a body into which you had carved.
When I stepped out of your house, I had a careful tempo of a walk,
a quick stroll worthy of the fifties that categorized my dress.
I knew the smell of mints that someone had left on your coffee table,
the way the velvet indoors of your rented American car felt.
I walked outside, after having sat by you in a fabulous chill,
and stood erect in the perfect position of a woman you summoned.
I swayed my feet to the sound of Sinatra's *Something Stupid*.
The porches were all whitened; a few lights came out of houses.
I walked and saw my city in miniature, and me, miniature pin-up
with ragweed in her hair, roughed up skirt and bruise below the knee.
I walked and my sweet mind was forlorn, away from my lips,
being ravaged, being kissed, back and forth in the trailing street.
I walked and the Canadian night sang, the breeze up and down the curb
and into back yards. I clung to my walk, infatuated, a brand new dollar,
hawk-eyed poetess of a girl walking home after being with you.
I walked in a space called night, and my city revolved in the dark,
the coffee table, my golden limbs against your pale white arms.
I walked with my face looking up, with a blue smile of glamour,
not feeling sleepy, in a familiar street thrown out of spin and hollow.
I was carried away, smooth, alone and wrapped up in riot.
I had the feet of a brunette in a television film, brushing against the
cold checkered tiles of a diner floor. I stepped outside your house.
It was just an ordinary city crushed in night, the tranquil order of us,
eyes like wide camera movements and me, walking down my street.

Sierra Leone

You imagine blue roads in the dirty green leading to the village.
The faint screeches of tires that lead to a silence full of panic.
The cabins' roofs are distorted by the lens or the heat or the void
and soldiers in washed out uniforms, bogus soldiers, bogus rebels
of a bogus war inspect villagers with fingers glued to Kalashnikovs.
You imagine sick mockeries of heart shapes in the nearby trunks
made by rocket leftovers. You see soldiers looking for a mission,
possibly dazed with cocaine, soldiers that you can't understand,
their war like a snake swallowing its own tail to stave off hunger.
On one side are those who have nothing.
On the other are those who have nothing but are armed.
You see the soldiers and the impression gets blurred by normalcy
and press reports and the time to eat and practice human games.
I am astounded that I have to concentrate to care fully.
Sierra Leone. The name hovers over dinner time and television
and all the faces that are caught in distress in war photography.
These faces are the slap given to our millennium craze.
This is where my festivities snap: they fire and I am concentrating.

Hotel Rooms

For Brent Stirton

People are standing by their windows in hotel rooms
all over the world. Standing like beautiful pieces of chess,
unaware of strategy and cunning. Looking out, trying hard to
understand dusk and its implications. An arm folded in their back,
their silhouette curved to the thought of something past.
People are standing by their windows in hotel rooms, looking out.
The surfaces are shining with all the ghostly presences that are
wiped off each day. People stand amidst what is caught in mirrors.
Hearts go unheard in absolute silence.
And yet, sometimes, one or two meet in hotel rooms and
the sheets are suddenly warm and stained with red. Mornings
look like nights and time never seems to rest. People share bathrooms
and bend for one another. Television sets glow in a darkening afternoon,
the sound set on mute, its message diluted. All the television sets in all
the hotel rooms in the world absorb more life than we will ever know.
The moonlit movements, the silent gazing, hands opening on clothes.
People are standing by their windows in hotel rooms.
There is red blinking on telephones. There is blue above the space
outside. They know they are free. They know it doesn't mean a thing.
People mess up the cleanliness, create havoc in a beautiful place,
do it over and over again. They listen to the next room with expectation.
The water fills bathtubs in several places. Wires never get crossed.
People speak all of their languages. Little rituals of trust are broken.
Others are honored with a trace of the sublime. People are people in
hotel rooms all over the world. They stare, suspended high above cities.
Millions of cells are evolving in the void.
Modern life is very ancient. The longing is the same. Nothing is learned
through the times. People are standing by their windows and television
sets and bedside lamps and marbled floors, and they know this.
Their eyes follow the traffic. The blood in their veins runs perfectly still.
It all comes down to nothing if sheets aren't clung to.
People are standing by their windows. Something about them isn't simple.
They are heartbreaking presences behind glass. People acknowledge the
passing of the day. The sound returns on television sets. Screens are ablaze.
Murmurs are eloquent. Desires are simplified. Propositions are softly
voiced. Nakedness becomes less important, almost beside the point.

all from Anatomy of a Love Affair (My Life in the Movies) (2007)

PHILIP FRIED

Big Men Speaking to Little Men

Slowly the black snake severs the path
all four feet of him with forked
tongue that constantly tastes the world
sentinel to the length of the body

laying bare the interval
between the hell-bent trail-bikers
and the big men speaking to little men
conspiratorially in the forest

sotto voce there are places
the faintest trails created by lines
of desire an elsewhere interwoven
with here and everlastingly now

the doors they lead to are oddly chamfered
open to admit the random
molecule in or out the bit
of information no one sent

to anyone this clearing's a wild
field the universe may have been
someone's orchard overgrown
now with herbs and loosestrife

the big men say use this scattering
build cities from the strewn seeds
until the infinitesimal
sings to us in unwitting chorus

these are the carriage paths that lead
out of the nineteenth century down
into the ramifying great
wilderness of less and least

big little men stroll secretly holding
the world at bay but at any scale
confused with the day's late shadows a black
snake comes and takes itself away

from Big Men Speaking to Little Men (2006)

The Kibitzer

My name is the chair I've sat in all my life
while the games spun by as if on a lazy Susan:

scrabble, fast-pitch softball, seven-card stud.
In physics, which gives us the rules of the house, it is written,

Irresistible forces encounter the kibitzer.
(Sir Isaac tutored the apple all the way down.)

So the jiggles and jukes, the rules and the statistics
are grist for my godlike witness and niggling chorus,

and with twitchy omnipotence, I'll give you the scoop
on shuffleboard: propel the cue then stop

... the disc will glide then hover over the well
of emptiness beneath the painted numbers.

Calm down, my nervous father coached. He knew
that Yiddish has as many words for anxiety

as the Inuit language does for types of snow.
And the play could always drift into the stands. I know

and bring a foul mouth to the game, but also a glove.

from Big Men Speaking to Little Men (2006)

Short Line Driver (in the Garden State)

Not God but the lead-footed, combustible
Bus-driver steers our destinies—
No appeals except to the wheel.
So bouncing in potholes, no matter the wobble
in the spin, the wandering poles, the rifting
plates, we ply our cosmic commute,

with *her* keen eye in the rear-view mirror
to check out reckless comets, ensure
we leave no litter, just a molecular
flurry, little stuff, when we leave.
Her uniform, custom designed by the Line,
features gilded cuffs and crescent-

moon-shaped epaulets like scythes
at the shoulders; it's a pleasure to wake
each working morning to find her driving
us to work, but what a temper:
the chatter of billions, stuffed with banality's
weightless luggage, drives her crazy.

Good thing there's a fraternity
of drivers, the jocular shock-absorbers,
kidding on two-way radios
about asteroid traffic, mocking the daily
fool, some soul at the bus-stop
confusing your local run with the time-

warp express to the end of it all.
She smirks, they all do, at this poor
petitioner who appears at her soon-
to-be-shut door, smirks from the official
condescending height of her gritty
weather-streaked vehicle and croons,

"Honey, it's coming in twenty, just
hang on." Petty sadism, yes, but
who else will speak for combustion, exhaust
gases, thermal cycles, imperfect
reactions, inevitable losses,
residue? Who else will get us through?

(First appeared in Terrain.org; nominated for Best of the Net, 2006)

ERLING FRIIS-BAASTAD

The Strait
for Raymond Carver

I walk beside the gray strait
and study on the far shore
Port Angeles, USA, where you
once walked and peered out
under the risen mist
at my beach in Canada.
One of these days
I will cross this tossed
water in my own boat,
visit your old house
with all my friends.
It can be a small boat.
I haven't been sober long
and have saved few friends
from my drunken storms,
just Dave and Greg.
Though I have some new friends:
Pat, Eve, Rhonda, John and Joan.
I love them as I love this strait
in a wind which sets all
the exotic ducks to rafting
beyond the breakers—
scoter, pintail, goldeneye—
yet launches the winter gulls.
They remind me of poems by
Wallace Stevens and Hart Crane.
But that's as far as I'll dare
love today. I won't be taking it
further, to some bar, won't
be dragging my love out,
swallow by drop, to the dregs.
Tomorrow, I'll set off from here

again, beside the strait, early
before the crowds,
with the gulls and poets
stride part-way
to wherever their metaphor
would take me.

from The Exile House (2001)

Exile

Again I have summoned the word
exile. How many decades must I waste
at laments before coming to believe
my long exile has ended, is served?
True, it is cold here at the northern-
most frontier of my wandering. Winter
has arrived with October. Last night,
I heard geese taking their leave.
This morning, trumpeter swans deserted
at first light. Was the map too simple
to comprehend? My final memory
of the South is surely distorted
by some recent adventure in this land.
A slow summer walk with Elizabeth
among huge oaks has become
a quick hike with Patricia
through yellowing poplar.
I have confused magpies with mocking birds
and river willow with sumac too long.
What I recall as endless possibility
was just a young man's boasting
and greed. I will indulge myself
with no further talk of promise.
I was called to walk this high place.
Around me lies all the bounty
one could ever hope to spend,
a home hidden only by snow

from The Exile House (2001)

Arboreal

i.m. Gennady Aygi

I spend the first
hours of each day
talking trees
with a dead Russian

G. and I sit around
my coffee and say,
birch. For both of us
birch has served

as punctuation and
as a sort of travelers'
rest between Eucharist
and soul or soul

and Father. However,
it's a cautious chit chat
of leaves and twigs—
we are too polite

to come right out
and mention
the quaking aspen
just yet, or admit

to spruce boughs
cracking, breaking off,
and even falling
in the great wind.

First published in 2River View

PAUL GENEGA

November

Of the many nightmares I've made,
The worst, I think watching the cold sea,
Is the one in which I discover myself
Changing, not yet changed, but changing
Into something not-quite human, some-
Thing of the shadow world, where the wild
Romp and randy about with themselves.

In that dream sometimes I have horns,
Not even stuck in appropriate places
Like a nice old myth, but at shoulder blade
Or abdomen, a clump at the top of the hand,
A whorl of calcium on the bottoms of my feet...

What I've done to the body,
What I would do to the body,
What will be done in indefatigable time
Seems so very sad now standing on this bluff,
Sea air softly purring, the waves
Gently licking the green fur of the beach.

from Striking Water (1989)

141

Descent and Sentiment

The plane makes its descent on
the city where I lived once, flickering
Interstates, cloverleaves and loops,
as if Omaha, exploded, had strewn
its ruby innards from sea to shining sea.
Still, there is the roc egg of the Capitol,
floodlit—there, Washington's white cock,
things recognizable amid the squat
flat-top office buildings, all built
since I've been gone. I remember D.C.

Southern—waxy magnolias, ornate columned
mansions of mustachioed ambassadors,
unbreathable summers, and you, dreamer,
drifter, odd-jobber, first honest love
in a rowhouse long ago. I remember that
whole summer beneath your sloping roof,
laughing at nothing, drinking too much
wine. We spoke three words through August
then firmly shook good-bye. Me, back
to Nebraska; you to Virginia, I think.

Now, here, buckled to my speeding seat,
I search, despite myself, for our
rowhouse gable, for the window strobed
with candles and moon, though surely razed.
Of course I cannot find it, more than count
these lights, the beds I've known since you.
By landing the runway is just a blur
of blue. Then the wheels touch, touch down
firmly, and the dim dishonest longing
for the long gone bursts in flame.

from That Fall: New & Selected Poems (2001)

Wolfie's Tavern

in memory of Bob Fuchs

Shadow home,
lair, the dark
place your sick
body honed

in on. You ate
verboten burgers,
nursed lager,
excuse to pontificate

on the tv news,
to extol, to pronounce,
opine and renounce—
as you would say: schmooze.

What the locals
thought of your
New York jaw,
what the yokels,

as you called
them, felt
about your purpled pelt
cannot be recalled

but at that moment
you were top shelf,
the Alpha wolf,
and you lent

your jejune know-it-all
to the un-impatient masses.
Blotched with rashes,
a thrall

of skin and bone,
you bristled and scowled,

yelp-howled
on your bar throne

as if bluster and bray
could pass for folks talking,
wit's fangs keep stalking
death at bay.

FRANK GOLDEN

Death the Invisible Accomplishment
i.m. D.F. Golden

From within a cream-ultramarine kiosk
    Overlooking Aughinish Island,
I saw the water between shore and shore
    Churn dark, the sky bleed greyly,
The land winter its mortal green.
    The black mouthpiece like a dark body part
Bobbed in the slim chamber
    Echoing my mother's whispered words—
The news is bad
    The deep scan of my father's body
Had pictured lesions on his stomach wall,
    Shoals of growths which devoured
His appetite and fed death's dream.
    My eyes trawled out to sea
Through middle currents and uncharted banks
    To seals on the misting rock of Deer island
To boats and the carriage of a wish
    To the tidal sea taking and offering.

On the storm road by the Flaggy Shore
    I walked in witness to your end,
Loosening the line linked
    To your migrating self.
On the shores of Loch Muirí
    A swan for each of your years
Clustered the terrible blue water,
    Their sometimes whirring wings
A chorus to your vanishing.
    Through the pores of soft stone walls
A south wind blew inordinate and warm,
    High over Black Head
A sudden cloudswell broke,

A page of rain fell seaward
Shedding the memory of a life—
    A life inscribed upon a filamental sheet,
Decoded to the sea,
    Subsumed in the eternal afternoon.

from The Interior Act (1999)

Eve

Walled rain, gold light and you,
Soaking the soft wet in a dance,
Your cobalt kimono fleeting
The drenching grass,
Your eyes on the copper crisp beach,
Your leaf-tongue sipping
The lightest sustenance.
Dark swan, Blue Fox in rain,
Eagle wings trailing the wind
In Coole's fat historic spaces
Strangely, magically present,
With clouds of women
In florid white dresses,
And sharp men in London suits
Declaiming Revolution and Poetry.
We see an otherness,
A world of mirages,
Fraily real with vaporous
Echoes, musics, whisperings.
Past things curving back,
Fluttering upon our necks—
A velvet breath, a kiss,
A silver girl in a golden kimono
Diamonding a square of glass.
You are an animal inside,
You run in fox.
Wisest of us all,
Knowing you can die
In a minute and switch forever.

from The Interior Act (1999)

In Veronsk Palatou Trabant

We met again and again
Photographs prove it
Stations in Veronsk Palatou Trabant
Meet me she would text
3 days from now
Dress in white
No socks
Over the years I learned to drop everything
Sickness to evade work
Trips to betray a lover
Our final destinations always reachable by train
Sometimes she would be waiting for me
Sometimes I would be waiting for her
Years might pass and then a call
She was always recognizable
The shape of her head
Her standing posture
Her disdain for the conventions of the world

They merge
The stations of the world
A cold stone annex
A vaulted arch
Glass and oxidised red tiles
Men in blue serge uniforms
She coming towards me in the early morning
The train tracks snaking towards a bleak corner
She taking my hand
The light electric for a moment

There is an eloquence to the loss you cannot name
A kind of frailty that instils allegiance
Breath requiring breath
Needs that need to feast
Need as oblique gift
Touch as total sustenance

In the green shuttered room
She whisked the walls to stunning flowers
And breasted the blue window's filmic light
Pressed my soles to her belly
Bathed my feet
Sexed until her body blurred
And talked until her talk became as natural as breath
And our past was not reconfigured but the present

MICHAEL GORMAN

Cresting the Wave

The saddest man in Sligo
With black, ringleted hair
Wore a heavy coat all summer long,
Stood still for hours
In the Nazarene field
Where his mother was buried.
Shadows from the narrow streets
Of our town followed him.
Whenever the sun came out
Or went in behind clouds,
The change in light
Terrified him.

He knelt down in Wine Street
And cried like a baby;
"You have me heart broken,
You have me heart broken."
Tears streamed from him so freely
He became a tourist attraction
Known to all the sundry
As 'Laughing Eddie'.

A day in the early seventies,
May coming into June,
A grey-haired man named Bruen
In a dark grey, pin-striped suit
Came into Saint John's school
To talk about the I.D.A.
He spoke of the golden future
Opening before us all.
Economics moved in cycles,
We were the crest of the wave.

Some smart fellow at the back,
Toolan from Coolbock,
Shouted up at Bruen:
"Well, if that's the case, sir,
What about your brother, Eddie,
Has he not heard the news?"

Bruen completely flipped;
"That delicate vessel,
He nearly broke me.
I was decent to him as any man
Who ever put a hand
Out through a coat.
Deep Heat, Algipan,
Sloan's Liniment, Ralgex,
Pulmo Bailly's Cough Linctus,
He was never without a tablet.
If you want to know me, son,
Come and live with me."
And forgetting all about Economics,
Bruen took up his briefcase and left.

I was talking later that day
To my special friend and confessor
The Reverend Owen Mac Glone
Who had high hopes at the time
I'd become a fisher of men
In Cedar Rapids, Iowa,
A place where he'd lost his thumb
In an automobile accident.
The priest was in a funny mod.
He "my childed" me this and that.
All he wanted to talk about
Was nocturnal emission,
What he liked to call
"Wanking Practice".

"It has to come out some way,"
Fr Owen said to me—
"Concerning the two brothers,
Bruen from the I.D.A. is easy.

If ever things go wallop,
He can start again in the morning
As though nothing has happened.
So far as the other fellow goes,
It's a lot more complicated
For anguish has no memory
In the mind of 'Laughing Eddie'.

Then he waved his hand in the air,
The one with four fingers on it.

from Up She Flew (1991)

The People I Grew Up With Were Afraid

The people I grew up with were afraid.
They were alone too long in waiting-rooms,
In dispensaries and in offices whose functions
They did not understand.

To buck themselves up, they thought
Of lost causes, of 'Nature-boy'
O'Dea who tried to fly
From his bedroom window,
Of the hunch-backed, little typist
Who went roller-skating at Strandhill.
Or, they re-lived the last afternoon
Of Benny Kirwan, pale, bald,
Protestant shop-assistant in Lydon's drapery.
One Wednesday, the town's half-day,
He hanged himself from a tree
On the shore of Lough Gill.

And what were they afraid of? Rent
collectors, rate collectors, insurance men.
Things to do with money. But,
Especially of their vengeful God..
On her death-bed, Ena Phelan prayed
That her son would cut his hair.

Sometimes, they return to me.
Summer lunchtimes, colcannon
For the boys, back-doors
Of all the houses open, the
News blaring on the radios.
Our mother's factory pay-packet
Is sitting in the kitchen press
And our father, without
Humour or relief, is
Waiting for the sky to fall.

from Up She Flew (1991)

I.C.U.

Lying there at our mercy
You're getting all the news
Whether you like it or not.
The home place is so quiet now,
We can hear a car change gear
From a mile across the fields.
Can you remember the flapping
Of pigeons' wings early in the morning
On railway platforms, the shudder
In the launderette before the machine's
Final spin?
It was Cockburn's turn today.
The Albanians ran along Brindisi pier
Faster than children in any playground.
In Omaha, Nebraska, a man is selling his eye
For 10,000 dollars.
You were right about most things.
Eaten bread is soon forgotten.
Money refuses to grow on trees.
But the man who made time
Did not make plenty of it.
Least not enough for you and me, Joey,
Not near enough for us.

MARK GRANIER

Lines For The Diceman

i. m. Thom McGinty

Good to know you might turn up
in the frieze of faces on Grafton Street,
familiar stranger surprising us
in something from your wardrobe-gallery,

a walking painting say, holding its own
gilded ornate frame, the face
a white mask, Mona Lisa
in a black cat-suit, cracking a murky smile.

Dead-slow, solemnly careful
among eddies of Christmas shoppers, summer dawdlers,
tourists, street-traders, Guards...
mindful of each sound-proofed step, sure-

footed as an acrobat, spaced in, treading your own
high wire. When we looked
at you looking through us
we took in the joke that jumped—a spark of silence—

eye to eye, mind to mind,
across Grafton Street's canyon of swirling clockwork noise.
You're gone now forever (back
into the box with Jack)

and scanning the quickslow, giddy, sedate
everyday street-portrait—its procession
of invisible masks—the eye misses you.
Old Master, Diceman, conductor

of the ungrooved thought, catcher
of the thrown glance, are you still there?

from Airborne (2001)

The Mission

A stroll off the N1 beyond Swords, and its grip abruptly
loosens: back roads, lanes over-
hung with tall leaning hedges where it's easy

to find a likely field, an acre of anywhere
with a tree for a backrest, a half
of Paddy raised to the low sun: *Here's to no one*

but my own sweet fucking self
and the bastard miles we've done
blazing till the boot-soles crack,

from the fringes of the grey Pale —
skyline cocked with cranes, Millennium Tack —
to the black north, the raggedy west, my mongrel trail

(skirting the glare and the money
streaming to nowhere) back, back, back
over whatever it was I forget walked on me.

from The Sky Road (2007)

At Sea

i.m. Neil O'Brien

His stated wish—to be scattered at
the Forty Foot—was carried out

with difficulty. This wasn't a day
suitably in mourning, empty.

The weather was fine, the place rife
with splashes, laughter—life

(the kind of day Neil might have sprung
into the *great sweet*, like Mulligan).

On the road above, some of us gathered
to murmur a few words,

while we kept our eyes on that rowboat
ferrying his urn to a remote

and suitable distance. I looked for
the unlidded cloud (clay poured

like water) but could make out only
something they let fall, gently

as a life belt.

ROBERT GREACEN

Night in Dublin
January 1944

Stand easy now, while the world spins: look inward,
See yourself walk stammering towards the heart's defeat;
Watch the last surrender of the vagrant lamps,
Each ebbing, flowing into unregenerate night.
We are the defeated: all men are the defeated,
Especially the conquerors—they are the most defeated.
Especially the man who finds ambition's terminus,
Especially those who lived without perilous aim,
Who dribbled out their little lives in safe retreats—
All these are of the dark conquered.
And what of those who lived beneath the unhalting shadow,
Whose wounds were newly-salted day marching on day?
What of those who clung to their small living
Not because of any quality of life
But because they feared to think of death?
(O sweet annihilation, bride and mistress ...)
Were they all too of that defeated class?
No one answers the insistent bell,
No doors swing open into radiant halls,
No footsteps clatter on the uncarpeted stairs ...
Choose a bright morning for your questioning:
Sun still is sure although the night be obdurate.

At Brendan Behan's Desk

Full seven years I've sat
And scribbled at this desk:
Cards, letters, poems, autosnaps,
Diary entries, shopping lists,
While Beatrice down below hoarded
Memories of Brendan in a clutter
Of paintings, posters, photos,
With, for company, two dogs.

To Brendan's ghost I must confess
My orderly grey days.
At moments I'd like to be out
Emptying glasses in the pubs
Of Dublin town, blarneying
To actors, poets, drunks,
Then taxi-ing back to Cuig*
Not earlier than three a.m.,
Rousing the solid citizens,
Telling an uncaring world
How 'that old triangle
Went jingle-jangle
Along the banks of the Royal Canal'.

Instead, I sit at Brendan's desk,
Reading, scribbling, drinking coffee—
A Protestant without a horse.

---

* At Brendan Behan's Desk, line 15: 'Cuig' in Irish means 'five';
here it also is to be recognised as a street address.

Alliums

If I had a garden I'd plant
Some great-headed alliums,
Each a soldier one metre high,
Defenders of the floral world
Standing erect under huge heads.
In clumps or on border duty
They flaunt their summer uniform.
But is all this sheer romancing
Since, as I say, I haven't got a garden?

If I had a woman in my life
I'd take her by the hand
And lead her into the garden
That I haven't got and hope
She would admire the alliums.
'They're gorgeous', she'd say
And I'd believe her lying words.
But am I just a daft romantic
Since there's neither woman nor garden?

all from Robert Greacen: Selected & New Poems (2006)

ANGELA GREENE

Terrorist's Wife

A phone-call takes him
into the dark for weeks.
In the mornings, his absence
fills me with dread. I thin my eyes
to watch for cars that come to wait
down in the street. All day
I move from room to room. I polish
each spotless place
to a chill shining. Fear tracks me
like hunger. In the silence,
the walls grow wafer-thin.
The neighbours wear masks—
tight lips, veiled looks, such
fine tissues of knowing.
My mother doesn't visit. I drag
my shopping from the next town.

Once, putting his clean shirts away,
my dry hands touched a shape
that lay cold and hard. I wept then,
and walked for hours in the park.
I listened for his name in the news.
When I looked at our sleeping son
my sadness thickened.
His comings are like his goings—
a swift movement in the night.

At times, he can sit here for days
meticulously groomed; primed,
watching soccer games on TV,
our child playful on his lap.
But scratch the smooth surface
of his mood, and how
the breached defences spit their fire.

Now, when he holds me to him,
I know I taste murder
on his mouth. And in the darkness,
when he turns from me, I watch him
light a cigarette. In his palm
the lighter clicks and flames.
Balanced, incendiary.

Silence and the Blue Night

Here is the place
you would want to arrive at
after a long journey preceded
by grief and much delay.
There is a brown mountain.
Lavender clouds roof a sea
so wide and level the image
blanks the mind. Night is falling.
From the terrace you see a farmhouse
with ochred arches lit
from within. Its beasts are settled,
folded into rest. It is a scene
of domestic tenderness
offering its warmth.

But
it is too artful a backdrop
for the mother
calling anxiously to her child.
He has wandered off
beyond the rocks to the sea
leaving his blue bag spilling
its contents over the red tiles.
She calls his pet name, twice,
but the third call becomes
a frail and exotic sound—
some primitive bird's perhaps?

She risks the rough ground, mind
racing, she is
already elsewhere her torchlight
a flame plunging through lakes
of blue air. Now the clouds are
deeper purple, agitating darkly
to loose and grab at the moon.
In hot dust, among dry stones,
she stumbles; lizards
crackle in the scrub. The rocks
are full of shadows. The sea is a
hiss on distant shingle.

Again she calls but her cry
falls in thin and difficult
echoes and is absorbed
into the mountain. Is the name
really a name, or a memory
unravelling inside her skull?
Is she calling her child
or is she
the child being called?
She has forgotten where she is.

        She stands.
Night deepens, merciless.
The lit farmhouse, the terrace
with its globe of light
are out of reach now. Like ships
becalmed on a sea of dark,
they are remote, inhuman. She dips
the torchbeam. Around her
the indigo stillness glooms.
Silence and the blue night
engulf the boy
whose pale limbs she is desperate
to arrange in sleep.

Ancient Garden

To this ancient garden I am
a future ghost. A pale shape
in its tiredness that waters and weeds.
A warm pressure on the wintry earth,
a kneeling form bedding in plants
hopefully, like a pilgrim at a shrine.

It is aware of me, in its own scheme,
and tolerates the changes caused by my
succession. Feels, itself, wearied
by the seasonal round—the prunings,
the mulchings. A spate of wilderness
tangling its fragrances and it will know
that I have passed on.

It will be lost, of course, but slowly,
and not in my time. A beech tree
or a haze of blue-bells survives
for generations. But my devotion
will fall from it, evaporate. My
excesses and mistakes will run
riot to clog its furthest edges.

Though the clipped yew trees
those Victorian enthusiasts shaped
stand vigorous and green at any time,
a frail woman, her life grown thin,
would petrify if she did not move.
Would whiten among their harled roots.

all from Silence and the Blue Night (1993)

MAURICE HARMON

In those days, in that place

On Sunday afternoons we would sit outside
by the public road, fifty yards from home.
Ready for anything: Numidians, Chinese hulks,
Duffy's caravans in cavalcade; lions, tigers,
trapeze artistes, cyclists pedalling on their hands,
stiltmen walking with God above the telegraph wires.

Sometimes we had a yacht race off Skerries,
angelwings flitting about the buoys.
We never knew who won or if winning
was in anybody's mind, so gauzy their pace.
Enough just to be serene. From where we sat
the ocean was a glaze they floated on,
cotton motes, thistledown. Why think
of being first or last? The middle
might be best, motion gauged by slow drift,
twinkling companions in a milky way.

Winter gales bent trees in two,
reclaimed roads, smashed walls,
kept us at bay, dredgers of roads
where ships shuddered and died.
Tellers of old tales, revivalists,
we sank our heads in the sands.

In summer emerged again to see
pilgrims wading slowly through iodined air,
filling their lungs. Mothers exposing
their babies' heads to the wind-balm
and sun-chrism of this coast.

A bee mumbles in a grassy maze,
a ladybird feels the line across my palm,
a seabreeze softly stirs,
while on a whitened bough a chaffinch
sings the beauty of then and now

from The Last Regatta (2000)

The Long Haul

I'm here for the long haul, an old dray-horse
has done his rounds. They taught me to walk, taught
me to halt, snaffled spirit, bitted soul.

No more. I've taken a shine to unmarked ways,
forgotten paths, unapproved roads, lanes
I knew before the halter age, rampant

From lack of use, one went to the national school.
I roam about, see life in a frayed branch,
kick up heels, drink from the waters of reverie.

It looks like aimlessness but that's the key.
In time the dunce in the corner misses nothing.
I'm sometimes asked 'how do you put in time?'

I shy away, refuse fences, escape
the stop-watch mind. I've set aside bridle days.
From where I lie it 's a clip-clop to eternity.

from The Doll with Two Backs and other poems (2004)

The Gentle Years

They never told me what was wrong with you
Just took you off in the dark to that ugly ward
where you lapsed at once into a silent place
Neither doctors nor nurses could infiltrate
Where you closed the shutters of your mind
On guard against intrusion, let them do what they might
Let them peer and probe, tap chest and back
You kept your counsel, held your peace, even
When I sat for hours beside the bed, silent too
We had no need for words, not now, not ever
Respecting your decision to opt out, to dwindle
Softly out of sight, no need for fuss, that
Was not your style, nor mine, like-minded
Until one day I found you wide awake
And smiling, happy to see me, ready to talk
I said, 'wait here, don't go away, I'll get
Maura', and hurried off to bring my wife
Your gift to her as to me, time for parting
Time for love, for thoughtfulness, before the end
Before you went back into that silent place
And I resumed my quiet watching by your side
Until once again in the dead of night
They summoned me and Authority at the door
Questioned my rite of passage and I felt the rage
Bursting, it drove straight out of my mouth,
I told him savagely I was going upstairs
To see my mother die, that shut him up
And there you were breathing softly still, dwindling
Down, in need of nothing, little Red Riding Hood
Come quick, the woods, the shore, breathing while
I watched and waited, we needed no one, in
our secret place, dug-out of memories, until
reminding me you scrunched your face, not liking
the taste, and quietly went. I waited a moment
then went to tell them they could run in now
with book and candle, clatter about the bed
do things you did not need, your soul was safe
and had been so through all our gentle years.

CLARINDA HARRISS

Veronica Asks

Q. He came on like Dylan Thomas
only more height and less paunch
and of course not dead but spreading
poems thick as Irish cream
all over me and the whole bar
so of course I took him home. Imagine
my shock. Turned out he didn't
drink a drop of booze hung
his clothes on hangers made love
as if he'd known my every fold
and crease his whole life long.
Didn't seem to mind when I untwined
his arms and legs to answer the phone
a few times. Get this: Rose
at six insisting he wrote best
before noon. Kissed me and went home!
What can you do with such a man?

A. Put an old desk in the back room
where the east window looks out on
a birch tree pink in the rising sun
and lead him there with a kiss at dawn
next time he comes. If he comes.

from The Night Parrot (1988)

"Scrimshaw"

Hunting for the word I get
Scriabin, scrimmage, sabotage,
skittles, Scaramouche, skeedaddle,
mawkish, mishmash, skinflint, rickshaw—
I can never find the word itself
when I most need to name
what you have written on my bones
and, naming, tame the memory
of how the flesh with which you entered me
shot out a stylus
shocking as a switchblade.
How it etched my whitest places—
pelvis cup, hip-balls and ribs—
with pictures: little wooden ships
and Chinese gardens, castles, mountains,
whales, and whale-like clouds
above a stylized sea.

When I strip completely (and these days
there are damn few I take my skin off for)
they are amazed: "How weird,"
they cry, "a tattooed skeleton."
I'm looking for a coinnoisseur
who'll know at once,
and never once forget the word,
that all this scrape and scribble at the bone
is art, and cost me
my life's savings to collect.

from The Night Parrot (1988)

Mortmain

Gravity or Mother's soft little hand,
which one tips the pictures to all angles?
Which to be more scared of is hard

to say. Knowing a giant magnet herds
every legged thing by its ankles
is not without a subtle horror,

but to know Mother's been here,
dead and boldfaced as an Ingres
odalisque, to handle what's hers—

what's left of her weird hort-
i-culture, viney climbers inching
up the walls, those gilded, hirsute-

looking frames with familial harpies
trapped inside, abandoned by their angels—
it chills the healthy hormones

she also willed our way, Who can whore,
how happily give in to the ancient
pull and fall, when the witching hour

belongs, as it always did, to her.
She over-waters the spider plants
before she leaves. Every lover hears

the walls close behind her—hardly
the click of a husband's shotgun antsy
to kill, but still sufficiently horrid

to crumble to dust their hardest ardor.
They stumble into morning, shrunken.
Energy plays matter like a harp.

ANNE LE MARQUAND HARTIGAN

Tarte Apple

Woman who goes to the tree
who climbs the tree
becomes the tree   becomes a bird
becomes a monster becomes dead.
Become herself   she does not change
she changes   disappears   she is invisible

becomes virgin   becomes child
becomes apple   becomes pip   becomes grass
becomes the dust   becomes a path   becomes the road
she becomes the fruit   becomes the savour
she is the bite

from Immortal Sins (1993)

A Tint of Madder

You talk of Rose Madder,
You talk of love.
Madder and madder;
And the rose.

Fugitive.
Who is running running,
Do we run from love
To become madder and madder?

The Rose is fugitive.
Opens wide, dying in its love cry
To the sun and bee.

So we will talk of the fugitive
Rose. Not love.

No no, we will not
Talk of love.

Or dye like the fugitive Rose.

I will paint your spectacles
Rose Madder with love.

NOTE: Rose Madder is an oil paint;
a semi-permanent, fugitive colour.

from Nourishment (2005)

At Christmas

The old ghosts come out of the
cupboards, brushing off the dust.

They glimmer with hate.
They shiver with love. They own.

They have bought you before
you were born. A down payment.

The slammed coins
on the table. The money hurled
across the room. Someone

grovelled. But you were
innocent in your pre-birth
dilemma. And Christmas—this
moment of innocence.
The moment of greed.

Money is an innocent
substance. Love is never
innocent, but money is pure.
As pure as lust.

So memory creeps up loaded
with buried tears. Childhood
tears. Brimming. The pools,
the holy wells. The Benedictions.

MICHAEL HEFFERNAN

Manchild

Green thickets hiding me from all but joy
or night alarms that raised me up too far
toward enmity against particular
embodiments of the everlasting Why
left me at last with slumber in a dry
confusion. Thunder, birdsong, rainfall were
divine ideas of an earlier
redemption in the skin. I was a boy
of seven underneath. Multiple sins
against the sacred idiom of desire
cried out to be expunged. This joy I mention,
it was like candy-drops in little tins,
like tiny coals nesting inside the fire,
the look of larks taking a turn in sunshine.

What did you mean by that, madman? Whatever
it ends up saying is the thing I mean.
I mean to say precisely what the lover
says when he finds beloved words again
to make beloved talk for his beloved.
Nobody's reason for the things I do—
as I continue moving in the vivid
kingdom the likes of me can hardly know—
bears any likeness to the things I see.
You call it what you will—call it insane—
call it a temperamental vanity
of heart and head—call it the utmost sign
of something rampant in the poor man's soul
and ugly as a rat in a sewer hole.

But these were larks and these were elms as well
and tulips yellow, pink and lavender,
and here were squirrels facing each other
around a plumtree by the garden wall

and yes, I kept on thinking, yes, of all
the other lovely things to tell to her
including certain wonders that never were
except in nightsongs once the quiet fell
and I could listen to the silences
between words, where the words were hidden fast.
And when this knowledge came on me at last
that she might hear me if I said she was
the one bad woman that I ever knew
worthy of praising, maybe that would do.

But what is this you're up to, madman, now?
But me no buts, Alonzo, said the Friar
in green organza riding his gravid cow
with gaudy yellow horns that read DESIRE
on banners purply curling from them both.
One might do worse that ride a cow's backside,
crowed joyous Harry unfolding his face beneath
two eyes that roamed a virginal forehead
winsome and white as lily-petals fallen
upon a lawn where languid ladies strayed.
Let me be lethal, let me be sullen,
the captious Captain bragged: Nobody lead
the likes of us till I arise and come
from the holy city of Delirium.

Nobody knows the trouble that came then.
It wasn't long before I rose and went
and left behind the scent of all that pain
and sped to find that cubby in a tent
of hedgerows leaning green and difficult
beside a yard where other children sat
by toys their stranger mothers found no fault
to let them play with, and I looked at that
thin strip of grass between the dirt and walk.
There came some footsteps falling, and I saw
a lady wearing lady-clothes. Her talk
was plain: Boy, she said, if you do not know
the one thing that I told you, listen again:
Learn to disdain the things that want disdain.

I got up toward the breaking of the day
to take my bearings from that broken dream,
but all the streetlamp gave me was a room
much like the one I slept in as a boy,
except the buses didn't run all night
and there weren't any ships braying upriver.
Out where the planets were was dark as ever
for all my lack of motive to look out
and wonder anymore. Whatever they said
was there I took for granted, what was not
was not, and what a man could do I did
about the things I had some say about.
Anything much else was in the mind of God,
even the daybreak, what there was of it.

from The Back Road to Arcadia (1994)

Flood Watch

I'm going out to lie down in the rain
beside the peachtree you and I put in
the summer after the second baby died.
Before you left, you showed me where they were,
above the creek beside that old man's garden
he left to run to weed. It's all those things
you always knew about the dead and dying.
I saw everybody dead that belonged to me
and I fell over. I could not get up.
You got up and you left. Not too long after,
I knew you were gone for good. A night like this,
it isn't hard to think of lying down
and disappearing in the dirt. The creek
is swollen and the road is under it.

from Another Part of the Island (1999)

Cattle Seeking Shade

In Patagonia, where a friend would take
her lover's hand in marriage
under a wild tree that she knows is there,
though she's never been in Patagonia,
love blossoms bountifully and makes its vows
to no one. It can pronounce
the round vowel of the moon over the Pampas
or the black curse of an old galoot
on a nag galumphing up a curl of dust
to the hitching-post in front of the cantina.
Nothing mysterious
in Patagonia. I was transported
when a bird stepped off the top of the cherry tree
I planted twenty feet from my neighbor's wall,
which is a gray abyss the lacy disks
of the wild carrot where my peppers were
stir into spots of incandescent white
between the river meadow and my eyes.
They match the cloud puffs. They decry the grin
of the inflated yellow brontosaur
my other neighbor's grandkids come to splash in.
The news the light brings can be bolstering.
Even the noise of death sweetens the mind.
This often happens before midday.
It took me nearly seven thousand years
of the deepest sadness known to humankind,
not to mention loneliness and starvation,
to find this place so I could celebrate
these patient voiceless things. Nothing unspeakable
in Patagonia. When the afternoon devours
the blue above the mystical green below,
a field of cattle traipses
to the one tree in view. It is cool there.

First published in *Poetry* (September 2006)

KEVIN HIGGINS

Some Cold Water Morning

As downstairs the old man fades,
our days here seem suddenly numbered.
In a matter of months the developers will come
and throw all of this—these rooms
where MacNeice and Mayakovsky
came back to life—into a great big skip, as we
make way for solid types
with planning permission for wives.

The future is as enigmatic as ever,
as unpredictable as the price
of oil in two thousand and twenty,
but, terrible to think, that we might
one day wake and find
the last of the poetry drained from life,
be stuck there, some cold water morning,
glancing endlessly back as the door finally
shuts on all the great times.

from The Boy With No Face (2005)

I am Ireland

after Pádraic Pearse

I am Ireland:
I am the love-child of Brian Keenan and John Waters.
I drive Lebanese terrorists and Sinéad O'Connor bonkers.
I will go on forever.

Great my glory:
I am Enya's next album
and Michael Flatley's other testicle rolled into one.

Great my shame:
I am Frank McCourt's next book
and, even worse, I'm his brother.

I am Ireland:
I am Louis Walsh waiting for the Milli Vanilli to hit the fan.
I keep a hyena in my front garden and I am ready!

from The Boy With No Face (2005)

St. Petersburg Scenes

August. The small white cat
in the Winter Palace courtyard
is grabbing all the summer she can get;
as a woman takes time out
from her big loud ice-cream to tell
what looks like her husband
that the Smolny Institute is a place
where someone did something once,
but now it's a girls school. Later,

an old man plays chess against himself
at a bus-stop on Nevsky Prospect;
as the guide book reliably informs us
that above the hotel opposite
sits a plaque: *Leningrad, City of Heroes*
but all we can see
is a Coca Cola sign. And

on the other bank of the Neva,
as the day whitens, a man, whose
role in his own Bolshevik fairy tale
has long-since earned him a place
on the FBI's least wanted, waits
at the window of Lenin's study
for the disposable camera's
immortalising click; fumbles
in his pockets like a best man
whose mislaid that speech, and gazes
meaningfully into the past.

MICHAEL D. HIGGINS

When Will My Time Come

When will my time come for scenery
And will it be too late?
After all
Decades ago I was never able
To get excited
About filling the lungs with ozone
On Salthill Prom.

And when the strangers
To whom I gave a lift
Spoke to me of the extraordinary
Light in the Western sky,
I often missed its changes.
And, later, when words were required
To intervene at the opening of Art Exhibitions,
It was not the same.

What is this tyranny of head that stifles
The eyes, the senses,
All play on the strings of the heart.

And, if there is a healing,
It is in the depth of a silence,
Whose plumbed depths require
A journey through realms of pain
That must be faced alone.
The hero, setting out,
Will meet an ally at a crucial moment.
But the journey home
Is mostly alone.

When my time comes
I will have made my journey
And through all my senses will explode
The evidence of light
And air and water, fire and earth.

I live for that moment.

from The Betrayal (1990)

Dark Memories

Sitting in a dark room, she'd ask me
Not to turn on the light,
That her tears not be seen
We'd know it was like that
For, earlier she might have said,
If I was starting out again,
It's into a convent I'd have gone,
Away from all the trouble.

Or she would have spoken
Of lovely times in the shop, drinking tea
And eating Marietta biscuits,
Or taking a walk with her little dog,
After playing the piano in the sitting-room,
Over the shop where soldiers
Came and bought more biscuits,
When life was easy in Liscarroll,
A garrison town: before my father
Blew up railway lines and courted his way
Into her affections.

She stood straight then,
And, in a long leather coat,
After her mother died
She packed her case, left and joined him
A full decade after the Civil War.
And she had loved him in her way.
Even when old Binchy placed a note
Behind the counter in his shop in Charleville
Stating that when all this blackguardism was over
There would be no jobs for Republicans in his firm
Or anywhere else, for that matter.

Now bent and leaning towards the fire,
With blackened fingers holding the tongs,
She poked the coals; and we knew,
It best to leave her with her sorrow
For her lost life, the house she'd lost,
The anxious days and nights,
And all that might have been.

We ran outside and brought in turf
And did our lessons and vowed that we would listen
To what she said, of cities where always
There were voices for company, and churches
Close by, if never cheap.
We would listen to her story
And vow that, for her at least,
We, her children, would escape.

from The Betrayal (1990)

On Making the Three Decades
(For Alice-Mary)

Time will never make a boundary that could contain,
Nor space enclose,
Those moments you turned to gold
With a light that will always be your own.

It is your special gift
To see the need for joy,
To muster a courage
So far beyond the ordinary,
To make of friendship
Something sacred,
And feel the need to break the silences
That mask oppression.

These are no ordinary achievements.

We who were blessed with your presence
Did not measure it in time
Or confine it to any space
Nor do we now
Put boundaries of time or space
On all we wish for you.

May that which you never measured
Come back to you in love.

May the friendships you cherish multiply
And we are grateful
For all those moments of dark and light you shared
And placed in our indelible memory.
May you never be alone
In what you seek,
And may you live to see the decades brighten again with hope,
Beyond the darkness of War.

And when spirits lift
Behind banners
In all those decades to come,
It is a source of the greatest joy to know
That you will be there,
And in the quiet times too,
Plotting even greater things
For all humanity in ceaseless celebration.

RITA ANN HIGGINS

Poetry Doesn't Pay

People keep telling me
your poems, you know,
you've really got something there,
I mean really.

When the rent man calls, I go
down on my knees, and through
the conscience box I tell him,

'This is somebody speaking,
short distance, did you know
I have something here with my poems?
People keep telling me.'

'All I want is fourteen pounds
and ten pence, hold the poesy.'

'But don't you realise
I've got something here.'

'If you don't come across
with fourteen pounds and ten pence soon
you'll have something at the side of the road,
made colourful by a little snow.'

'But.'

'But nothing,
you can't pay me in poems or prayers
or with your husband's jokes,
or with photographs of your children
in lucky lemon sweaters
hand-made by your dead grand aunt
who had amnesia and the croup.

'I'm from the Corporation,
what do we know or care about poesy,
much less grand amnostic dead aunts.'

'But people keep telling me.'

'They lie.

'If you don't have fourteen pounds
and ten pence, you have nothing
but the light of the penurious moon.'

from Goddess on the Mervue Bus (1986)

Higher Purchase

We saw them take
her furniture out,

the new stuff
her kids boasted about
six months before.

The Chesterfield Suite
the pine table and chairs
the posh lamp
the phone table,
though they had no phone.

When it was going in
we watched with envy
she told her kids out loud
'You're as good as anyone else
on this street.'

When it was coming out
no one said anything,
only one young skut
who knew no better, shouted,

'Where will ye put the phone now,
when it comes.'

from Higher Purchase (1996)

The Immortals

The boy racers
quicken on the Spiddal road
in Barbie Pink souped-ups
or roulette red Honda Civics.
With few fault lines or face lifts to rev up about
only an unwritten come hither of thrills
with screeching propositions and no full stops—
if you are willing to ride the ride.

Hop you in filly in my passion wagon.
Loud music and cigarette butts are shafted into space.
We'll speed hump it all the way baby
look at me, look at me
I'm young, I'm immortal, I'm free.

Gemmas and Emmas
stick insects or supermodels
regulars at 'Be a Diva'
for the perfect nails
eyebrows to slice bread with
and landing strips to match.

They wear short lives
they dream of never slowing down-pours
while half syllable after half syllable
jerk from their peak capped idols lips.
Their skinny lovers melt into seats
made for bigger men
Look at me, look at me
I'm young, I'm immortal, I'm free.
The boy racers never grow older or fatter.

On headstones made from Italian marble
they become 'our loving son Keith'
'our beloved son Jonathan,' etcetera etcetera.
On the Spiddal road
itching to pass out the light
they become Zeus, Eros, Vulcan, Somnus.

JOHN HILDEBIDLE

Lamppost and Child in Autumn, Northfield Mass.

As if afloat on leaves
the pointed house looms

windows blanked by glare
lined by tree shadow
empty, lifeless: late autumn,
the distant hills barren
gray with dead grass, weathered bark

the near trees, huge twisted elms,
bare too, dark except where
the pale mark of limb-pruning shows

and alone she stands, looks out
dressed like a seamstress's pattern doll
hat, cape, gloves, sombre expression
only the alert black dog to protect her
alone, not a sign of footstep

she can't have walked there,
can't have been set up like an ornament
grew there, burst up from the rocky lawn
the leaves cover entirely

or was only thought there
to deny the empty house, the bland grey sky
the trees like hands splayed to hold off the light
the lamppost a thin gesture against dark

from Defining Absence (1999)

To Accompany A Gift of Flowers

still, for Niki

'Something new,' you said; 'Not roses.'
So I picked out these, nameless to me,
streaked pink, orchidean. I suppose

you'll centre the table with them: three
spindle-stemmed flowers, stamens stretched
toward the sun, tentative, lewd. We

speak, sometimes, this bloom-language,
more sensible to you. And if it tells
more than I mean, less than I want, that's

much of the point. You've trained me well,
and it's no little wonder, given my
wordy reticence. Out of these small

unknowing habits maybe a love is built,
O flower of my life, O nearest bloom—
keep them until and after they wilt

and keep me longer, in the absolute
centre of your wide heart's room.

from Defining Absence (1999)

A Modest Disquisition on Bovines

You'll have been persuaded
they're quiet and rather dim.
True, they don't look very wise.
Still, to have contrived such an easy life
(fresh air, no work, ample food)
is, speaking in evolutionary terms,
a sign of considerable perspicuity.
And as for silence, given the chance
they are prone to croon, in a baritone
audible for miles, all from
the sheer musical delight of it.

As for foot speed, it's true they seem
to prefer a stately, head-down amble.
But urged by some impulse
or a lad with a switch or riding herd
on a bicycle, moving down the roadway
say from one pasture to the next,
they can muster
remarkable, if inelegant, speed.

Far too large to make likely pets,
and expensive as well—you'd be shocked
to learn the pasturage
it takes to support
even a single milch-cow.
But they offer such fine companionship,
superior listeners that they are.
And those large, dark, liquid eyes!
It's neither accident nor insult
that Athena was called "Ox-eyed,"
and Jacob's beloved Leah, "Cow-eyed"

RON HOUCHIN

The Clairvoyance of Earth

It's not just that everything
on the busy planet was becoming
something we could worship or use;
not just the red circumference
of the apple, shaped for our hand
and mouth; or the lamenting moon's
face holding our tears in dust and stone.

It's not the electric day, able
to ignite our brains; or the night's air,
just the temper of love; and
not the canyons of light
stacked around like Christmas
for our eyes.

It is that everything's here,
and anything; that, like Mother,
the Earth knew us before we did;
that she bothered to make the gestures
and wait for us to find out.

from Death and the River (1997)

The light from childhood

shows growing up to be a lake
you row out to the centre of
and wait until you are bored
enough to look over the side
and see yourself changed.

Or it shows you running in the woods
until you forget that you are not the wind.
Eventually, you stop and see all
the trampled leaves under two tired feet.

When you were small, says the light,
everything larger than you was God
and everything smaller was a pet
that went into your pocket.

At one time, not seeing over the fence
turned all distances into fantasy,
so you walked in circles in the yard.
Later, light lifted you so far over hills
and seas, you were unable to return.

The wind that comes now from the once
friendly trees sputters your lantern
down to a fireless wick. And the only
face you see in the lake is the moon's.

from Moveable Darkness (2002)

197

Translating Water

(Mt. Nebo, Arkansas. 3/21/07)

What's it trying to tell us, with its sinuous fingers over rock,
organization of leaves in gullies, vapors in our breaths?

That it seeps into the coffin too as our bodies sigh Decay,
leaks from our eyes when we look down at the hole
dug in earth,
oozes through the cellar walls when river
stretches its arms again,
trickles along windowsills looking
for the rotting spot from the last rain,
dribbles from the cup rim when we are
too hungry for its return,
soaks all the towels at our feet,
leaches through the woodpile
sprinkling it with white fungus,
bleeds from twigs ends to
the rabbit's lips,
percolates in the creek
and foams up steps to
escape into our living room?

The first syllables of rain
make their way down to
our faces hissing the same truth
we heard under every passing
car tire on wet streets.

Just now ghost water fogs the valley
turning all memory into
a fading mountain.

BEN HOWARD

Holy Water

Was it a drink I wanted? Walking past
The public benches and the public toilets,
The roses in the garden, worse for wear
But still exuberant on trellises,
I turned into a churchyard, where the stones
Took on the slanted light of early evening
And voices softened, not in reverence
So much as confidence or privacy.
Strolling through the shade of the cathedral,
I found myself positioned by a wall
From which a faucet jutted, featureless
But for the metal sign above the spout.
Holy Water. Not a caption, really,
Nor yet a cataloguer's designation
But something more insidious than that,
A sort of invitation to a party
Or more respectfully, a gathering
To which I had no conscious inclination.
Speaking in Roman characters, it held me
Long enough to wonder where it came from,
That latent spirit cloistered in a pipe,
Its fluent cadence silenced by a valve
Though primed to be released at any moment.
All it would have taken was a turn,
A counter-clockwise motion of the hand.
What was it stopped me? Say it was a sense
Of something tangible behind my shoulder,
By which I mean no priest or risen ghost,
Much less a stern protector of the State,
But something I'd brought with me to Tralee,
A figment of a once and future longing.
Would that it might sustain me or be gone.
Would that I might pass and leave no trace.

from Dark Pool (2004)

199

Remembering Galway

That city where the streets are sinuous
and wind, as if predestined, to the river:
why does it come back to me this morning,
as though its smoky pubs and crowded shops

were daubs of paint, and I were but a canvas
receptive to the gestures of desire?
Even now, the sight of swans returning,
their stable forms afloat amidst the cups

and sticks, their necks recumbent on their breasts,
could be the mere projection of a mind
replete with specious emblems of repose
and freighted with its own uncertain notions.

Yet even now the memory of gusts
on Claddagh Quay, the reek of salty wind,
and the one red house—distinct among the greys
and bobbing in the water's undulations—

take on their own solidities and causes.
That was an artist's house, my friend explains.
The artist moved away; but what remains
is hard as glaze, as real as painted vases.

from Dark Pool (2004)

Leaving Tralee

What better place to set down furtive thoughts
than here at the Imperial Hotel
on Denny Street at seven in the morning.
Not so much imperial as mellow
and darkened by Victorian décor,
this dining room is vacant but for us,
that harried-looking waiter and the one
he waits on, namely me. As for the page
I'm writing over tea too hot to swallow
I see it as a sieve, through which the pungent
odor of last night's fish, the kitchen clatter,
the muted talk of patrons in the lobby,
and all the sights I have or haven't noticed
are passing to their final destination.
But even as I mutter my lament
for all things unredeemed, unrecognized,
I'm thinking of the Sunday afternoon
I pulled a yellowed journal from the shelf
and found in it the features of a dream
of which I had no other recollection,
no tension in the limbs or in the heart.
If it survives, that story of a ride
through cobbled streets in someone else's car,
it's in those sentences, themselves imperiled.
Lift up your voices, cries the aging hymn.
Lift up your cameras, your pens and notebooks,
lest the images that flash and fade—
those taut inflections in a fleeting voice—
be no more lasting than a passing thought
and no less formless than a jotted dream.

First published in *The Recorder*. Reprinted in *180 More: Extraordinary Poems for Every Day*, ed. Billy Collins (Random House, 2005).

GERALD HULL

South of Ulster

Snow covers red hills like a bandage as
we cut broken soldiers from Tyrone.
They shuffle fields below South Ulster.

Look north for tunnelling, switchblade
tracks, masks in pines. Sudden sighting,
bad blood, the clandestine.

No landscape here for drama. Plain life.
Winds paint out texture, geometry.
The Midlands, and then the Mid-West

(Longford untouched by Cherokee).
Parade the desperado's waistcoat
ridiculously. Poor reward:

Art grows cold with commerce on the
trees. The flat run of Volkswagen, stone,
cattle sours any Achilles.

Green met gold, family colours. Jones
for Wales. A country settled; danger a
Jacobite; remonstrance a brother. Skills

for a traveller. Money matters. The good-
natured man; a sizar at Trinity, placed
forever, scratching a window pane.

Grubbing in congeries. Dublin, London.
Low friends in high places. Geese, pigeons,
burgundy. Yellow gin, Anglican graces.

Decent men and straight roads. Meadows in
tidy sets. So safe this open country it might
be Hertfordshire, or Middlesex.

Written for the Oliver Goldsmith Festival at Pallas/Abbeyshrule, Co Longford 1997.

from Falling into Monaghan (1999)

Confronting Friends

I read of death (the slow drain of cancer),
hear tell of a move south. Another's left his
wife for one whose sullen girl's a dancer.

We men send out cards every other year,
the jokes tired but hearty. Plain pulses sounding,
now grounding. And few words to spare.

We who roared pale-chinned, threw out a toast
of curses then walked pierward. Fought in pubs
over tough verses that didn't work. The idle boast.

Wild nights at loose ends. Fitzgerald, Sartre.
Confronting friends, spilling poor coffee and the
heart out. A last cigarette for the martyr.

Now settled for the liberal wing, the Easter bonus.
(And the Standard for local sport: 'Dance Cancelled,'
'New Promotion,' 'Meat Factory to Close at Clones').

Yet still lionhearts in kind; tough on bills
but not domestic seekers. Hard on news, managed skills.
Eying that break through the pass to alien hills.

from Falling into Monaghan (1999)

Heronology

for Tom McIntyre

You dream two ghost rivers. Call off traffic,
its light and noise, ivory lurchings staining negative.

You sense music, birds scratching jigsaw hedges,
slate. Call off the wind. In the back of beyond roads
flesh-out land, vegetate.

You feel jolts of early rain in a powder sky. Call off
the long walk: live ibis, flamingos, fight with cloud
as condors die.

You own the light fantastic. Spin over chapels, halls,
the jackal tractors on the roads, their cartilage of cars,
crustacean, twitching pursuit.

You know loughs are mirrors (furred with ash). Wetlands
lisp cormorants, insouciance a drowning fisherman nobody
notices.

FRED JOHNSTON

The Angels Of The City Fold Away And Sleep

The angels of the city fold away and sleep
the last taxis mutter and dissolve beyond
sheets of rain and gutters weep—while
the summer constellations revolve and wheel
lovers dreaming dream of what is real
and of losing what they cannot keep.

'Bus-stops gossip of what they've seen and heard
the neon cafes blink and then go out, behind
naked tables wiped clean of every word
late lovers dropped about like gems
true for no-one else but them
the rose they offered turned into a sword.

The poets of the city smoke another cigarette
composing to their muted radios, while
insomniacs like you and I forget
how much we've learned of love and still pretend
to play a midnight game of being friends
each holding all the cards, afraid to bet.

from Song at the Edge of the World (1988)

True North

Hearing for the first time that my grandfather's
Brother had drowned edging round Cape Horn

A sort of want starts up, as if the axis of the known
Had tilted. One more small thing needing a place

To fit. Boxing Day—above a snug wee graveyard
In a sloping field a man walks, rifle broken, with

His son. Time paces itself, a slow mist danders off.
The headstone names are local, a carved roll-call

Of certainties and what's what. I do not possess that,
A rooting gift, but clamber up to touch something like

It through the rigging of my doubt, feeling with every pitch
And squall the need to let go, fall free into what will

Absorb me, drown me. My True North is always shifting,
A few degrees from far off marks a considerable distance up close.

from True North (1997)

Inkscratch

for John Moriarty

One day more desolate than the rest
He climbed into the mountains and felt
The child-hug of stone upon stone.

The stone is warm under the rain,
The roads of the hurried world are
A long way below, varicose, narrow.

And how to describe a lake, grey
As sky, light as air, an absence in fields
Of gorse, a blow to the cheek, whitening?

The scribes are in their cradle-huts
Plotting the end of poetry. The heron is
Patient. If words come to him here, he'll

Borrow them and speak them to a small
Room. There is a soft line of track
Punctuated by droppings, a paragraph

Beginning itself in sheep-bleat
Higher up, a page turning in heather-lick:
The sun, drying the inkscratch of his days.

JOHN KAVANAGH

Solveig's Song

for Columb McBride

Each morning I go out before the kettle sings
and scan horizons not knowing if you will come
— whirling dervish, Arab sheikh or aged cripple
bent over a gnarled stick.

I wait for you high up where the air crackles
surveying forest and valley that stretch
before me to the sea, listening for the low swish
of gull's wing as she comes to my outstretched hand
— two of us mutual in our longing
nesting high above walls of stone and ice.

I search for traces, for tell-tale signs of difference,
disturbance on the blanket-top that stretches to forever,
broken only by the hard green thrust of pine
or the slow lean of bared birch white-wigged and still.

But all is as before, as it always will be here,
savage in its stillness, barbarous in its silence.
I pull on a strand of hair loosened in the hard wind,
the gull flutters momentarily before settling again
her dark beak careful on my open palm.

We are two, tired and thin-worn from waiting
What does that say of you?
What does it say of me?

from Half-Day Warriors (1999)

Daybreak In Arhus Forest

Day breaks in faint, yet insistent silence
just audible beneath early morning sounds
— bird flitted air streaked with the dip and twist
of wing flash and dive as grub hunter
and insect gobbler go to work
reaping the night's rewards

darting between stretched strings
of gossamer spooled from branch and stem,
flashing threads of glass hair
that belly and bulge in breeze breath
that tickles branch and leaf into undulating dance.

Overhead towering birch weep elegantly
downwards into the damp bluing air,
cloudless but for the unravelling spiral
of a pair of early morning jet plumes
and a cotton fleck of cumulus
sitting where the blue settles onto the sea
or blankets the sloping roofs of faraway houses.

from Half-Day Warriors (1999)

On Your Way

for Pat Sheeran

Coffined now—the *puer aeternis* glow fled,
A bloodless sheen settled
And fifty odd years suddenly nesting
In your tallowed face

Your necktie knotted in that off way
It is when done by someone else,
Recalls a mother's final twist and tug,
An expert swish of fingers through your hair
Sending you on your way to school.

That russet wildness lies flattened now
And just like your tie—not quite right,
Coaxed into acceptable mis-shapeness
Ignorant of true flight and fall
Of fringe and part
—an undertaker's flick handed guess
Before sending you finally on your way.

ANNE KENNEDY

With One Continuous Breath

I have stepped out
onto that same patch of grass
a thousand times,
it is my Heraclitean stream.
You, jingling your car keys,
me, wearing the low-cut lilac dress,
eager for the Italian meal,
unsure, always unsure.
Only your hieratic gestures;
tipping the head waiter,
calling him by name,
assure me you too are uncertain.

Up on the hill our house
dissolving in a sea of lights,
under chaparral, granite decomposing
our oranges slightly sour,
more lemons than we could ever use,
the jacaranda;
life in such profusion.

Again and again I step
out of the car your father gave us,
too posh
too grand for newly marrieds.
The grass springs sere under my lilac sandals,
petal sleeves, beehive, eyes absurdly kohled.

With one continuous breath
I absorb the pungent night air,
never dreaming
that from all our years together
this moment only will sting.

from The Dog Kubla Dreams My Life (1994)

Cairo

Rain straifes our city bus.
Beside me, a lady with tinted glasses remarks
she has no umbrella,
she lost it months ago in Paddington Station,
that cave of bears.
No doubt some station master's daughter
is sporting it through London's seamless streets
or, knowing how they clean the trains,
it lies still furled in a corner of the luggage rack.
She can see it lying there;
(she'd give anything to have it back).

'Oh, I've had other umbrellas,
a green one once with a broken spine
that I couldn't lose in a fit,
but this umbrella was special
because it doubled as a third leg.
I need that, you see, a disguised walking stick
and the handle, a carved bird.

Ah, but one takes one's comforts
in the ordinary little courtesies.
Just today a lovely man gave me a lift
when I asked directions
to a furniture showroom out the road,
'Hop-in', he said and I was young again,
I was twenty and life was full of adventure.

I've bought myself a little house, you see,
and I want to furnish it.
Today was a very lucky day for me,
asking directions,
but nowhere in the world have I met people
who know so little about where they are—
the men are desperate but the women are worse.

Is it because they live under their
husband's protection?
Women do that, you know, they follow money,
they do, you know, they really do.
Myself, I'm a tough old bird, a wanderer, solo.
Did you know the French are building
a tunnel under Cairo?
Must be bread and butter in it.
The women here wouldn't even know
where Egypt is.'

The fierce low sun bulleting in
the scumbled bus
lights up her purple-tinted glasses.
I am hurtling beneath baking city streets;
I see Cairo.

from The Dog Kubla Dreams My Life (1994)

Buck Mountain Poems

1.

The road to Buck Mountain
ends at my cabin.
From the cliff it appears
to travel underwater and surface
as the lights that fly up the ski run
above Vancouver.
Last night my road sliced the sky
all the way to the Arctic;
my neighbour called it the Northern Lights.

2.

If you doubt the miraculous,
watch from my window
for snow in summer.
In the old snag
blackened by lightening,
a bald eagle is devouring a seagull;
feathers float past our open sill.
The white flash of discarded wings
breaks my reverie.

3.

This morning my neighbour
rushed in to report another marvel:
a ship sailed behind "The Two Sisters"
and never reappeared.
As soon as the fog lifts
I stare and stare from the porch
until the rocks themselves
begin to move.

4.

After a quarrel
lying on a stone above Buck Bay
I am surrounded by otters
tossing flounders, joyous sport.
They don't see me lying there
still as the land curve
that vanishes north.
I long to slip in with them
and float among the reeds.

5.

In search of trout
I walk up a steep logging trail.
The spring air spins out a frail heat.
Halfway up Buck Mountain I discover a pond
and catch dinner.
When my neighbour later boasts
he owns my hidden pond,
"man-made and routinely stocked,"
imagine my dismay.

6.

Walking home I'm mesmerized
by the glittering caps from beer bottles;
their fluted edges press deeply
into the muddy path,
companions of pebbles and shells and spouting ferns,
machined symmetry
amidst the crazy chaos of the ordinary.
If my neighbour ever stops drinking,
this brass trail will vanish.

7.

Last night my neighbour
menaced his wife with an axe.
He smashed the windshield
of her Cadillac in a drunken rage;
we heard their screams up on Buck Mountain.
This morning I saw them in their row-boat
quietly fishing for cod;
their knees were touching,
she was wearing his cap.

8.

The blackberries we bring down in pails
from Buck Mountain have caught
part of the summer;
leaves and drowned wasps tumble
into the enamel colander
to be washed away in a river of juice.
All through the short days of winter
we will spoon this wild fruit
from sky-blue jars.

9.

The summer visitors have all left the island;
we gather rosehips around their empty cabins.
The North Shore is ours again
and no one comes down the road
without reason.
Even the mailboxes look abandoned
except ours,
which creaks when I open it
in the cold morning air.

10.

When my lover goes into the forest cutting firewood,
he brings along a young friend and a volume of Schopenhauer.
The friend cuts wood for his own stove
and listens to philosophy all day.
At dusk my lover returns
without kindling
maintaining he was too busy to log seasoned timber
and all the young birches
looked like "widow-makers".

11.

A lightening storm knocks out the power
so I bathe by candlelight;
a bowl of oranges
glows with an oily luminescence
on a Persian tin tray.
No need to pull the curtains,
who would call by
on such a wild night?

12.

For days I have lived
in a landscape of Scriabin,
thirteen hours transmitted by the CBC;
Scriabin is blowing in the pines,
coming in with the waves;
Buck Mountain receives Scriabin
like a long-lost friend.
He is here among us,
diving with the osprey.

13.

Last night the wind blew from the southwest
taking the forest by storm.
Roots braced against northeasters
gave way in the rain-soaked earth.
So many trees blew down,
not even the rolling clouds
filled up the empty space.
Morning light
dazzles my eyes.

14.

Morning sickness rises in my ribs
rolling up into my throat
in salty waves.
Behind my head my neighbour's face
peers in the leaded window
looking for company.
When I jump up to put coffee on the stove
the springs of my old iron bed
seesaw a rusty song.

15.

For days now, the sun has not risen
above Buck Mountain
yet it lights up the rest of the North Shore.
We built this cabin in summer
in a spot full of foxgloves and daisies
never dreaming
that for months on end
we would live in a cleft of shadow.

16.

The pond at the foot of Buck Mountain has frozen over
trapping two mallards in a sheet of ice.
Knowing the neighbour's pups will venture out
and kill them for sport,
we risk the ice in our heavy clothes
and bring the helpless ducks
back to the cabin to thaw.
Releasing them later at the lake,
they are lost in a cloud of birds.

17.

My lover and my neighbour both hate holidays,
yet on Christmas Eve they speed off down the switchback
intent on cutting a perfect tree.
Six saplings later they roar back,
chain saws rattling in the empty flat-bed.
My youngest daughter brings home
a mossy branch from Buck Mountain
clustered with dark berries;
glittering frost seeps into the floorboards
beneath it.

18.

Except in high summer
it takes a fool to live on Buck Mountain;
smoke no longer rises from the chimneys
and frost splits the alders.
Only the generous moon
throwing a thousand fractured stars
into the frozen rain barrel
breaks the gloomy spell.

19.

Branches breaking at midnight
too loud to be rabbit or racoon
or the surefooted deer
moving with ease
on the steep slopes of Buck Mountain.
After drinking so much beer
has my neighbour lost his footing
and fallen among the crackling ferns.

20.

On a morning when our breath hangs between us
I say goodbye to my neighbour.
We are leaving Buck Mountain
for a sun-swept farm on another island.
Warming his hands over the glowing stove,
he offers to buy back the cabin
confessing he always knew the pipes would freeze
and that for months
we would barely glimpse
The sun.

Buck Mountain Poems. First published in 1989, with illustrations by Allison Judd.

THOMAS KRAMPF

The Brown Hat

They have taken my hat.
I know they did.
My brown hat.
The one that has no shape.
And that I got from Bolivia.
And wear in the garden.
Somebody came in the house.
And took the phone off the hook.
They were sitting there in my brown hat.
Making calls.
I know they did.
They left the receiver on the floor.
In the living room.
Who were they calling?
I hope it wasn't long-distance.
I know they did.
In New York you take the phone off the hook.
So the junkies can't call.
The line is busy.
Maybe they want to find out.
If they were really there.
I know they did.
Then they walked out.
In my brown hat.
The one I got from Bolivia.
And that's made from Alpaca wool.
And that I wear in the garden.
I know they did.
And that has no shape except for a tiny sun.
Rising in the hat band.
And that barely fits over my eyes.
I know.
I know they did.

from Taking Time Out: Poems in Remembrance of Madness (2004)

The Glass Slipper

Only the soul can walk in glass slippers.
Only the soul can slip its toe into the blown glass
shaped like a bottle.
Only the soul can walk up and down on the earth
like lovers.
Only the soul can know death and live.
Only the soul can resist the bulldozer's teeth
and the journey between kingdoms.
Only the soul has a glass buckle which is chipped.
Only the soul doesn't ask why the poet has buried
the slipper with his fantasy.
Only the soul knows the lover can give no answer.

from Taking Time Out: Poems in Remembrance of Madness (2004)

Downpour

for Françoise

Sometimes the rain falls
in a state of grace

On the daffodils
for the wrong reason

And sometimes the rain
falls for the right…

But the tether of the sky
loosened long after midnight
the daffodils don't care

As long as the rain falls…

from Poems to My Wife and Other Women (2007)

JESSIE LENDENNIE

Father

The first thing, crossing that bridge;
Tennessee into Arkansas,
the first thing I thought
after all those years:
where were you when I left,
when I said I wasn't coming back
what were you doing when I left?
You never said, I never asked
never saw you to ask ...
and years and years ...

I always wonder what they mean,
what does anyone ever mean by saying
'we grow old, time passes before we
know it.'
What do I mean now, to come back,
cross the river,
knowing all about symbolism
and the myth of rootlessness.

If you were alive would you tell me
what I want to know and allow me my life,
if you weren't dead would you meet me
at the next bus stop.

And maybe when you were young
you could smell adventure
and your heart would break over it—
to be free and skimming a highway
that you'd never see the end of.
Maybe you just wanted to be free,
and wasn't that all you wanted.

Oh, how I would love to see you a whole man
and know you had thoughts of greatness
and maybe you were too great, too free
to be a father,
and I could forgive you that.

Only now I'm so very far away
and it's so long ago
and no one to say right or wrong except me
and I say it, mixed with everything
I ever thought I was
mixed with what, most likely, will never be.
And, if I could think you were a hero
that you stuck it out like I wanted to,
would I do these backward journeys
would I run away again?

Here, as this yellow-grey light seeps
at 8:00 in the morning
another year is starting
and there is a drift to the wind
sounding low along the ground
and this light deceives me with movement;
the sea, from my window might be a stretch of field
in mid-winter;
and the day moves and the words go round in my head,
place names: David Acres, Promise Land, Clear Lake,
names that write themselves for me
in the rhythms of an earlier speech.
Clear Lake road—
didn't your family have a farm out the Clear Lake road,
and didn't your mama have 13 kids,
you the youngest and turned out a drunk like your daddy
and most of the others.
And grandma lived to be 85 and was as tough
as any woman in Arkansas
when once I believed that she'd died young
worn out from her husband's troubles,
but didn't she outlive him by years,
a Blytheville farm matriarch with a sadness
in all her children.

But daddy, can I speak to you now—
something in me believes that you will hear,
do you remember that bus trip from Florida
and in New Mexico the Indian bracelet I wanted
when all you wanted was a drink.

Why do I think this is all about love
and how you didn't know how to give it,
but left me with a craving for things
impossible to possess;
and I'm sure that you didn't want to be poor
with rich America all around you,
how you must have hated it in your heart
but blamed the drink and your Irish blood,
and when I left I could only be an immigrant
unable to live with your shadow in my path.
But I've come back daddy,
I'd even speak to you now if I could;
Ireland, I'd say, would suit you,
I see you there all the time.

Exile Sequence

Vision

and I wake again
at 4am

and from the back door
in a slip of light
I watch a black outline
against a neighbour's wall
marking the night

and later I dream
floating about the Florida islands
whose shining bridges
form one great Key

and the vision is a vast shape of water
coloured like neon cities
and the brightness,
which I had not remembered,
makes me, in my shape as air,
in my very being, a foreigner

America

Where were you going when you took up the stories
of all those lost people
and laughed across acres of fresh ploughed land
rolling, as a train through the desert ...
where were you going in that hot dust
your words burning the air
choking the breath of trees ...

Oh, I will always be here
where the smell of the wind become loss
and the turning of a simple leaf
the end of a lifetime.

And where you are now, how is it?
Do you still hear the tales from those who cannot
repeat your words, as I never could?
Am I silent as the sea, would I follow you ...

would I look beyond memories
because I have only these of you—
strained toward the horizon,
covering the mountains ...

and I see you as I must see you,
sea and air, mountains and dust,
and the people who are your people
are not mine, not mine.

Displacement

Seventeen years, and you didn't go back,
not once—
no, never

and not going back now
but backwards.

Is this a settling, as into old age
not longing, but boredom for my time
which was just too late?
Landscape?
Oh, yes, I miss the landscape ...
who would forget Great Salt Lake
or the Greyhound bus station at El Paso.

So many images, yes, and they haunt me ...
haunting as any puzzle or paradox
as any bus station at 2am

I didn't choose. The choice, however it was made,
came as thinly disguised as a sentence of an exile

when there is no native land.

The Search

This is Galway in 1988
and I'm near the sea at last
and I know the tides.

There are no hills here,
but a river through the town
river to the sea.

And here I am at last
on a grey day, in an old house
and the children skate past the door

and there is the sound of birds
and the hum of years,
as I sit here

and the children's voices
might be the voices of birds
taking the Atlantic wind
on their wings.

I could be gone like the wing tip
of the Heron,
vanishing far, far off.
Back to what has been replaced by a struggle
for a new speech
replaced by a language which is spoken by no one
but mid-water creatures seeking flight.

all from Daughter & Other Porms (2001)

JAMES LIDDY

The Apparitions

Sixteen poets (sixteen dead men?)
pose on chairs in front
of the restored Thor Ballylee
as maidens in national costume
(the last screech of the Pearse logo)
deliver mead to us on trays
I the junior on the last seat.
Colum gets up to sing the
swan song to the tower and crowd,
(Yeats's cobalt is turning tourist)
he recites rather lilts
the lines about the truth.
where the poet's lamp has shone.
I believe only what I believe
Yeats had a great churn
and made beautiful butter in this countryside.

Our arboreal Paddy Kavanagh
on scotch baking soda in Dublin
is not invited, too dangerous, too tall,
might say anything to that wall.
Paddy had authority like Yeats
in his face and arms and golden rudeness,
but the comic thing that happened
this afternoon was the Panamanian-Irishman
Tony Kerrigan falling down the stairs
of Glynn's Hotel breaking
a glass case in Lady Gregory's town.

Retrospectively: could I have been
a member of the poetic nation
instead of singing, dancing, and
courting in Wisconsin?

Rubbing shoulders a difficult business
but what spirited me away?
The silver and gold of my own mind,
and the half-bliss of ordinary life.
I can only describe what flew out of the trees
fringed by the poets, Austin after Padraic:
down the road past the cottages
Mammy and Daddy walking in the late marriage,
they had driven from Kilkee, the Peugeot
is parked up above. I fell
on them, this was surcease.

from Gold Set Dancing (2000)

Gold Set Dancing

It's the figures in the set, what they do,
how they execute their wins and weave
they come a little closer than you imagine,
how they start being great friends
thanking/being thanked for attentions.
The walls belong to them and me.

The feeling I had in 1940-something
hurtling out of the Paramount cinema
having heard Delia Murphy singing,
how a whole country could empty its throat.
I would move with boys-in-dreams through
that landscape, shawls, spinning wheels, masts,
a band of soldiers including myself.

For me at the beginning,
never a towered elite hermit,
the gold of Ireland did seduce
then I arrived in gold rush
town San Francisco;
mouths, limbs, kiss-talking,
I replaced home mind,
emigrated to god and play.
I burnt love down to the ground
then we lay there.
Dancing starts again, the ground
is lustrous, all gold leaf.

Happy those stepping on the floor.
If I, woman and man
as my poetry mouth suggests
a sweep from both sides,
take the dancers' hands and kiss them
their ringed fingers turn to gold.
I find now I'm in a set with you
(I'm in love with a man who's just married)
whose movements elaborate ....
Your sense of operations your midnight colour
unalterable by heat or moisture.

from Gold Set Dancing (2000)

What Does A Man in Love Have To Do?

A man in love: makes moan and labours to an understanding. A man in love has to take shelter in institutions conceived by history or philosophy. A man in love protects himself from the banality of love expressing itself (dosage).

In prayer for solace a man in love moves towards the temple. He trembles in guilt and hope because he has had a great experience. He wants to find out how he can give himself. Temple flowers are watered the candles are lit before the images.

What are the correct procedures? How are the safeguards for the beloved set? Divinity has discovered love first. Man has been handed it on a plate at a banquet. Perhaps what he feels has taken place before he was born. It is part of a retrospective exhibition.

But there are two temples. First on the moon in spraying light questions about love are debated basically its origins. Love is rehearsed and performed in a landscape that is like a nightclub. Participation is clarified. Do not make haste to the wedding. Clothes do not count. Wherever you are you may look on the beloved.

The other temple is the church where there is an altar for sacrifice. This is where we pray for each other whether lovers or not. For a moment we hold each other's souls. Sins are forgiven because at last something amounts to knowledge but sins are also forgiven because of attachment to specific people. The priesthood of lovers does not pass away.

Rules can be reversed they are similar for lovers and beloveds.

DAVE LORDAN

The Boy in the Ring

Where is the boy?
The boy is in the ring.
And where is the ring?
The ring is in the school-yard.
And what makes up the ring?
The ring is made of other boys.

What kind is this ring?
It is a spinning ring, and a jeering ring
a hissing ring
a rhyming ring
a kicking ring
a spitting ring
a teeth, tongue and eyelid ring, a hair and eyes ring
a snot and nostrils ring, a knee and knuckles ring
a fist and boot and mouth and ear and elbow ring.

Who is the god of this ring?
The god of the ring is unknown.
Jack O the Lantern maybe
or the scarecrow with the two axes
or a wailing midnight wind
or a sack of smashed glass.

What is the boy doing in the ring?
The boy is looking
at himself in the ring.

He is sitting down
and crying
and looking at himself
in the ring.

Why did the boy go into the ring?
The boy never went into the ring.

When will the boy get out of the ring?

Explanations of War

See all those bright lights whizzing around in the sky—
They are only the stars throwing a party.
And the shaking you feel beneath you,
The shaking that jars your teeth and your bones—
That is only the way the earth dances.
And the bangs and roars, the cracks and blasts and booms—
These are only the sounds of little spirits tuning their instruments.
And the horrible wailing that rises and falls, rises and falls above
the buildings—
That is only the rooftops shrieking their envy that they cannot fly off.
And the high fires that climb above the rooftops—
These are the rejoicing souls of our city flying to heaven.
And the black clouds of smoke blotting the beautiful woman of
the moon—
These are our dark acts evaporating.
And you my child, lying still in my arms,
Lying stiff as a mould of ancient clay,
You my child, you are only sleeping.

Driving Home From Derry, Feb 3rd 2002.
For Catherine

After the hours retracing
Bloody Sunday's route with thirty thousand,
from the Creggan Height right down to the basin of the Foyle,
through all those ordinary, downtrodden, every-streets to Free
Derry Corner.
After the speeches, the clapping, the marching bands, the mourning,
the silence, the wind in the flags; after the names were joined—
Derry, Palestine, Afghanistan—
time came for five to hurry back before the frozen road
would stay us for the night.

Out we drove towards Aughnacloy
past the union colours painted on the kerbstones,
past 'FUCK THE BRITS' and 'UP THE UDA',
past the watchtowers and the listening posts,
past election snipers and billboard hunger strikers,
on over a sudden blizzard's leftover slush and ice,
on and on towards the invisible line,
on towards the republic of signs.

When "See that there" said Brid, the driver, to Zack from Gaza,
jabbing through the windscreen at the Greco-Roman night.
"See that there, that's Orion. See the three bright stars across,
that's his belt
and see the two small ones down on the left, that's his sword
and see his big head and shoulders, see them?"

"Aha" said Zack behind her—half-asleep and dreaming perhaps
of diving as a child into the starlit Nile to catch a fish between
bare hands
or of the Gaza stars his father fished beneath
and of the stars his father's father saw before him.

And in the back seat our heads lolled at the frost-glittering stars,
seeking out *Hercules, Cassiopeia , Perseus, Andromeda...*

And in the back seat I got to dreaming
about how when the war is over,
when the curse of blood and soil is done,
we'll both lie naked and brave under a starlit sky
stretched on the fine sand of a phosphor-shimmering bay
somewhere out there in the wide world,
and how one by one, we'll tear the gods down off the sky
and hang new names for the constellations, you and I.

all from The Boy in the Ring (2007)

CATHERINE PHIL MacCARTHY

The Opal

The jewelleer in New Hampshire
turned opals on his palm,
focused a telescopic light
strapped to his forehead
on milk-white, blue-green, crimson,

like a miner at a seam
exploring a vein
along its length with fingertips
or working deep in the hill
to touch cracks in ironstone.

One he called fire
showed a hair-split
invisible when turned in the light
as the ocean bedrock at the Flaggy Shore
impinged with sunset

where we sat against the wall
kissing in the warm dark.
The air was silent assent.
A chain slid on my neck
and you retrieved the clasp.

I looked downn
knowing a day might come
when I would turn
to see half the opal gone
or the entire stone.

from This Hour of the Tide (1994)

Touching Down

When your flight touched down
did I ever tell you
I was coming out of Bartletts
antique shop at Ringsend Bridge
that Christmas after buying
five black and white
china kittens for my niece?

The street trembled with
jet noise. A seagull lost
altitude and buffeted,
went into a perfect glide.
Clouds over the city
turned to brine.
A juggernaut roared by

reminding me of Tenth Avenue
and Eighteenth, a flat
on the corner, shaking
to the foundations
into the night.
I tossed and turned unused to
intense heat and noise.

I leaned over the waters
at Ringsend and closed my eyes
to imagine you standing there
and my feet moving against
the earth's pull.
For a whole minute I held you
in my arms, hold you still.

from This Hour of the Tide (1994)

Child of the House

                 The headlights of the car
that dropped him late in the yard,
lit branches of the ash
splayed across the sky, as it slipped,
down the passage. Black patch

over one eye like an old soldier
he stooped at the door,
pitch of the night on his shoulders,
cleared rheum from his throat and spat,
then made his entrance—my mother
already winding the clock for morning.

Crutch to one side on the floor,
he sank into a wooden arm-chair,
propped on the seat of another—
the worn trouser gleam—
stump of his right leg.

               He'd come for whiskey
and restoration and from the safety
of my father's arms, stricken
I eyed our intruder, winks,
jokes, mock grimaces,
as if he found in my eyes,

fault with his own reflection,
my face unable to hide—

what the adults couldn't bear to show him—

through the dumb show of peepo,
all there was to know
of the colossal wreck of his body,

acrid odour of skin, faint whiff of urine,
his teeth stained with tobacco—
clay pipe in his hand still smoking
that would eventually kill him.

Our game, a tired distraction,
gave way to that ear-to-the-ground,
soon to be well-oiled divagation
on land-prices or cattle,
the cost of buying-in hay
or animal bedding, our flooded meadow.

It taught me something of friendship
and something of sorrow, an old seer,
chief in that territory,
bred on hardship and marrow,
our winning greyhound of a country.

Soon carrying me to my cot,
my mother let me wind the key of the clock
like my small train, set the hand
for alarm guided by her fingers.
As a parting shot he opened
his pocket watch, the second hand
skipping, tick-stop-tick
in even beats like my heart,

his one eye fixed me, a tawny eagle
seeming to say,

damn it all for a story
I am still the man I used to be.

JOAN McBREEN

Willows
i.m. Anne Kennedy (1935 – 1998)

> *"No, plant me,*
> *like my Grandmother's blazing dahlias*
> *in the subsuming earth,*
> *where I can be lifted,*
> *where there's a chance of resurrection".*

One day in March you lined up
willow cuttings on your table, stems wrapped
in foil, a gift for each of your friends.

"These will take" you said,
"they will take, I promise,
like no other tree you've ever known."

I placed mine in water
near the light
and waited for the roots to appear.

Even when they did and white fronds
filled the jar, I feared transplanting
my willow into the dark.

In September you left. The first frosts now
lie on the grass and on the willows
whose disconsolate leaves blow around us.

from Winter in the Eye: New & Selected Poems (2003)

243

On Reading Your Letter in June

June and the hedges are drenched with hawthorn.
It is evening. There is a silken rustle
in the beeches. I sit with your letter; the wind makes
the whispering sound of lovers' laughter;

laughing I wore a blue dress at the water's edge,
your fingers stretched out to touch me. Nothing
kept me from you. In the morning there was
lavender on the window-sill and to this I return;

returning each time to find it startles like something
that is itself. Nearly midnight, I stand
in the open doorway. I speak to you
but your back is turned. You are painting a picture;

picturing a stone cottage, alone and exposed.
Two people have arrived from another place.
Over a bridge. You have painted trees the colour of rust.
You sign the painting with your name,

your name that no longer catches in my throat.
Look at you wrapping yourself up in your dark coat.
See how the trees have darkened. The town lights
have come on and each house holds a woman.

The two in the painting survive. I finish your letter.

from Winter in the Eye: New & Selected Poems (2003)

Montbretia on the High Road, Renvyle

Between hedge and house
Montbretia flares.
Slow rain falls. September.
Season of stillness,

of hoarfrost
and early dusk. From here
at the edge of the world
summer's birds take off

from rowans laden
with fruit. When you left
absence and distance
became companions, familiar

as the curves on the road
and Tully mountain
in the kind of light
only this landscape knows.

I will begin again.
Montbretia bulbs
send out white roots
in water, on a window-sill.

JERI McCORMICK

Miners' Morning

From hillside porches they emerge
in firefly hats with carbide glow—
fathers, brothers, sons, who breathe
the river's mist and walk the rail-
road ties, a squadron of phantoms
who cross the dark bottomland to face

the chilling descent they'd never choose
if miners believed in choices.

Deep inside their shafts, the miners
forego Kentucky's curve of morning,
its warm ministrations that wake
the wrens, the willows, the common
blades of grass. For those encased
in coal's hard cycle, day itself
has dropped to dusky hearsay.

from When It Came Time (1998)

Your Mother's Grandma

for Celia Mary Whitaker

One of your uncles, Roy or Clinton,
would drive her up from the country;
she'd step out of the coupe in snow,

a woman from another century, in ankle-
length skirts, thick stockings, bun-pinned
hair, and you'd have to change your ways

for weeks—share your room, likely your bed,
hide your lipstick, listen to hillbilly talk
of folks you'd never known or ceased to care about,

go elsewhere to meet your smart city friends;
but she'd grow on you, listen in ways no parent
could, tell you things that almost mattered, and when

it came time for her to go home, leaving water
spigots and light bulbs until the next time,
you'd help iron her aprons, wrap her one good

brooch for the suitcase, wave goodbye
from the driveway, and hurry upstairs
to cry your mixed-up emigrant eyes out.

from When It Came Time (1998)

A Girl Running, 1847

She materializes alongside our carriage,
    a girl of twelve, we surmise, barefoot
        and garbed in a man's tattered coat.

Keeping the pace maintained by our horses,
    she focuses ahead, the coat fully buttoned,
        hands crossed to clasp wrists, cantering

unswervingly at our side. I tell her to save
    her breath, that we will give her nothing.
        Traveling here on business for the Crown,

we cannot furnish alms in this bogland of need;
    nor can we condone coins that are not contracted
        through honest work. Still, the girl runs,

never looking at us, never speaking to us,
    on and on in that garment of encumbrance,
        her thin face reddening, hair a moist tangle,

she moves with undiminished speed on naked legs
    that spin like spokes in uncanny harmony
        with our wheels. At a rise in the road

near Killaloe she acquires a rattling cough,
    sputters and hacks through the Shannon mist.
        My associate frowns, leans forward, pulls

a fourpenny from his pocket. I forgive him.
    A sprint for survival means something
        in these times. Some would even call it work.

This poem was the second place winner of the 2001 Davoren Hanna Poetry Competition and first appeared in *Writers Have No Age* (Hayworth Press, New York, 2005).

STEPHANIE McKENZIE

This Side of Acheron

i

Trees grow dense. The foreboding
smell of pine needles
like heroin, Hastings.

I cling to arbutus in showers,
remember a west coast
warning: they're full of ticks beneath.

I confess to Carr, her vicious and angry totems of paint:

ii

I was conceived somewhere
in the mid-Pacific, in deep
water. I am the salt-born

child of the drowned
and drowning still,
those who come up for air,

surface three times before
they sink beneath the weight of promise,
those who, with hearty strength, dig

their way to shore with fig branches
and anointed oil looking for dry land.
I wish to write a prayer

for my nation, though I am uncertain
where the gods are. Old Woman, Old Man,
old stones, will you bless our Maple Leaf?

Give reason to one caught between blood and the promise of snow.

from Cutting My Mother's Hair (2006)

Entries Missing from the Logger's Dictionary

i

The souls of old trees
will not give a wince
to spurs ground

deep. Red cedar, white
pine explode. Guts turn
to dust. Trunks send

friends to her door,
pronounce her love
caught:

between air's splinters, the forest plays poker with trades.

ii

Stumps clog our throats,
push out little cedar apples
on the bellies

of our necks. Days, we wish
we could plant
ourselves in lungs of women,

whisper then the wind.

from Cutting My Mother's Hair (2006)

Misplaced Couplet for Dead Loves

'Do these jeans make me look dead?' she asks.
'It's not the jeans', I say. The hip bone, skeletal,
demands a French cut, lined to the curves of flesh's
memory. Pin striped the arteries heave holographs
out from an absence of thighs or down by the calf
you once stretched, and it is the moulding death of leg
warmers, maggoty round your ankles that would tempt
me to grow you a dance. For him, I will all blades to lie
quiet in embracing grass: *Let me suck marrow from the teeth
of your zipper; don't get me wrong, you're not a dead fuck.*
I like my dead friends better than the living, though perturbed
by life's little twists and turns. Pockets betray hollows of sockets
seeking love, the banished of forms creaking husks
like armadillos too slow to make fast roads.

ETHNA McKIERNAN

Alzheimer's Weather

*"I think sometimes it's as if a storm were going through
her head and she doesn't even know it."*
—my father, on the telephone last night—

At first the weather was mild,
scattered showers at most
or the occasional dim hint of lightning.
She'd laugh when she'd forgotten
where she parked the car,
and so would we.

Lately now it seems a kind of static's
playing havoc with her brain
as small gaps of time explode into oblivion,
the way the weight of January snow
snapped the one brittle branch
off the burr oak last year
and suddenly a space blank as loss appeared
among the tangle of black branches.

All my life I've been afraid of thunder,
hiding, once, under my desk at 2:00 a.m.
in the old place on Selby over Captain Ken's.
I don't know why she doesn't reel or jump
the way I do when it booms through the sky,
or whether it's just one more sound
added to the clamor humming there
between her ears.

How I'd like to hold her as the slow tornado
approaches, how we'd all like to save her
from the darkness of the storm.
But her children have become remote

as third cousins, blurred shadows
indistinct as any raindrops
splashed on summer windows.

The burden of memory is to feel pain:
I pray she doesn't own it. Let her mistake
me for her sister and I'll gladly answer
in the present tense; let my father's banter
serve as courtship once again. Let
her small world keep her safe from any harm,
and in the stillness of amnesia
let her never know the sting or fury
of the desert wind.

from The One Who Swears You Can't Start Over (2002)

Addressing The Voice That Says I Can't

Like learning to walk again,
the first awkward stumble of shoes—
but harder now, since once you did it well.
This conscious movement is a gritty effort,
pride and dust weighed in equal measure.

Talk to that voice, the one who swears
you can't start over. Do not soothe it
with silence; it is a swarm of dormant vipers,
years of whispered lies hissing in the brain.
And will not go away until addressed.

A small girl's utterance: *Daddy, I can't.*
Not good enough, not smart enough,
not brave enough to cross the bridge alone.
Not enough. And so the voice travels
to adulthood, until risk becomes a frozen thing
reduced to mute inertia.

Listen: culture has teeth, has guard dogs,
big batons. Cross the bridge, my darling,
you are the woman it has weathered storms
for, refusing to rot. See, the greying planks
hold their old shape, yet.

Pet their dogs, tame those stiff hairs soft
with your touch. Perfect your twirl,
if necessary. Or bite back. But put your shoes
on. Learn and do. Keep on going, one foot
leading the next. You can, you can, you can.

from The One Who Swears You Can't Start Over (2002)

The Men in the Basement

The men in the basement are tired,
they say, of working without a contract.
I've heard their low grumbles in the evenings
as I read by the stove, and the word union
has slipped through the floorboards once or twice.

It was easier when there was just one—
mild, handsome Jake who fixed the faucets
when they leaked, bled the radiator pipes in Fall,
hung paintings on the bedrooms walls
and was happy with a plain pork chop dinner,
desserts a few nights a week.

Then Ted knocked one night, his bag of metaphors
slung on one shoulder, the whole bright alphabet
spilling on the threshold. Because the house repairs
were caught up and because the poem
I was working on was a little bare, I let him in.
We talked till dawn in the kitchen, and I swore
I'd only borrow what I needed from his bag,
then made another bed up in the basement.

These days it seems a little servicing
will only go so far. The philosopher complains
I no longer help him wring meaning
from the stars, the accountant disapproves
of the red ink in my books, and my handyman
threatened to move on today when he found
the poet in my bed tucking images inside my pillow.

The trouble with fantasies is that
they become unwieldy, swelling into great,
lumbering bears with large paws
who outgrow their downstairs beds
and begin to roar for more food, more
attention, more me. I hate to add
a locksmith to the mix, but
I need one for that basement door.

(from a forthcoming collection Sky Thick With Fireflies*)*

TED McNULTY

The Tenor—New York 1941

That night rain put a shine
on New York as we passed under
a filigree glass marquee,
doormen bowing to our tickets,
my mother and father so proud
to show me one of their own
singing the melodies of Moore,
the great tenor, hair shining,
his tuxedo with the green sash
in the gold of Carnegie Hall,
a place good enough for Rockefeller
my father nudged me to remember
and now I see his eyes full
as if suddenly he was a millionaire
who had come from the land
where the road to Ballyduff
was made of marble
and a Count sang in the square.

from On the Block (1995)

The Immigrant

The Yank in me
rides the sound
of loose chippings
on a Cavan road,

a neighbour
taking me along
to the cattle auction
in a shed of wet coats

where I'm the stranger
in a ring of men
but close to the creatures,
smells old as straw.

Driving back, the radio
plays 'California Blue'
as I go in two directions,
neither of them home

While road stones crackle
the hard words of immigrants,
telling me now I must livle
in the cut of myself.

from On the Block (1995)

Talking To Keats

It was enough
to read city streets
until you came after me
like a little teacher
down the aisle.

You were the smudge
in my school book
that started the doubt
I wasn't to smart.

By the lip you had me
while you spoke
the one languge
never heard in New York.

The way your words
were above me—
I was the immigrant again
outside iron gates.

Today I read
of the red spots
you'd find
on your pillow,
and now we're level
no words between us.

MÁIGHRÉAD MEDBH

Threshold

no matter how broken
the ground will transport me
through lashings of colour to light that consumes me
holes in my body and all of them gaping
to haul in the bleeding / to heave out the blocking
the rocking is starting / i'm shaking and spitting
my head is split sideways too rough for my sleeping
a roar from my chest and the singing removes me
eyes thinning out and my soul staring down me
the prince of my bed-foot is streaming around me
he's waited through days for the chance to embrace me
we're rushing through spirals of picture and sounding
and feelings too free for a flesh understanding
through flurries / through battles
through love-making / haggles / hassles
hauling / bleeding / screaming / smoking thatch
the withering / cloud / crowds
thinning eyes
i rise

from Tenant (1999)

My Day

March 1845

i sit up in our bed of straw and listen to the birds
we're a wild bunch of bodies all the same
—straw over, straw under—
mammy shuddered when i wondered
if we're kindred to the animals with no souls
she crossed herself and cathal frowned and i stuttered
to explain—
we're in the same byre, walk the same miry floor,
we eat together, sleep together in our clothes
the connors children run out naked
not just summer, winter too
even them that's in the bigger places
under gowns and mirrored faces—
well i never finished out my say
cathal went 'you better not' and i was on my own again
thinking things that turn me into something wrong

there's she's up and by the fire like she always seems to be
like an israelite waiting for the word
the boys are on their straw, daddy's in the loft
they're asleep but it's never silent here—
hoo and cluck and grunt and chew and the sounds that
blow in to us
people passing, children crying on the road
with the slit of window light and the brightening of the turf
i can see that she's looking at me straight
she gives her sunday of a smile
—you know i'd see it dark or bright—
and i make out what she's holding in her lap
it's my only good bodice that i stitched up late last night
so i'd cut a dash like any at the wake
'rena, girl, she says, you're a fine young woman now
i was thinking this must be your birthdate'

she says i needn't wish for more than this
the birds gone mad with spring
potatoes in the pit

myself pink and healthy and fourteen
i get water from the well and look closely in the pail
splash my face with my reflection, comb my hair
i'll be watching for the man who'll know i understand
who'll whisk me like a story far away
a poet or professor or a travelling prince
i'll be pretty, simply waiting for my day

from Tenant (1999)

Unified Field

For one moment when you express the air,
when the hard chatter of your tongue
turns to silver silk and slides you to the wind—
for a moment when the air inhales you
and you rest in its transparency like a
thought you don't know you're thinking—
wouldn't you liive this jacketed life?

For one moment when saffron bursts from your belly
like a lesser sun, and you know how it feels
to be a hundred spears of light—
for a space out of time, the ocean of all the tenses
beneath you with its nonchalant waves,
and you a cap on those waves, blowing off—
wouldn't you stick this sucking earth?

And when, in the last heave, you've gone to ground,
scattered, ash or dust, down with the ocean-bed bones—
isn't that the same as expressing the air,
supersonic sil, thought without thinking,
morning saffron, the absense of tense,
a cap taken by a breeze?

JOHN MENAGHAN

All the Money in the World
(for R. V.M., 1954-1980)

Four thousand miles from the last place
I saw you alive, a drunken young girl
on a London double-decker in Camden Town
who's spent the last five minutes mouthing off
at everyone and everything she sees
suddenly cracks the window at her high perch
and shouts at the top of her range to someone below:
'Ray! … Murphy! … Ray, you fucker! …
Murphy! … Ray! … Hey, *Murphy*! … Ray!'
It takes every last shred of sense I've got
not to look down, hoping to find you there.

I cruise a record shop for cheap cassettes
and find Ry Cooder's Paradise and Lunch.
It looks familiar somehow; I recall hearing it.
So I buy it, take it home, play it all night.
Until it comes to me you'd owned the disc and
suddenly I'm missing you unspeakably while Ry
sings 'Ditty Wa Ditty' or 'Fool About a Cigarette.'

In the mail this morning a note from my mother
reminding me it's five long years you're dead.
That means you're gone nearly as long as I knew you,
choked on poison fumes when a Camel slipped
from your callused, weed-stained grip in
New Orleans, conked out on the couch as it
smouldered to flame. They found you dead
beneath the bathroom window—smoke, not burns.

I could say you were just a fool for a cigarette,
or hope you're having lunch in some paradise.
Instead, I fill a tumbler with Jameson's,
listening as Ry sings a chorus you used to love:

Feèlin' good, Feelin' good
All the money in the world
Spent on feelin' good

I let this *Uisce Beatha*, water of life,
coat my throat with its warm, deceptive glow
and echo that girl in a whiskey-hoarse whisper:
Ray ... Murphy ... Ray, you fucker ...
Murphy ... Ray ... Hey, Murphy ... Ray

from All the Money in the World (1999)

What She Wanted

She wanted to paint
and she has painted
but too little.

She wanted to wander
and she has wandered
but too little.

She wanted to dream
and she has dreamed
but too little.

She wanted to love & be loved
and she has loved & been loved
but too little.

She wanted to live
and she has lived
but too little.

She never wanted to die
yet she has died
little by little.

from She Alone (2006)

Busaras Encounters

I.   In the Waiting Room

Alone on a bench
when an old man
sits down beside me
and after a minute
starts to chat.
I glance at him
briefly but look
away as quickly,
thinking it's money
he'll want in the end.
He goes on for a bit,
then senses my
detachment,
guardedness,
lack of response.

He stares intently at
me for a moment till
I turn and meet his gaze
resignedly, and move my
hand toward my pocket
searching for change to
send him on his way.
His eyes grow sad then
and he says imploringly:
"Don't mind me now;
I'm just an old man
with no one to talk to."

My heart rises to my
throat and my eyes
mist ever so faintly
over as I croak:
"You're alright so."
But whether he's read
my mind or said

his piece, he rises
now and says
goodbye and goes,
slipping down the row,
then out the door.

I sit, abashed, and stare
at all the lonely faces
floating through the room,
waiting alone and chastened
till my coach is called.
Then rise in turn and
gather up my things
and take my leave
of no one as I go.

II.   *In the Travel Centre*

I ask for the young woman I've never met
but need to see about a refund, all our exchanges
up to now having been conducted electronically.
She's off to my left, helping an old lady
book her trip. The old gal seems
a little scattered, and I ask myself
how long she'll likely be, what remains
of youth's impatience rising up in me.

The young one's patient, helpful, but not warm.
"All the cheap fares are gone for Monday, love,"
she tells her customer, who looks alarmed,
breathes six shallow breaths, but then decides.
"Tuesday, now. Would that be better?" she asks.
"Tuesday, Tuesday, let's see, yeah,
Tuesday's grand. Tuesday to Tuesday
is it then?" A long pause, then "Yes."
The young one looks up from the screen
just to be sure. "Yes, Yes," the old one says
to reassure them both. Then starts to stuff
a stack of papers back into her bag.

They're badly folded and so hard to stow.
She tries three times and fails. At last
I say: "Can I help you there?" Just then
she manages to shove them in her little sack,
then smiles at me triumphantly. All seems
well until she tries to slip arms through the straps.
"Could you?" she asks me with another, shyer
smile and turns her back to me. "Of course,"
I say and slide the second strap up her thin arm
till the pack rests between her shoulder blades.
"Thank you," she says. I smile in turn.

The young one hands her up her printed ticket,
turns to me. "Hello," I say and tell her who I am.
Her face lights up then and her voice sends forth
the warmth I'd wished the old one could enjoy.
"Give me a minute now, till I find your file."
The old one turns and says: "They know you here,"
a mix of puzzlement and pleasure on her face
that a Yank should get a warmer welcome than herself.
"They do," I say, embarrassed, then explain.
"It's just because I spend a lot of money,
taking my students out to Newgrange, Galway,
and the like." This satisfies her curiosity
and seems to soothe her ruffled feelings too.
"Enjoy your time here," she says as she moves away.
"And you your trip," I say as she drifts to the door.

"Now, then, how are you," says the young woman,
back with her folder, "are you keeping well?"
"I'm grand," I say, who've learned to talk the talk.
And I'm glad for her warmth and friendliness,
and for still being young enough to notice
that she's cute, and wonder if she's spoken for.
But my mind's mostly on that old one's trip,
which from the look of things might be her last,
and on my parents smiling down at me
who taught me kindness was the great virtue,
and like all virtues its own sweet reward.

ÁINE MILLER

Brown Stew with Dumplings

—*The October clay of sky,*
oncoming rain, migraine—

She sieved white flour
Watching it float and fall.

Saw this evanescence
Thicken into balls,
Pastecoloured,
On a kitchen plate, a summary.

—*Whey face in kitchen glass,*
buttoned-up, coarsegrained—

She put a lid on them, trusting
The air she captured
In that first free fall,
A little warmth.

from Goldfish in a Baby Bath (1994)

269

The Art Class

Trees are terre verte with a fan brush,
shadows indigo. Wrist flicks create
delphiniums or a laden hawthorn bush,
and there's no more to primroses than
some cadmium splodges with a late,
pale stroke for centre. Anyone can

paint a sky, a flower, a pool, be mistress
of flat strokes, broad sweep, what seems.
A thing's true features, loved face, is less
a subject than the space it fills, the role
the shape and colour plays redeems
its imprecision in the mass. The whole

class raised their brushes for May Garden.
Lawns and sky swam onto canvas
as deft filberts dabbed in margins,
orange wallflowers, white falls
of clematis through stippled cyanotis,
and yellow daubs for dandelions. All,

save one, had pictures full for framing,
when the sun crossed the wall. She stood,
like Adam in the act of naming,
assailed by petals, the clamouring of all those
grass tips, pistils, leaves, bite of lion-toothed
dandelion, sally flails, and chose

a daisy. Cupping its face she would know
its lineaments before she made a start
on canvas. Painstakingly she will show
each petal and the two hundred and fifty
three yellow flowerlets at its heart.
It is done. She calls it *Refugee*.

from Touchwood (2000)

Sloughing

Her eyes scrunch so she cannot see
the selves the shower is sluicing,

selves who make an unforced entry
in the unbarred hours of sleep.

Her gloves exfoliate last traces of
that commune they have become,

squatters in her House Private.
Preoccupants, they rise to greet her,

shadowing every movement.
They are too familiar, her familiars,

eliding her voice, sharing her clothes,
sharp-eyed slivers winking at her

in the fluid dreams they brittle.
She fears them. They are after her

secret, pushing the rights of kinship,
blood ties, matching DNA, best buddies,

they would swallow her whole.
These glimmer women heatseek her core

till she cannot wait to surface
to rucked sheet, the duvet's damp embrace,

a count-up of night's erosions.
The shower scours all memory.

She closes its door on them,
on the last long groan, the quartet of gurgles,

and shrugs on the robe of day.
Damp prints trail her away.

PATRICIA MONAGHAN

The Butterfly Tattoo Effect

Does the flap of a butterfly's wings in Brazil set off a tornado in Texas?
—Edward Lorenz

Charlene was fifty when she got it:
one small butterfly, perched on
her right shoulder, bright blue
with stipples of pink. Everything
in her life seemed safe by then:
husband, children, house and dog.
She wanted to be a little dangerous.

When she left the Jade Dragon
she called her oldest friend, Maggie,
in Florida, with the news. A tattooed
gal at fifty, she bragged. I ain't down yet.

Maggie laughed that throaty laugh of hers.
An hour later on her way to work,
she stopped on a whim and bought
a gallon of red paint for her door.
That night, she didn't drive straight
home but stopped for a drink at an old
haunt from her more dangerous years.
No one she knew was there, so she talked
awhile to Flo, the bartender, told her about
feng shui and red doors, and oh yes, she
mentioned the tattoo just before she left.

It rested in Flo's mind all night as she
uncapped the beers and mixed the drinks.
She was warmer than usual, sassy and loud.
Things got wild. There was dancing.
A new woman stopped in and picked up

one of the regulars. Washing up past midnight,
Flo thought of her old friend Paula, who
lived in California. It was still early there.

Flo picked up the phone, right then,
and called. Somehow the subject of Charlene's
tattoo came up. Paula had been thinking
of getting one too. Why not? Life marks us all,
why can't we chose our scars just once?
They talked till late. The next day Paula
walked into a dealership and bought
the reddest car she saw. By nightfall she was
driving fast, towards the south. And the next morning

the world awoke to news of seismic convulsions
on every continent brought on by
the simultaneous shifting into high gear
of millions of women in sleek red cars.

from Dancing with Chaos (2002)

Fibonacci Stevens

Chaos
is
the law
of ideas, of
improvisations and seasons of belief.

And
yet
relation appears,
a small relation:

This
object
is merely
a state, one
of many, between two poles,
so, in the metaphysical, there are these poles:

Nothing
exists
by itself.

Ramon
Fernandez
tell me
if you know
why, when the singing ended
and we turned towards the town, tell why
the
glassy
lights, the
lights in the
fishing boats at anchor in

the
harbor

were
falling
like notes
from a piano.

Thus
the
constant violets,
doves, girls, bees
and hyacinths are inconstant objects
of inconstant cause in a universe of inconstancy.

from Dancing with Chaos (2002)

A House in Renvyle

We pass the hours measuring the weather:
the Twelve Bens emerge and then dissolve
in mist and pearly cloud; a storm will gather
over Tully Mountain, break above us, then resolve

itself in light mist on the Diamond's crest.
We watch the sun illuminate the lake
which dulls then to a sheen of gray. Just west
the sea, invisible from here, makes

all this happen. At night the waiting wind
tests every wall. Within, we dream
of animals reincarnating as our kin,
of spirits rising from the bogs like steam.

NOEL MONAHAN

Candle

Milkrush at evening
Show me your shadow
On the tallowy field.

Leafspear of light
Trembling in the dark
Cradle my fear.

Waterlily at midnight
Pillow my dreams
In your oily well.

Snakeroot of smoke
At daybreak
Incense the morning.

from Snowfire (1995)

The Funeral Game

That winter we came to terms with death.
Every shoe-box was a coffin
For anything small and dead
And we wrapped them in calicoes, velvets ...

We grabbed hats, coats, umbrellas,
From the hallway to dress as mourners,
Someone struck an iron girder in the hay-shed
To sound the funeral bell,
John Joe beat the dead march on a saucepan.

We held wakes, issued death certificates
To old crows, kittens, chickens ...
Lined the graves with stones,
Erected crosses with ash sticks.

We pretended to cry, struggled with Latin prayers,
Filled the wet graves in the clover field,
Genuflected in the direction of a whin bush,
The rain pelting down,
We left by a side-gap,
Back to the hay-shed for tea, bread, butter ...
For all who travelled long journeys.

from The Funeral Game (2004)

Boochalawn Buí

The wild bee tosses my yellow hair where
I reside along a closed railway line
Since government surveys mapped my decline,
From that day forward pain was always near
Living as I do in mist, fog and fear
Staggerweed, stammerwort, names from outside
With their intended power to deride
Can't rob me of pollen and nectar here.
I love the risk, pleasure of the abyss
I am the shomeer come out of darkness,
Forsaken, I close my daisy yellow eye
On the grey incontinent Irish sky,
Whisper my name whenever you need me
Boochalawn, Boochalawn, Boochalawn Buí.

ALAN JUDE MOORE

Heading into darkness outside Athlone

Heading into darkness outside Athlone,
stolen segments of parchment, the landscape;
farms and various apparatus for hanging
names on scraps of people and places.
The roads and river look old, planted
beside an automated transportation depot.
Some horses stand mouths gaping open.
Likewise, after a hard night of drinking,
heading into darkness between Athlone and Moate;
battlefields, externalised historical centres.
Tiny pities of the aristocracy still roll down hills
to mingle with the smell
of bogwood and treacherous bog.
In rooms where no-one laughs,
(or has even come close to a tear for some time),
sentiment is wrapped in a paper bag
of title deeds and co-operative agreements.
Through cat's eyes, a service light or EXIT sign,
heading into darkness outside Athlone,
a city waits like a sentinel hung out to dry.
Seated nine rows down on a private coach,
heading into darkness outside Athlone.
History coils around my leg
and begs I believe the future scheme of things
is not decided by horses or men; insects
crawling up the window fall back down again.

from Black State Cars (2004)

Lord Pembroke

Kavanagh and Greacen had breakfast together
in a lodging house around the corner,
off Pembroke Road. Years ago.
Pembroke Road, these days, finance
and tailored shirt tails.

Move on.

Baggot Street is a tower turned on it's side.
It rolls it's people from doorway to doorway
like loose change. There's a girl in a coffee shop
who I saw once five years ago in a park.
I suppose she's moved on by now.

Strange, I met Greacen last week

and walked by Kavanagh's house this morning.
Now this face from five years ago;
this face I never said two words to.
I can't blame either man for that—

the address I wanted, on Pembroke Street.
My fault, and the aristocracy of course
for mapping out the world and quickly
naming it before they leave.

from Black State Cars (2004)

Passing the Telegraphs

Clouds open over the line
and fires burn somewhere across the flat topography.
We are crawling through the snow like an endless hunk of metal.
When we get there I will have nothing to tell you.
Only that along the way we were seated in carriage number five,
drew breath through the door that would not shut completely
and drank beers with a girl from Peter.

Trees continue across the plain.
It is deep out there in the space between us.
A dog lay down on the platform at Tver
and maybe on kinder days was fed sausage by old ladies.
It's harder now to look into peoples eyes
and reprimand them for having left
another living thing half dead and alone.

Bursts of daylight exhausted like neon explosions.
Night falls past the silent tapping of telegraph poles.
Having sold themselves across the Empire,
the women of the Kavkaz gather up their bags
and sit for a while beneath fluorescent lights.
Fires are burning somewhere on the flats;
we are waiting for the station to take us in.

TOM MORGAN

Walking the Dog

The lake is in November stillness,
swans ripple the cold glassy blue;
a dog sits still against the wall of a bridge
and plastic bags kill the blackthorn's view.
Pigeons arc like V's in the air and
boys aim stones at ducks in the lake;
Cavehill to the north is capped with clouds
and drunks on the verge are on the make.
My dog pulls tight past a woman walking,
her smile all teeth in the shadowed light.
I put one foot in front of the other,
read words of hatred scrawled in the night;
watch four schoolboys chased down the road,
their feet echoing with 'Kill the Fenian B's';
their cursing and yelling rising upward,
past the barracks and the spectral trees.

from In Queen Mary's Gardens (1991)

Tooneenvalley

for Nancy, Matt and Zach across 'The Abyss of Tears'

Between the loaded fuchsia and the broken fir,
the moon rides where the road meets hedges.
Fields carry the mountain and brace Atlantic
and time is laid to rest in flooded meadows.
There is no time for cowards and the shuffling badger
yearns for wheels of cars in silent badgers' corner.
Below the clasai snow is heaped on snow and
my love lies there with charcoal in her mouth.
Let water turn to mist and teach me to persist
like the mad blind poet with pots on his bag
and holes for seeing in his happy wrinkled eyes.
Or my blind pet seal under the table lifting his
head sniffing air and going under before storm;
his comic flesh moving from the lighted lantern.

from In Queen Mary's Gardens (1991)

Mullanfad

I do not see myself
carried the long street
of a town or village,
past grocer and baker,
the jaundiced face of a publican,
under flags and bunting
of any denomination.
After the furnace has eaten
plain wood and handles,
I would be put in an urn
and my ashes scattered
on a dead day
over my hardest making;
the septic tank, its strong smell
under concrete lids
to keep bacteria in,
cloying Summer air
as a handful of poets—
no masks supplied—
read poem after poem
under sycamore and ash,
not looking for rhyme or rhythm,
for that will be my will:
the big sea-captain first,
maps and territories next,
and "look at the stars" third.
I was confined in the urn
but now I am mobile,
waiting for wind to blow me
past this wasteful energy
up mountain paths and fields
craving the sky.

JUDE NUTTER

Alex Corville's *Seven Crows*

Perhaps the birds do inherit
the loveliest part of what we are. Every day

the crows unclose for us
like the lips of the dead:
under occasional sunlight the slick-hard
kiss of each body simply unlocks
as they break from the forest. Perhaps

we travel forever in that thin boat
of ribs, cradled behind the dark, busy

hearts of the birds. And maybe this
is how the dead unfasten
toward belonging, shot through
with irregular fire. Maybe this

is how we all get taken, one
from another. Are you ready to believe
that the soul would ask for this airy cathedral

that is the body of a bird, for a final body
more perfect than any you imagined
which rises off the earth at dawn and at the end
of each day comes back to settle
like a leaf on the roofless world?

from Pictures of the Afterlife (2002)

The Afterlife

So, linking arms like schoolgirls, my mother and I wander
all afternoon from store to store without finding
the one eye shadow she is counting on to complete
her outfit. *Try to remember*, I suggest, *the name
of the shade you want. I don't need to*, she says: *I'll know it*

as soon as I see it. But that night she decides
to name her own hue; so, in her darkened kitchen,
in our dressing gowns and slippers, my mother and I
invent the possibilities together: *Paradisio,
Smokey Rose, The Last Unknown Location
of the Soul*: wild names that made us grateful. When she dies

I will stand over her grave and repeat these words down
into the soil, because these are the words women use
to name their love for each other, in a kitchen
after midnight, while a gale rattles
the roof tiles and the shipping forecast blooms

from the radio so they can't help thinking
about those men out on the vast smear of the Atlantic,
dressed in oil skins and damp wool, playing cards and smoking
below deck, while the first mate stands in the unshared
silence of the pilot house navigating
the dull physicality of this world. Sometimes

there's nothing better for a woman
than the loneliness of one man, the weather itself

the only cause for alarm. But my mother is afraid
she won't recognize my father in the next life. *This
is my biggest fear*, she says. It has replaced whatever dread
it was that kept her moving between my brother's room
and mine as we slept our way across the vast country
of childhood. I think of her wandering forever, tired
of immortality, because what hope is there,

even in a world beyond this one, without love. *How*, I say,
could you fail to know him, thinking she will simply slip
between the burdens of the familiar world into an evening
of light rain, with her collar turned up and her best gloves on,
to find my father trimming the privet
with a pair of well-oiled shears, wearing the jacket
she once patched at the elbows with ovals of dark leather,
the top button of his shirt securely fastened; that he will

come forward, an unnamed shade only she will recognize,
the colour of sea wrack and surf, with the coarse dirt
under his fingernails and the scent
of something feral—badger or fox. And crushed grass.

from Pictures of the Afterlife (2002)

The Helmet

"Under the wind's cold roof we are lost and homeless,
And the flesh is flesh"
  Loren Eiseley

You have been lying so long with your face
against the earth that the dirt beneath your cheek
is warm and your teeth have a coat of grit
and dust. In your body, a great heaviness.
As if you had swallowed your own grave. So it's true:
in desperation a man can eat a shallow depression
in the dirt and get his head just below
a sniper's line of fire. Hour after hour the artillery
and the mortars coax dark mouths to open
in the duff and the muck, and there are times
when a man-photos, long bones, muscles, hardware-opens
with them. While fifty yards away,
where the light is whole and the trees unbroken,
you can see the wind's white shoulders moving
through the unspoiled grasses. And how
many times, in the life you had
before this one, did you cross, without thinking,
walking upright and whistling, a distance
of fifty yards? And which life is best: a long
life full of nightmares in which the blood of the dead
won't keep its hands to itself, or a handful of hours
in which each second is as long as a lifetime?
There are times when the mind almost
abandons the flesh, brief moments of reprieve.
When the man right beside you dies you know it,
without looking-at the heart of the barrage,
beneath the cough of mortars, enveloped in flame
and slaughter, you feel, far off, on the inside
of your body, a new loneliness. First
there is nothing more than his great stillness;
and then, around his head in the dirt, the long-
furled banner of his blood appearing. Under the skull's
curve, inside the heavy meat of the brain, the rooms
of his mind, their doors blown open, stand empty.

You notice his hair, darkened with sweat,
a fold of skin above the collar of his battle dress,
and how the sunlight is thrust like a dowel
through the tidy stigmata the bullet has punched
in his helmet, which has come to rest beside you,
now, on the battlefield. Alive or not,
each man here is equally dead, so, in a lull,
behind a screen of smoke, you slip on his helmet, aware
that a helmet pierced by a bullet will help you,
until the danger has passed or until the darkness falls,
in feigning death. And so the mind begins to rehearse
its own oblivion.

Long before he knocks off the helmet and presses
the cold, narrow rictus of the Luger against your temple,
you smell the breath of the barrel. He is your age—
no more than twenty, and his eyes are ransacked, empty,
the windows of a mansion gutted by fire. But after holding
your gaze for the briefest moment, he steps back

and holsters his pistol; and flat in the dirt,
in a fever of grief and fatigue, you are no longer sure
if he is real, or a dream with a heart made kind
by carnage and darkness, or even which possibility
you might prefer. Either way, after holding your gaze
for the briefest moment, he stepped back
and holstered his pistol. Either way, he has passed you over.

JEAN O'BRIEN

Flying East to Carthage

The ancient name resonates,
images of Phoenicians astride
white stallions galloping.
The 'ping' sound as our captain
instructs us to remain
seated. What would Tanit
have thought of our approach?
She who first sighted Carthage
from the prow of a ship
as it plunged forward in a sapphire
sea, her robes wind-wrapped
like winding sheets around her,
the tradewinds behind her craft
hurrying her forward to port.

Speeding inland by coach
we pass a family standing in tableau—
long gowns covering their limbs,
her face in shadow under the rim
of a wide dish balanced perfectly
on her head, two children motionless
beside their still father, around them
not a breath of wind touching
the sand and scrub-covered field.

I saw no sign of hut or tent, just a wide
tree where they stood, as if forever.
The tableau was splintered by the bright voice
of our guide—'The people here are not
poor, they just look that way.'

Oh carthage, once proud Phoenicians,
Tanit, your angry tears would flood
this barren desert if you could see your once
bustling port; ships sheltering in the low tide,
filled to the hold with cargo of salt, linen,
leather, fruits and rum; peopled now
by beggars and tourists and the only ships
pushing out from anchor, full of day-trippers
weighted down with cameras,
gee-gaws and the like.

from The Shadow Keeper (1997)

Census

A Census taken in 1837 in an area of Donegal with 9,000
inhabitants found that they possessed in total 10 beds.

Stones like steps on the road,
heavy, hard and hungry.
The hedges stripped of haws and berries,
fields once full of yellow dandelions,
hung ears of corn and swaying wheat,
all bare like my children
standing in their shifts,
their petticoats
bartered for corn bread.

Before us the road goes nowhere.
Behind, the cottage is tumbled,
bedding itself down into the hard
acres. I have no furniture to speak of,
just one copper pot given
on marriage by my mother
tied now with twine about my waist,
echoing like a bell in empty space.

from The Shadow Keeper (1997)

Knitting

You came home delighted
they were teaching you to knit.
From some back cupboard
I produced my hoard of needles,
ragged balls of wool. All colours.

I showed you how to cast on
pull the wool over your fingers
until you had a row of pearl,
such riches. Your hands had trouble
taming the leaping needles,
subduing the gamboling fleece.

Each day it grew, this knitted
cats cradle, this knobbled,
nubbled nest drawn together,
intwined, a Marcel wave of wool,
the odd stitch dropped.
The lines advance.

CLAIRR O'CONNOR

Great Aunt May

She came for a week
but stayed forever.
An old squaw,
plaited hair
and pleated skin
Great Aunt May
in the best bedroom
in the house,
My parents camped
in the box room.
Her trunks took
up the attic.
Sepia photographs—
men and women
in fifty year old
fashions.
Old party dresses
with underskirts
of frothy lace,
hats with feathers
moulting now
sad birds
sleeping.
Her long white nighties
smelt of lavender.
We fetched and carried.
Earl Grey tea in bone-white china
American cigarettes—
peace or war signals
according to mood.
Head of her tribe
though childless,
she was "at home"

on Saturdays.
Cousins came
anxiously
to visit,
scared she'd forget
them in her will.
Vain of her hands,
lean and phthisic,
age spots
she girlishly
called freckles
she fed them
cream at night.
I read her
the obituaries
after school.
Enlivened
by the deaths
of so many
of her contemporaries,
she cackled.
Squaw Longyears,
the most venerable
in the camp,
her fingers busy
with a new lace collar,
the pattern intricate,
delicate as a spider's web.
When she died she was laid
out in white,
a curious Christian
squaw, plaits
to the end,
her money left
to Tridentine nuns.

from When You Need Them (1989)

Aquamarine

Birdy Mathews, the druggist's wife
has disappeared. She left her clothes
at the edge of the lake.
Children playing there at the time
said she shouted, "I want to swallow
the sun," then dived.
The photograph Don Mathews gave
the police shows Birdy, smile
petrified, wearing a snake
at a druggists' convention
in Indiana in '81.
"Lilith's Store" say they sold
her their latest dress
in aquamarine that morning.
Apparently, she tossed her old
jeans in their garbage and put
the dress on straightaway.
They dragged the lake
but she wasn't there.

from When You Need Them (1989)

Mountain Man

Restless as a husband,
he was much-married
before calm descended.

Tired of his runaway year
in the city he moved
back to his mountain
and continuous snow.

When he caught
his eye in the thorn bush
he said to his current wife,
"I do not want to look
at a blank-walled house."

That was some time ago
and the doctors did what
they could.
The glass eye is a perfect match.

He used to be a man of determined
unhappiness but these days
he laughs a lot.

His dogs were kennelled
except for the hunt but now he feeds
scraps to them from the table.

He no longer intrudes on the farm
manager as he has taken up folk
dancing with his wife.
They travel huge distances
to tournaments.

The kitchen clock stopped
at twelve midnight last
Christmas Eve and he hasn't
noticed yet.

HUGH O'DONNELL

Maol Íosa Ó Brolcháin

d. Lismore 1086

They testify to this in cold faces
paving the decades with starlight:
speaking a language of night, voices
in shadow, Deus meus adiuva me.
At all hours, light is on upstairs,
his grace before death in a sick-room,
"I thank you for what is not a pleasure",
stone-blind, turned towards the wall.
Nine centuries on, our theme the same,
our closeness to clay—"it is six months
from yesterday that I have been lying
on my sick-bed…" We reach for his words
that bear the imprint of love,
like verse in a psalter lost in prayer.

from Roman Pines at Berkeley (1990)

Airing Blankets in Donegal

Now they are galloping with the wind up
and the sun on their backs; such Cossack
fury, horse and rider impossibly one;
snorting and kicking, hanging on for dear
life, a flogging will release the itch
of dampness from their veins. Ears pricked
among the stony hills, their bright colours
excite with thoughts of giant bats coming
in squadrons. Will they ever settle down
to lying comfortless on a bed after the chase
and the effort to edge even half a head ahead.
Now with their tails up, I haven't the heart
to take them in, although I fear they will
carry grudges with them to the grave.

from Roman Pines at Berkeley (1990)

Miracle

"Was he ever here?" asks mother
as an after-thought (meaning my father)
and we sift through the evidence.

After the check-up, she sits him down,
"God bless your hands", then,
lighter than cherry blossom,

she drifts from the Eye and Ear
having seen for herself at first hand
what no eye has seen.

MARY O'DONNELL

My Father Waving

In the New Year, we drove away.
I glanced back at the house on the hill.
It was shrinking, shrinking,
encased in ice, fragments of Christmas
in winking fairy-lights.
My father waved with both arms,
like Don Quixote's windmill.

On the brink of motherhood,
I saw lives swept almost to oblivion,
scuttled on reefs of the present;
then a processional, those quiet generations
moved through evening ice the colour of Asia,
described the entrances and exits—
parents of parents
like Russian dolls re-entering my body,
telling what was never told anyone,
announcing it now to my unborn girl.

The unstill past entered, forgotten
ghostlings and wanderers fussed
and made ready for the future—
one step ahead, bridging dawns,
afternoons between birthdays and Christmas.
The vision displaced the crammed wells
of fear, fed my courage.
In the New Year, we drove away.
The child turned beneath my ribs,
the parents of parents waved.

from Unlegendary Heroes (1998)

Unlegendary Heroes

'Life passes through places.'
—P.J. Duffy, Landscapes of South Ulster

Patrick Farrell, of Lackagh, who was able to mow
one acre and one rood Irish in a day.
Tom Gallagher, Cornamucklagh, could walk 50
Irish miles in one day.
Patrick Mulligan, Cremartin, was a great oarsman.
Tommy Atkinson, Lismagunshin, was very good at
highjumping—he could jump six feet high.
John Duffy, Corley, was able to dig half an Irish acre
in one day.
Edward Monaghan, Annagh, who could stand on his
head on a pint tumbler or on the rigging of a house.

—1938 folklore survey to record the local people
who occupied the South Ulster parish landscape.

★ ★ ★

Kathleen McKenna, Annagola,
who was able to wash a week's sheets, shirts
and swaddling, bake bread and clean the house
all of a Monday.

Birdy McMahon, of Faulkland,
walked to Monaghan for a sack of flour two days before
her eighth child was born.

Cepta Duffy, Glennan,
very good at sewing—embroidered a set of vestments
in five days.

Mary McCabe, of Derrynashallog,
who cared for her husband's mother in dotage,

fed ten children,
the youngest still at the breast during hay-making.

Mary Conlon, Tullyree,
who wrote poems at night.

Assumpta Meehan, Tonygarvey,
saw many visions and was committed to the asylum.

Martha McGinn, of Emy,
who swam Cornamunden Lough in one hour and a quarter.

Marita McHugh, Foxhole,
whose sponge cakes won First Prize at Cloncaw Show.

Miss Harper, Corley,
female problems rarely ceased, pleasant in ill-health.

Patricia Curley, Corlatt,
whose joints ached and swelled though she was young,
who bore three children.

Dora Heuston, Strananny,
died in childbirth, aged 14 years,
last words 'Mammy, O Mammy!'

Rosie McCrudden, Aghabog,
noted for clean boots, winter or summer,
often beaten by her father.

Maggie Traynor, Donagh,
got no breakfasts, fed by the nuns, batch loaf with jam,
the best speller in the school.

Phyllis McCrudden, Knockaphubble,
who buried two husbands, reared five children
and farmed her own land.

Ann Moffett, of Enagh,
who taught people to read and did not charge.

from Unlegendary Heroes (1998)

Café Terrace at Night, 1888

The waiter at Arles is white-aproned,
Tray in hand before a solitary, hatted man.
At other tables, women sit beneath the awning,

Heliotrope yellows above and behind,
On a deck that skims the cobbles.
These sitters are un-posed, indifferent

To the artist painting some distance
Up the street, familiars, drawn for
Coffee, absinthe, or conversation.

The invisible is touched on, feet
Toe gently at the floor beneath a chair
Where no-one notices the telltale movement.

To the right, a couple is about to vanish
Down a street where night has fallen
And frugal rooms are lit. They

Have somewhere to go, footsteps intimate
Beneath wavering poached-egg stars.
This morning I want to be devoured

By those yellows on Van Gogh's café terrace,
Toeing the floor of the unseen,
Atavistic, darkly cottoned, like

The woman with the red shawl,
Head inclined like a bird
As she listens.

MARY O'DONOGHUE

The Textures

for John C

I am velvet.
Smooth nap,
But rub me up
The wrong way
And I bristle,
Growing hackles
Beneath your palms.

I am moire.
Metallic skin,
But scan me
Under lamplight,
See silk
Shot through
With routes of tears.

I am tulle.
Lively bustle,
But gather me
Between your hands,
I rustle,
Murmur,
Settle.

from Tulle (2001)

Why I'd Rather Germaine Greer
Didn't Visit My Home

"By the millennium housework should have been abolished [...] People who said that they enjoyed doing housework or needed to do it or that doing it made them feel good would be known as addicts"—The Whole Woman

Wholesome Woman,
Don't come to the door;
You may find me buffing
The parquet floor.

Confession to the sisterhood:
I have forsworn sluttish ways
To haul hairs from the plughole
In drowned mouse gobbets
And once shoved my paw
Into the S-pipe
Without a rubber glove.

Wholesome Woman,
Don't ask me why
The names 'Pledge' and 'Jif'
Bring a gleam to my eye.

I like to raise a bit of a rumpus
Smacking pillows back to plumpness,
And wiping tannin faces off teaspoons
With a bit of spit and Brillo.

Wholesome Woman,
Don't bother with the speech;
I've an appointment with mildew
And some pump-action bleach.

Ye lady gods forgive me:
I know well what I do!
Begging for his trousers,
Shirts, and boxers, too

And planing out the rumples,
Coasting my iron into pockets and sleeves,
Stotious in a fug of laundry steam.

Wholesomest of Women,
Don't name me drudge or freak,
Just because I hop for cobwebs
Every other week.

from Tulle (2001)

Thanksgiving in Florida

The giant roadside orange
might be full of children
packed vesicle-tight together
cheek to small fat cheek.

At a bar reclaimed from the water
a dead ringer for Oliver Reed
blears his details, wipes them clear:
His girlfriend.
Is coming.
From Gatwick.

We skim over swamp in a boat
made of tin. Routed birds scarper,
filling the air with a blitz of black paper.
We chunter close to alligators
who test-click their teeth
like just-fitted dentures,
and eyeball the day
like it's bothering them.

We visit the place where you
were the neighbourhood rascal,
shrugging off the door locks
of your mother's great terror,
running down the way down,
galloping right the way down,
stopping short at the drop
to the Indian River.

(First published in the *Journal of International Women's Studies*)

CIARAN O'DRISCOLL

Heliography

It's out of the question that we don't
pull ourselves together now chaps
for various Muslim and Hindu reasons
also reasons of State, various
longterm goals but above all
because of the task in hand namely
fixing this blownup length of track.
To which purpose, it almost seems, rebels
have been deployed in the country round—
those flashes of light up on the hills
are not chance reflections, it's called
heliography. I thought that would
be able to concentrate your minds.
Well it's all together then chaps
for the Empire and the young prince
in the carriage happily absorbed
collapsing houses of cards.

from Gog and Magog (1987)

Roads

(for Margaret)

Where is the road to Wigan Pier
which I set out upon last May
with labour's bread, with heart of fire,
with factories that mounted higher
on each side in the dawning day,
and at my side this child so dear?

The dew rang out where grass grows sweet
from fertiliser tractors spread,
and cattle grazed where buses run
transporting manpower by the ton
to where the complex has been laid;
and this child climbs on tired feet.

I walked the road to Wigan Pier
where factories send up their smoke
and metal gleams in hardening light.
White-coated teams came into sight
in glass-built plants; and then I spoke
to spur my child whose blood is dear.

'All energy the task demands
is gladly given, freely spent,
since it is bread in the freshening breeze
to feed on what the warm heart sees
the little share of each, when blent,
can make to build what love commands.'

Where is the road to Wigan Pier
which I have tramped on all my days,
inspired by Larkin, Connolly?
This road leads downwards, to the sea;
and at the pier my boat delays.
But there remains a child so dear.

from Gog and Magog (1987)

The White Mule

The white mule's throat marks the passing of time,
an angelus braying. The tide has one tune for always,
a tune with a turning. Mussels in rock crevices
pray for the sea to turn its tune, to come back
swollen with nutrients, swill over them again.
The sky and the sea are quite an item, and lead
an exemplary couple's life: one is not bright
while the other is dark, though on some skyless days
the sea in the distance seems to laugh to itself,
as if not just the presence but the thought of the sky
could brighten it. The tide has one tune for always,
and the bray of the white mule marks time for the land,
its pale green fields, its hillocks, cottages and crows.
I would speak backwards as a child, into my throat,
and everyone laughed at the strange ebbing sound of words.

DESMOND O'GRADY

Kinsale

Cúin tSaile or *Ceann tSaile*:
Quiet of the Sea or Head of the Ocean.
Either way, home-haven. Here we all
live 'blow-ins': exiles, or exiles from
exile. And we 'love our ease, our idleness.'
You would too if you lived here among us.

The Bandon river finds sea exit here,
Atlantic spawning salmon entrance.
Kinsale origins flowered beyond the Ice sphere
which makes of Time and History a nonsense.
Here Celtic alternative order fought, died,
sixteen one; left us Ireland's modern divide.

We sleep side by side, together,
enjoying harmony's just measure
without weapons on display for war.

from Tipperary (1991)

Breakup

Fishermen give back to the sea
as they take from it,
leave old boats to the wreckage
of the waves that sailed them.

Far from you now,
on a deserted beach
I saw two ships'
skeletons in the sand
and a corroded anchor.

I stood reminded
of the two of us
our last winter together
of the sea's severity,
of sightless rudders,
lost anchors, timbers
breaking up.

from Tipperary (1991)

Olga Rudge Pound

on her one hundred and first birthday

13th April 1895 USA — 15th March 1996 Venice, Italy

Your vine of life fruits full againt this year
and vintages your best to share with us.
We'll taste and feast on your ripe memories
of past times and lives lived as time's guest.

At first light your birthday will dawn and shine
all day for you. All your love will radiate
response in kind. The stitch in time of your
first decade saved your tenth decade to knot.

In childhood we gather life's images
round us: places, people, those things that catch
our attention, please or displease all, as
they may do thereafter when they repeat.

In youth's dreams of adventures in new ways
of life we dare to broaden our horizon.
We work in happy hope through hurt and heal
to shape life in profession, vocation.

To live our love of life defeats mere death.
All live, all die one way or another.
What we make that outshines our mortality—
children, lives for others, art—examples.

Human history effects all life in peace,
through war. What we make well helps growth improve.
All love helps heart and soul survive through strife,
inspires each joyful flight of peace's dove.

The peak of life, when real, rejects all masks,
stands clear as truth. It may revive oldtime
values to live the age process with strength,
enliven each day's order with fantasy.

Aging matures, mellows our stress from struggle
and those who order time to live life well
find joy in age, comfort in nature's law.
Age's serenity transcends all that is mortal.

Physical passion spent, the mind follows
its own commitment. Now age resists,
declares its right to decisive seniority.
Our time flows on until our life drains out.

Keep an interest in the parts you've played,
your last act will demand, reward example.
Your last part played, exit with composure.
Those who applaud will follow your example.

SHEILA O'HAGAN

Taking Lily to the Tate

When Lily was two
I took her to the Tate,
in the sculpture hall
let her go her way

Saw her draw near
a woman full of augeries,
her head turned inside out
like a seethrough bird.

Lily tried to climb
into the caverns of her mind
but intimidated by her stillness

Found a mother shape
perfectly round
and more accessible

And another bird
of sold gold
a Maiastra
singing to the emperor
who inspired her

So she ran into the picture gallery,
on the wall
saw a large coloured spider
with square feet
unfolding itself slowly
from a sandbag

And with wonderful invention
she made her own spiral
dancing in and out, out and in—
I thought of a bee against a windowframe—

After this celebration
she came across
some desert flowers
so red they made her eyes revolve

And rested beside them
maybe hoping to absorb their red
but she could only manage pink
so in a little huff
she moved on and came to

A curious singing lesson
hanging in a corner,
tried to read
its joined up lines and circles,
made all sorts of up and down sounds
ending on a squeaky C

Then very tired
found the Rothko room
in all that dark maroon
remembered how it was
to nestle in a womb
(or so it seemed)
for she fell asleep.

from The Troubled House (1995)

The Wood Pigeon

A tree bends over you like Yeats' old thorn,
How desolate the day, your place in it.
I push the graveyard gate, walk slowly through
The gloomy avenues of fern and stone.
I buried you in the wrong place, the wind
Is softer from the west then from the east,
Your feet should face the sea like any Celt.
But I'll do what I can to clear your space,
Brush off the sodden leaves, replace the lead
Of letters fallen off your name, our name.
And I'll not ask what of you perished first
Yet hear the truth, that all is gathered up
In human love. I've left you some flowers.
Is it the rain or you who flays my face,
Or wind dements my hair? I turn to leave,
A wood pigeon breaks from the trees, a whirr
Soft as a ghost. I listen to it
As it comes and goes, comes and goes.

from The Troubled House (1995)

September The Fourth

At four am today my lover died
He didn't reach for me or call my name
Dreaming he would waken by my side
But turned his face and shuddered as some shame
Or haunting shook him and his mouth gave cry
To a portentous and unearthly pain.

Between darkness and dawn that cry of pain
And nothing warm has reached me since it died
Some ethos of cold starlight I can't name
Possessed my love while he lay by my side
Something strange, inhuman, born of shame
He had not said goodbye, called out or cried.

Some ghost or spirit left his mouth that cried
Out and he'd gone from me, had gone in pain
Into an alien world yet as he died
He drew my spirit to him, gave her my name
Something possessed him as he left my side
His face was turned away as though in shame.

I took his absent face and murmured shame
To that which claimed him, for my love had cried
As though some shady trafficking in pain
Some curse or Judas kiss by which he died
Unknowingly in another's name
Had come to term as he lay down beside

The one he loved. Perhaps lying by his side
Fearful in sleep, I had called up that shame
And he, my love, unknowingly had cried
Out in redemption for another's pain,
As though a chosen victim. My love died
Because some cursed spirit took his name.

For he was loved and honoured in his name
And I, as I lay sleeping by his side
Guarding his innocence, knew of no shame.
On the stark cusp of dark and dawn he cried
Aloud so strange my heart burned cold with pain.
Not one warm thought has reached me since he died.

Still I call his name. All hope has died.
My unspent love's my pain. I have not cried.
Such is winter's shame, all's bare outside.

MARY O'MALLEY

Area of Scientific Interest

On my first visit after the solstice,
delayed by a good storm,
the woman in the stone house spoke:
'I will rise and drink the morning
even this grey daylight
that is neither sunny nor beautiful
but stuck like a half-torn rag
on a holly bush, a plastic bag in a doorway
at the fag end of the century,' she greeted me.

'I will rise and eat the black clouds
that stick in my craw
because they are merciful and hide
the bloody necklaces of Kosovo,
the planes over Baghdad,
the cold faces of the subsidy-checkers in Dublin,
stemming what comes in on the tide
not knowing that flotsam and jetsam
is what keeps coastal people going. But I tell you,'
she said, 'they have lives of pure misery.
Such misery as you never saw—

halfpence and pence.'
She got up and took in gulps
of bad weather and dressed herself in tattered clouds
magnificent in her own way. Then we breakfasted.
She poured tea into elegant cups.
'I always liked fine china,'
and the fire reddened in the grate
and we ate the bad morning and it did us no harm.
'We'd make great queens,' she remarked,
'Or a damned sight better than what's there.'
We looked out over the waves. 'A big sea.'
She made an elegant arc of her arm, trailing cumulii.

'That is an Area of Scientific Interest
according to Brussels.'
'Did you ever meet a bureaucrat?'
she asked as if I might have unwittingly entertained
one in my home,
his pointy hooves hidden in patent leather shoes,
they being practiced in the art of surprise.
'Talking golf-sticks, most of them.
They wouldn't care if I was ten miles out past Slyne Head
clinging to a barrel so damn their souls to hell.'
We drank our Barry's tea.
Charity may be all very well for those
that lie on under the covers on cold mornings
but not for women in stone houses
at the edge of the sea.

from Asylum Road (2001)

The Otter Woman

Against the wisdom of shore women
she stood on the forbidden line too long
and crossed the confluence of sea and river.
One shake of her body on O'Brien's bridge
and the sea was off her.
A glorious swing from haunch to shoulder
sent water arching in the sunlight,
a fan of small diamonds flicked open,
held, fell. Her smooth pelt rose into fur.

He stood and watched her from the shadows
and moved to steal her tears
scattered on the riverbank.
Now he could take his time. He smoked.

She was all warm animal following the river,
trying her new skin like a glove.
He trailed her, magnetised by her power to transform,
the occasional bliss on her face, her awakened body.
Once or twice she saw him.
Her instincts were trusting on land.
They smiled. This took the whole Summer.

He took her by a lake in Autumn
a sliced half moon and every star out
the plough ready to bite the earth.

She left him on a street corner
with no choice and no glance back,
spring and a bomber's moon.
In between their loosed demons
played havoc in the town.

He pinned her to the ground, his element.
This was not what she came for
but what she got.
Soon the nap of her skin rose only for him.
It was too late to turn back.
She grew heavy out of water.

ii

Indifferent to all but the old glory
he never asked why she always walked
by the shore, what she craved,
why she never cried when every wave
crescendoed like an orchestra of bones.

She stood again on the low bridge
the night of the full moon.
One sweet deep breath and she slipped in
where the river fills the sea.
She saw him clearly in the street light—his puzzlement.
Rid of him she let out
one low strange cry for her human sacrifice,
for the death of love
for the treacherous undertow of the tribe
and dived, less marvellous forever in her element.

from The Knife in the Wave (1997)

Dreampoems Three

The First Dream

They walked through the empty city, past the shattered square,
the tight streets. The ghosts of musicians waved
along Quay Street and places where people picnicked on the grass
paler than ever and thinner. They made for the docks

the last ship out. No God would live here nor the hope of one.
From a lane, three clear notes, a blue cry from the belly
defiant bowstrokes. Tears come easily to the hungry.
then the rope trailing, the sun, blinding as they swam.

The Second Dream

As an army of houses marched dead-eyed
across the plain, annexing first Connaught
then Hungary, then Spain
the fat God laughed and his fat wife sang.

The Third Dream

In the first dream he phoned: I'd like to see you.
She woke happy. When was the last time?
Happy is a movie, a saxophone.
The second night there was a kiss, a token.

This old fashioned courtship could go on
for years. What of the third dream:
a lake, the moon, on the window an apple.
May enters and blues the world. A birch
two china cups on the table. Next
she wakes to a missing verse
the red rain of her dream fox
gliding across the late October grass
silent but for his sharp morning cough.

TOM O'MALLEY

Roots and Instincts

Grey-frigid, he stands out on a hard landscape
of streaked limestone, beside a glacial lake,
as stark as in some drawing by Edvard Munch.
He seems to lack all fruitful contact with rich soil,
tribal warmth or touch of a gentle god; and yet
he survives, absorbing sustenance like this ash
that persists, though stunted, in mysterious clefts
where no life is normally expected. I wonder at
the ingenuity of these roots, their prospecting instinct
that can suck up food from some secret source. What
brute will lives deep in both their natures
that can give them energy to live though warped—the ash
in its dwarfed ashness, he in his stark humanity.
And yet, both endure and somehow proclaim life
where white rock is chill even at high summer.

from Journey Backward (1998)

Spring Cleaning

for Anne

Often things have to get worse before getting better
as now, when you blur your side; I, mine.

You polish the windolene into the glass;
and I shine and shine until my blur is gone.

You point out some small imperfection, my side;
I point to a small speck on yours.

Again, we each shine away our observed blemishes
until at last one pane stands perfect between us.

from Journey Backward (1998)

Meath's Lost Railway

Where limestone bridges leap a gap
Between twin Meath fields
A railway track has disappeared.

Like stoats with arched backs
Hindlegs/forelegs at a gallop,
These bridges cross/re-cross rich pasture.

Where oaken sleepers lay in gravel
Chestnut horses frisk and start;
Cattle graze where a train ran.

With motte and bailey—castle,
Hill-fort, tumulous,
A railroad steams towards the prehistoric.

I ghost-ride a screeching train
Along fantasy's relaid tracks—
Get off at a vanished platform.

BARBARA PARKINSON

My Aunt

My aunt would start to fret
when the first brightness
stretched into the evening.
'Away ye go to the head of the road
and wait til ye see his car.
Don't forget
VIM on top and 375 underneath'.
I'd stand there in the pissing rain
a salty southerly slapping me
in the face
my gym-slip going crazy,
coiling up my waist.
How the hell could I even
see the bloody Volks
never mind
VIM on top and 375 underneath
why wasn't the slime faithful?
I learned a litany of curses
to pile high on his Romeo head.
Soaked to the skin
I'd flop in the door a sodden heap
and utter proudly through my teeth,
'yea, it's definitely him.
He passed by the head of the road
at half past five
on his own; straight from work
VIM on top and 375 underneath'.

Boston

(For Tony Conneely, my brother)

We eat breakfast like a habit
outside at the *Au Bon Pain*.
Our crumbs will never carry
much weight;
the pigeons, making the best of their time,
do justice to them.
Your pancakes slurping in 'Maple Syrup'
make me laugh across streets
where young boys play—
'Back Bay' where my last love poem
stepped out of the harbour.
'Any change for the Jugglers' you say,
three brass coins we give them,
dressed to kill, our love they juggle well,
well as we know,
Boston has been good to us.

Widowed Black

The way the wind is blowing
And is warm
Makes me feel good this day
Makes me feel it's time to burn
The cloak of married widowed black
Time to light a roaring fire
Brighter than a spangled sky
And burn to white ashes
The ugly black threadbare cloak
Time to move in flesh
Dance a Palooka across the emperor's head
To a first sense of life felt
In a cloakspan of time
It's time to burn the cloak
Of married widowed black
And blow the white ashes across the earth
Out of the palms of my hands

all from Any Change for the Jugglers and Other Poems (1995)

GWYN PARRY

Between Lands

Ship moves smooth
like sun floating morning
on steep mountain fields.

Air pegged by stone walls
shaped blue sculpture.
In the purple cloud shadow,
the small white stars
of my father's favourite flowers.

The ferry ploughs gallons
of wreck-green sea
propeller shadow-thumps
the sandy bed.

Leaving land
my astronaut suit is steel, rivet and paint.
I take a thread
tie it to the last red lighthouse,
take it across the waves
thread it through wingtips and raindrops,
leave a loose knot
on an eye-brow of island.

Achill Island

Everything around,
rotting brown,
the best taken,
burnt
on a simple hearth.

The wind wraps
its razor-wire
close to the skin—
the message of this place.

Lift a stone,
find nothing
but the black
sipping bog.

Bones stained
with the land's
nicotine.

Sky brings down
a fat grey gut,
smothering the living
in a swear of weather.

Women watch
their men
open the earth,
to find
puss-filled
potatoes,
and the future
derelict
on the hillside.

Kite

It would take a week
to persuade my father
to make a kite.

On Saturday
he would suddenly say,
find a broken umbrella,
coarse twine, newspaper,
a straight branch of willow
or beading
from an old chest-of-drawers.

Then
mix flour and water
into a sticky paste.
The balance
just right,
my father bent
umbrella steel,
a tense arc
over a thin
cross of wood.

Local newspapers
we'd paste taut
on the coffin shape
joining centre-spreads
together.

The sun dried our kite
while I plaited a tail
of bailer-twine,
dickie-bows of newsprint.

The wind, my father said,
would come from the west,
licking his finger
to test the air.

Harness complete
we laid out the kite in a field,
tail long as a girl's hair.
Dad held the kite above his head
and I ran with the line
arm straining
at the pull of the wind.

It was climbing
string thrumming,
burning
letting-out
through my soft hands.

With my father
I watched
as headlines
became foot-notes,
the kite
a small shimmering doorway
on a patch of sky.

all from Crossings (1998)

ANGELA PATTEN

Emissary

On a narrow road in County Kerry
a herd of cattle surrounds your car.
You turn off the ignition, swearing softly at the delay.
Cows' breath fogs up the windows
as curious cow-eyes bat their lashes at the glass.

Spellbound by that mild bovine gaze, you rock
back and forth between warm flanks
until a vision surfaces of skeletons straggling
these roads that wind downhill towards the sea,
of mouths stained green with grass stubble,
of eyes hollow from hunger and despair.

Why should that famine story in an Irish schoolbook
haunt you now? Why should those words,
in a language you were forced to learn,
reverberate like blood thirty years later?

Eventually the animals roll past,
udders murmuring of milk and straw.
You start the car and flee back to town,
the convivial meaningless pub-talk,
the reek of Guinness and fish and chips.
It's still potatoes and conversation,
the same trick of living between two worlds.

No part of this watery island is more
than sixty miles away from the sea.
The stories creep up like water in your lungs,
and you can't breathe for choking on the past.

from Still Listening (1999)

Thatch Pub, 1958

It was Grand National Saturday
and our father, never a betting man,
had put a shilling each way for the four of us
on a horse called Oxo. After his dinner
we trailed him to The Thatch to see the race
running a gauntlet of cap-shadowed glances
as the men looked up from their pints
to gawk at the strangers.

I think the world was completely brown then.
The smoke-filled air. The dun-coloured caps
of the drinkers. The dark oak of the bar
and deeper dark of porter
chased with a swirl of whiskey.
The smell you'd sometimes get
in the early morning after it rained
when you walked over a metal grating
and caught the waft of stale ale
and Woodbines rising up from the depths.

Our father, thin as a whippet among
stout-fattened neighbours, beckoned the barman
while we clung to his coattails. He brought us
Orange Crush poured sideways into tall Harp glasses,
and Tayto crisps tasting of smoke and beer.
The television blared from among
the dusty bottles on a corner shelf.
All eyes were glued to Oxo when our sister,
nervous as a thoroughbred,
clamped her teeth down hard and bit a piece
from the fluted edge of the glass.

Chaos then. Everyone yelling
don't swallow, spit it out, quick now,
there there, you'll be right as rain in a minute.
But what struck me then as now
was the suddenness with which everything
can change. One minute you're holding on
to your father, safe as houses; the next

you've bitten through some invisible membrane
and the world and Garret Reilly is shouting at you
while you stand there like a gormless eejit,
your mouth filling up with fizzy liquid
and delicate shards of glass.

from Still Listening (1999)

Preponderance of the Small

for John

Yesterday the little cardinal's pointed hat
caught my eye from the kitchen window.
Then the bluejay in his bright cockade
raced screeching across my field of vision
as I stood there at the sink washing dishes,
daydreaming of spring.

I noticed the strawberry pink stain
on the grey shirtfront of the purple finch
and the way the small birds blew about the sky
like coal smuts when the chimney catches fire.

Where I live there is a preponderance of the small.

Tiny paw-and-tail patterns etched across the snow,
the delicate hoof prints of deer among the rocks,
cavities created by that manic percussionist,
the woodpecker, turned into dwellings
for the red squirrel and the common vole.

But it's always humanity that intrigues me
for all its shallow cruelties,
its idiotic clinging to belief.
I can't resist its elegant hinged jawbones,
its complicated knees,
its half-truths and fabrications,
and this leaping music issuing from its mouth.

In the beginning, the Oracle reminds us,
one should avoid trying to fly.
The flying bird brings the message:
it is not well to strive upward,
it is well to remain below.

from Reliquaries (2007)

PAUL PERRY

The improbable flowers of Vizcaya

Outside, the fountains swallow the sun.
Again and again, I fall asleep
on Peacock Bridge
and dream of chasing kites

in my Italian childhood.
The living room replicates
a typical Renaissance room,
a high beamed ceiling,

a sixteenth century fireplace.
Plush coven.
Lumber room.
Loot.

The trees talk
in a prehistoric
gnarled and tangled
language. A two thousand

year old Roman tripod,
a fifteenth century Spanish
heraldic carpet.
Rococo ceilings

and two sixteenth century tapestries
depict the exploits of Hermes.
I want to sneak
into the butler's pantry.

No echo in my mouth.
Biscayne Bay, goodnight.
Beautiful Iseult, be with me
here, where the fishing boats

dawdle on the water
like small children
who should long have been asleep.
Here, we could walk

by the silk palm trees
with their gracious,
but improbable flowers.
You could say

you love me
and I would be Tristan
or whatever it is
you want me to be.

from The Drowning of the Saints (2003)

Slowly Home

take the third train east
use no whips or spurs
but a gentle whisper
to encourage the driver

say good-bye to all you've known
but slowly, you have time
don't talk to your taxi
or pretend to be someone else

if the old guy takes you
on a detour, say nothing
smile politely, if you should
arrive in a strange land

where people no longer talk the tongue
you once knew, simply nod
and thank your fare
do not ask for directions

the stars obviously are not themselves
the headlines you suspect are a decoy
people leer at you conspiratorially
if you walk the streets

and you do not recognise them
no matter, if you happen
to stumble into a back-garden
weakly resembling a photograph

you once carried in your wallet
welcome the place with open arms
and the family that come now to greet you
take them, too, as your own

from The Drowning of the Saints (2003)

343

Promise

You get off the train
in another no-where town
and are welcomed home.

The wind leads you
to a road and you start
to walk.

Where you came from
is no where like this.

A man is pushing
a bike. He tells you
the rain is on its way,
but you don't see.

He offers you
a place to sleep.

You keep going
to where there are fields.

Not far from a river,
someone is calling out.

A woman is standing in
the doorway of a house.
She sees through you.

In her silence,
there is something
of a promise,

something
which suggests
you could
if you wanted
become again
the person
you wished to be.

You can hear the voices
of children.
Their laughter.
You can choose to walk on.

You've been travelling
a long time.

Before you speak
the first words of the day
you can rest.

The world is waking.
And the morning is welling onto your lips.

Speak.
Say something.
You can still be healed.

MARK ROPER

Harristown Dolmen

We came in pale hawthorn light.
More cats than people patrolled

the roads. A horse pissed
in shadow. Haycocks were breasts

without nipples. The stones sprung
at the junction of three fields.

You said music raised them.
I said people lifted them,

inch by ton-defiant inch
people were forced to lift

this stone ear this stone vase
into which out of which pour

the nightingales of water,
the honeysuckle sweet nothings

of speech, the sweat and silence
of those who suffer and those

who build on their suffering.

from The Hen Ark (1990, Co-publication with Peterloo Poets, England)

Absence of Lilac

Easter Sunday and there's a skin of snow
across the allotments in Birmingham.
I have to cut down an old lilac tree,
so leggy it darkens the garden.

Falling branches splash the Sunday silence.
A vague guilt stirs as sap meets air.
This tree must have seen bombers darken sky
above its first fresh attempts at flower.

My friends doze indoors, tired from a hard night's
nostalgia. I've known them half my life.
Halfway through its span I envy their lives,
their quiet committed union work.

There's a discipline in these parcelled skies.
They'll plant vegetables in earth lit
and freshened by snow and absence of lilac.
The saw poses on the cut trunk.

The scene giddies out of history.
Cocooned in words I bear branches
like standards through the narrow grid
of Midland gardens and hurl them down

onto ashes, broken glass, rusty cans.
My native soil, my own backyard.
As dusk shakes the confidence
of Chamberlain's redbrick city I go

in to the warmth, wake my friends.
We head for the pub. Through the blurry mirth
continually comes the image
of a cut stump struggling to escape its ground.

from The Hen Ark (1990, Co-publication with Peterloo Poets, England)

Cut

So you drive to work
thinking of this and that
and suddenly find
you don't know
what road you're on,
you've never seen
these hedges before,
you look in the mirror
and there's that garden
those iris leaves
which cut so clean
you don't feel a thing
until minutes later
your skin parts
and the blood wells,
a cut as clean as that
of Saladdin's sword
on which a handkerchief
might fall and
continue to fall
in two halves still
thinking they're one.

TOM SEXTON

King Island
(abandoned 1958)

The carver used whalebone for the base
of his island where two figures,

so small they must be from another world,
climb into an invisible wind, a wind

that pushes the ice pack with its wandering
bears closer to their island.

Now they drag two ivory seals
toward an ivory house on ivory stilts

where a woman sits beside her seal-oil lamp
dreaming of greens she will gather

from the jagged cliffs come spring
in that pure light the carver has revealed.

from Autumn in the Alaska Range (2000)

Numen

It was cold enough for down coats and our
woollen boots from Norway that made us
feel like reindeer herders from the icy
steppes. A good night to stay inside,
but our old dog needed her evening walk.
The mountains that lift our eyes all summer
were deep in winter's glacial dark.
Cold enough for dark thoughts of a failing
mind and then of the random seal of death.
Still, we followed the path toward the lagoon
where the city cleared a rink for skating.
Near the bench where the skaters rest,
a fire was blazing in a fifty-gallon drum.
We heard music coming from the dark
beyond the fire before we saw the figure
bent at the waist and playing a wooden flute
as he glided in and out of the light:
numen of breath and wood and icy air.

*from*Autumn in the Alaska Range (2000)

New Poem

At Dusk 832 A.D.

AnIrish monk has drawn a small blackbird
with spindly legs and saffron-yellow beak.
It's sitting on a curving branch of gold
in the margin of his still unfinished Irish
copy of a psalm written out in Latin.
It's a sweet-tongued little Ulster bird.
The abbot will smile beneath his frown
when he sees it there in the margin.

Pleased,the monk turns toward the window
to watch the sea's white frenzied hair.
No Norse raider will come from there tonight.
There will be no need to tremble in his cell
or to quickly smother the tallowcandle
that warms his moving hand and sharpened quill.
September, centuries later, I close
the book before me,look out my window.

JANET SHEPPERSON

The Belfast Urban Area Plan (Revised)

I dreamed I saw the City Hall subsiding—
wavering like a drunk, its straight lines buckling,
its grey hide wrinkling, all its legs giving way,
till it sank down with a sigh like a cow in a meadow

full of daisies. The air was heavy with humming,
loud as a thousand bees. I passed the Lord Mayors,
stiff on their pedestals, straight-faced under pigeon shit,
respectable as only dead men can be,

and Frederick Temple, Marquess of Dufferin and Ava,
Canadian Governer General, Viceroy of India,
his chest a tangle of tassels and medals that must be
stunting his growth, the way ivy strangles a tree trunk.

When I rounded the corner, the ground was littered with fragments
like twigs, or prunings, smooth and grey and bulbous,
and the humming was louder. Women in yellow helmets
were ignoring the trees, and having a go at the statues:

their chain saw took a chunk out of a frock coat,
buttons bounced on the grass, a stern beard juddered
and went sailing through the air. *Stand clear*, they told me,
this lot are all coming down. There exists a shortfall

of recreational space in the Inner City.
Look at that fellow—you couldn't say he was exactly
recreational. Besides, he's rotten
inside, you hear him creaking when it's stormy

—if he comes down on your head, you'll know all about it.
We plan to plant small trees here, flexible
enough to bend with the wind, they won't strike poses
or preach or rant—the perfect Urban Forest.

The last I saw was Carson up at Stormont;
his hand, that had pawed the air for decades, quivered
as the hum of triumphant bees rose to a crescendo,
and he dropped his fingers and clutched his plinth as they came.

from The Aphrodite Stone (1995)

Tremors

The bomb exploded a mile and a half away
—our house twitched slightly, dust fell from the ceiling.
Two men were murdered at the Cleansing Depot
—for days our street was full of bins not emptied.

Always the epicentre is somewhere else
—only the tremors reach us, gruesome, banal,
like the Red Hand of Ulster at Mount Stewart
Gardens, set with tired geraniums.

It's the hand I think of. The woman who lost two fingers
in the blast. She appeared in the paper, nameless,
ousted next day by more casualties, more dead.
Patched up by plastic surgery, Valium,

and prayer, will she pull her life together,
picking her way through a web of absences?
I start to notice people's hands, as if
hers with its awkward gap—scars not yet healed—

is waiting for me. In the newsagent's
she's the one who can't untie a knot
to lay out a stack of papers. She hands me change
cautiously; a coin rolls to the floor.

At lunchtime in the pub, she balances
a glass, but can't quite manage knife and fork.
At the school gates she takes her children's hands,
flinching as they touch where it's still sore.

In church she kneels beside me at the rail,
holding her cupped hands to receive the wafer,
the fingers of one hand lightly cradling the other,
tilted slightly; trembling with the strain.

Everything she touches bears the print
of grief, bewilderment, courage. My own hands
ache in this bitter wind. My fingers itch
and then turn numb, as if they were already gone.

from The Aphrodite Stone (1995)

Warthog

I have brushed from his back and ears the mess of cobwebs
that grew as he sat in the dusty curio hut
near the Nyalazi Gate, dreaming of mud
and the soft hiss of rain. Now, swart and wary,
he sits on the glossy top shelf of my bookcase.
(He has kicked off all the other ornaments.)
He is carved from soft wood hardened and darkened by smoke,
with only his tusks left pale and vulnerable,
one slightly chipped in transit, one still sharp.

The room's too smooth. It has no antbear holes
for him to back into, hindquarters first,
watching me with suspicious piggy eyes.
When I go out, he gets down, rootling through
my too-sparse undergrowth of papers, searching out
anything small and sweet, perhaps decayed
and squishy, tasty juice oozing across
the dry unpromising floor. He wants to fatten
himself on succulence while there's still time.

With disbelief he views the tumbling rain
outside my window. He knows it can't last.
He remembers Umfolozi, years of drought,
the river Hluhluwe narrowing
then gone. Its bed bare rocks. The stranded boat
that should be taking trippers to the dam
roosting on dried-up mud. The thinning grass
brittle as straw. Palm and acacia losing
their soft green, shrivelling. Leaves tinder-dry.

He watches in alarm. It's happening here.
Leaves have curled up and staggered to the ground,
tawny and brown, the colours of distress,
but still they glisten, and tired winter grass
stays green. He can't look upward but he knows
the tight-stretched eyeball-hurting blue has gone,
replaced by endless permutating cloud.
Rain is like jewels, and mud is like salvation.
He sits back on his haunches, settles in.

JAMES SIMMONS

Ghosts and Beasts

1.

The people here know all the inside dirt,
a wife oppressed, an aspiring son hurt,
badgered to death. Was Frost so vain and bitter
suicidal, angry, mean ... and does it matter?

It does; but I don't for a moment turn away
from what he made of that life, poetry.

2.

A ghost haunted me.
Muddy footsteps up the corridor
came from the bathroom to my bedroom
and turned right to the cellar.
There was tap breath
as of a metal drum
up from beneath.

3.

And some bitter Irish
haunt me and hate me.
Will time find them out?
Or have they, as a Catholic colleague told me,
something to be bitter about?

4.

Now there was an educated man
with a good mind
from The Bogside; but you'll find
there was that time at Coleraine

when he failed to live up
to his mission of speaking out
for the underdog, cowtowed
to suave colleagues, connived,
and had to be badgered
into rectitude
by this liberal with his mild
manner and all the advantages,
who cleared up the mess,
the gerrymanderer's grandchild.

5.

Wild hyena and tame cur,
black bear and wolf;
they howl with stiff fur
outside my house
in an unhappy ring.
I invite them to my hearth,
but they will not sup or sing.

from The Company of Children (1999)

357

Ballycastle

for Medbh

I once came down here with Ernie Mann's 'Black
Songbirds,' after dark, from Portrush, this town's
big sister up the coast that lies on her stiff back,
open, exposed ... houses built on a spine of rock
sticking out, looking down on the broad
Atlantic, sharp like a bird's beaked head ...
Portrush is not dead stone, it shouts and sings,
leaning back, always. I remember the beaches flowed
whitely from her shoulders like stretched wings.

Everything shelters Ballycastle and looks down ...
the wooded hills and headlands. Driving here,
in daylight, you descend the glen by stages—three
spangled green tunnels of old trees—and suddenly
drop into the sheltered heart of the town,
down a hill of pubs, grocers and hardware
to the spired Anglican church, the market square.

I never looked till today—but it *is*
a market town with houses for families,
butchers, chemists, a substantial Catholic school
under the comforting, curved and nippled
grey breast of Knoclaide—the broad hill
I climbed with my first wife one crucial
fair day, when noise and pleasure rippled.

Boys from Portrush came down to the Royal Hotel
on Sunday nights for dances to raise hell
in a small way. Today I followed the one street down
out of the town centre to the sea: all
the gardens have high thick hedges crowned
with roses, safe houses for retirement, and space
for gapped ruins rented by trees and grass.

The countryside comes right down to the shore
to tennis, contested on top of the Dane's harbour,
the kept turf of the golf course that surrounds

the Priory. Herbs, crushed by our spiked shoes
in the springy grass, raise perfumes that confound
our senses like turf smoke and seagull cries.
Council improvement teams obscure the views.

. . . .

Glen's foot and river's end—
the curved shore is sheltered
by might headlands.
Under the cliffs, Medbh's house nestles,
not far out, but all alone,
in the sea's mouth broad Rathlin
is the big stone.

from Mainstream (1995)

Janice

My love, my softy, my brown swan,
swimming now in the brimming river
of my affections. Will you swim on
forever and forever.

My love, my freckled gardener
busy with balm and briony,
Americanly kind and conscious
of the limitations of irony ...

supportive to a fault, hurt
by local abrasiveness, our wit,
the winding up and putting down,
brilliance that has no heart in it.

I grow less Irish every year
with kindly love to lean upon.
Our home and garden is my nation,
my freckled gardener, my swan.

from Mainstream (1995)

JANICE FITZPATRICK SIMMONS

The Husband's Photograph

Behind him is the farmhouse
on a shoulder of land.
Muck's tail rises darkly from bright water.
I know that rocks in reflection move and change
on the surface, chimeras, nothing solid.

And in front of the background farm
is the dog leg harbour wall…
then all that blue. That blue!

The car park is empty,
the old boathouse is empty.
A few belated boats shelter by concrete walls
set in the base of a hill.

Here, in the centre of the photograph
my husband stands, his arms spread
high and wide in blessing and friendship.

He arranges the earth for me,
kindly weather and harvest,
crazy Borage rampant, as blue as his eyes,
in clusters about his feet revealing

his comic, vulnerable and priestly nature,
ordering obedience to vision,
attempting to juggle the family from palm to palm.

from Starting at Purgatory (1999)

Bird Song

I

The sun rises. Nations rise,
and the morning birds
lift their territorial song
over the day.
Purple Finches, Orioles, Sparrows,
the ornate Cockatoo, The African Crane
call out the day's activities.

This morning mothers rise
to pots and pans, droughts,
wars, glorious recreation
and sudden death.
Across the Mohave, the Andes, the Grand Canyon,
the sun rends
and crashes against the blinking eye
harsh as white-capped waves.

II

In this small New England valley
the poverty in the hollows lies hidden.
The sun falls in bright waves
beneath summer leaves.

And tourists come in Cardinal Red BMWs;
in Mercedes Sports Coupés
sleek as Peregrine Falcons cutting
mid-day sky.
Familiar are the indistinct blues
of ancient Chevys and the local habit
of descending on the dump

for plugs and wiring—
the summeer people's throw-aways.
The Blue Jay stays too;
all winter he raids and searches.

In the song-rocked forest
light falls through fast clouds
wave-like on the running water
where salmon follow instinct
to move against the current.

III

Night birds rise. Small towns and nations rest.
The long fast day has fallen aside.
The call of the Thrush, the Owl
fill dreams which rise

as salmon might from coldest water.
And over all the stars
that scientists plot and track
envisioning them to be our escape.
We might be whole flocks
that can take flight before a nuclear winter—
our call, the call of a thousand engines.

And still the nightmares feed the waking days
and the territorial and human song
falls like fire, pitifully, like rain after fire.

from Settler (1995)

Lughnasa

For Gearoid MacLochlinn

I've got the end of summer blues.
I've got the end of summer moving on blues.
I've got the end of summer not enough money to buy clothes blues.
I've got the moving on, moving into rented accommodation blues.

I've got the blues
I've got the end of summer not knowing a soul blues.
I've got the moving on love in abeyance blues.
I've got the end of summer blues.
I've got the end of summer moving on leaving the graveside blues.

I've got the end of summer getting older blues.
I've got the blues, the weather howling,
storm engulfed, autumn coming blues.
There is nothing for it cause I have
the end of summer, love in abeyance blues.

I've got the blues, the monoglot, want to be on
a beach in France blues. An end of summer
miss the poets, moving on blues.

I've got the blues, I am playing Joni Mitchell's *Blue*,
I am sitting in my blue living room with end of summer,
the end of summer, moving on, getting older blues.

ROBIN SKELTON

Two in a Garden
(Áe Freslige)

Lovers, we lie wondering
why our amorous leisure's
marred by spectres blundering
through our pastoral pleasures

under trees' tranquillity
blossoming boughs above us,
whispering futility
and names of other lovers.

Samhain

for Alison

(Droigneach)

Mystery attends the year when Earth confesses
and uncontrollable need of celebration
and each leaf in the Autumn orchard expresses
in ochre and bronze and crimson the conflagration

needed now the seasons are nearing transition,
the fire that is power and pride and supervenes
whenever the slowing sun threatens inanition,
pallid and shadowy over the evergreens

that still spire upwards, needles gaunt, unchanging,
remote, it would seem, from the earth's predicament.
There comes a time in the year when, rearranging
summer memories, colours rustling, resplendent,

the crisp dry leaves call out to us and, responding,
we build a fire of the broken and dismembered
fragments of earthly suffering and, extending
hands to the dead who are, in this blaze, remembered,

celebrate the riches we've known, the profusion,
the births, the deaths, the ever changing history,
finding in fire a vision beyond illusion,
welcoming the holiness and the mystery.

On the Moor

for Jane Urquhart

(Trian Rannaigechta móire)

A lone pleasure's
wandering where
purple heather,
haunting air,

appears to move
within the eye
as if a mode
of memory,

a kind of dream
that is a past
we nefver knew
and never lost

but keep within
the marrow bone
and feel it when
we walk alone.

All from Samhain and Other Poems in Irish Metres
of the Eighth to the Sixteenth Centuries (1994)

KNUTE SKINNER

The Bears

Not my father but my mother.
That's who you see on the footpath,
holding my hand while I look at the bears.

Old and overexposed.
The snapshot, I mean, not my mother.
About her, I can nothing say.
I was still in pipe curls.

I do remember the bears.
They were large and dark and I didn't like
their heavy, deliberate movements.
When one of them came near the barrier,
Mother tightened her grip and said,
"Do you see the bear?"

Mother looks like a bear herself in that long dark coat.
Of course it would make you think
that she was my father.

But it wasn't even my father who took the picture.
He was gone by then—somewhere in South America.
If he had taken the picture, it would be in focus.

from The Bears and Other Poems (1991)

368

Keeping Warm

"Doesn't life get shorter by the minute?"
I turned to locate the speaker,
impressed by the audacity
of the cliché.

What I saw was a spare old man
speaking into his pint
and letting our end of the bar listen in
as he talked to himself.

Outside a promising season had clouded over.
Inside a man in an unlikely Mexican vest
was urging on me a whiskey I only half wanted.
It was his birthday, he said.

Along the bar there were men keeping warm
in the company of laughter and drink.
Then a new one came in from the rain.

"Whatcha drinking, craychur?" the pretty
young bargirl asked him—
still dressed in her school uniform—

and "Mercy Bee Coo," she said to the birthday man
as he paid for my whiskey.

The spare old man looked up at her from his pint.
"Doesn't life get shorter by the minute?"
he asked her.

from What Trudy Knows and Other Poems (1994)

A Question for God

At the end of his life, Job got his cattle back and became a
Happy Man, but all Jesus got was the Resurrection.
   —from a student response to a test question

What were they like, Job's cattle?
Were they dry stock? milkers?
Did he scrutinise them with contented, proprietary interest
while complacently caressing spots
where the boils had been?
Did his comforters eye with envy
a Happy Man?
a man blessed with such cattle?

God only knows, I suppose,
so go ask God.
All He got was the Resurrection, of course,
but He's up there in Heaven with Himself
where He/They remember Job's cattle
and remember his boils
and remember those faithful who witnessed the Resurrection
believing, perhaps, in their limited vision,
it was quite enough.

JO SLADE

Someone Must Go Voyaging And Bring Back Other Ways Of Seeing

Someone must go voyaging
And bring back other ways of seeing,
Different eyes in new colours,
Yellow as dandelions or pink
And delicate as the common mallow.

My man bought me sapphire eyes
He took them from a Tibetan woman.
He laid his head in her lap
Inside a cool temple with gold
And silver mosaic walls.

Her beautiful mouth opened,
It was the sun rising
Behind a mountain, he said.
Now when we talk together
There is a smell of wild rhubarb

And where we sit the air
Is dense with expectancy.
It was my saint's day,
He came to celebrate, he brought me
Sapphire eyes in a velvet purse.

I said our first born would
Be conceived in the shadow
Of her mouth. He said,
Someone must go voyaging even
If the mountain is lost in dark.

from In Fields I Hear Them Sing (1989)

Semana Santa / Andalusia

For Pauline Goggin

Our Lady of Loneliness, Our Lady of the Red Earth
Mother of the Pure and the Impure Mother of Sorrows
Virgin of the Moon and the Stars
Black Virgin of the Sea in her winter house facing the storm
in her white church that rocks like a boat—
shelter for women who cannot grow old
shelter for sisters and talk of sisters.

Black Virgin of the Waves in her summer home
at the foot of the mountain
protection for strangers and the goatherd.
Compassion for the black pig who grazes
in the shade of the jacaranda.
Pity for women who have sons and daughters
and for women who don't.
Bless them with stars that dance on the water.
Tenderness for children. *Todas los besos.*

Songs for men who smell of the horse, *Toda mi fuerza.*
Prayer for the bull who remembers his daughters
and refuses to die, for his heart that beats into the night
and penetrates the joy of the crowd, that isn't joy
but fear of joy. Pity for bulls on the camino de tauro.

Virgin of Gardens, Our Lady of Blood
is the poinsettia tree in spring. Prayer for women who bleed.
Our Lady of Squalor Mother of Perpetual Help
Virgin of Horror swathed in snow. Mother of the Blind
Daughter to Anna, Virgin of the Unbound
Star of the Sea who is guide to the Father, remember me.

Our Lady of the Rocks in her dark cave under the earth
in her white shift smelling of dust—*toda mi muerte.*
Mother of all Deaths—Remember us.

*Todas los besos/Toda mi fuerza/toda mi muerta
(All the kisses/All my strength/all my deaths).

from City Of Bridges (2005)

The Painter

Chronology : Gwen John to Marlene Dumas

Indelible heart
fades beneath the skin
but not.
Baby hands
dipped at birth
drip colour out.

The snow its pure untouched
becomes a trail of wound—
a creature strayed
a winter bitch
a wolf perhaps.

R. T. SMITH

Bear Mischief

I am told a bear
can shinny up a honey tree
in an instant, can
force a fat paw deep
into the trove in spite
of sliding bark slabs,
gravity and angry bees.
I am told it is less hunger
than a love of sugars
and the joy of victory
and the clot of amber
on fur and maw. Also,
I have heard our ursine
cousin can run faster
than a Kenyan miler or
spy the flash of fish
in a shallow river, can in fact
catch what shimmers,
not because wild things
are enchanted, pure or
deserving, but because they
share with us a sense
of mischief, awe at the dance
of bees, ecstasy over
the cold fire of trout
in the river. These things
I am told at every turn,
and when I climb a hollow
tree or bend on stones
to plunge my hand through
the sound of the river,
I believe the hour of bear
has come round at last

and rejoice at kinship,
feast on elderberries all
morning, then look about
for a place to sleep till
all my humans yearnings cease,
give way to honey, speed,
rainbow meat and a bouquet
of claws to halt my sliding
earthwards before I'm ready.
Thereby this mischief ever
enchants me. As wildwood
ecstasy, it disperses all
sense of envy. It is a pure
immersion my best dreams
suggest I may yet
learn to deserve.

from Split the Lark: Selected Poems (1999)

Cardinal Directions

In the body of a cardinal
who hops along the tamarack limbs,
cathedrals are collapsing. Whole
worlds are falling, exhausted
stars and dialects no one left
can translate. This crested finch,
red as the last cannas
wilting, is famished. He scavenges
in a dry season for pods,
cold grubs, any scrap to sharpen
his beak or hone his sight,
and also within me the tree
of bones is giving way
to gravity, the tree of nerves
surrendering, memory's tree
releasing its leaves, though my
eyes are still seeds looking
for fertile soil, and the one bird
heavy in my chest, the cardinal
heart, still has ambitions
to forage, to sing the litany
beyond language, and fly.

from Split the Lark: Selected Poems (1999)

Dar He

When I am the lone listener to the antiphony of crickets
and the two wild tribes of cicadas and let my mind
wander to its bogs, its sloughs where no endorphins fire,

I will think on occasion how all memory is longing
for the lost energies of innocence, and then one night—
whiskey and the Pleiades, itch from a wasp sting—

I realize it is nearly half a century since that nightmare
in Money, Mississippi, when Emmett Till was dragged
from his uncle Mose Wright's cabin by two strangers

because he might have wolf whistled at Carolyn Bryant,
a white woman from whom he had bought candy,
or maybe he just whispered "Bye," as the testimony

was confused and jangled by fear. The boy was not local,
and Chicago had taught him minor mischief, but what
he said hardly matters, and he never got to testify,

for the trial was for murder after his remains were dredged
from the Tallahatchie River, his smashed body with one
eye gouged out and a bullet in the brain and lashed

with barbed wire to a cotton gin fan whose vanes
might have seemed petals of some metal flower, had Bobo
—as friends at home called him—ever seen it. And why

this might matter to me tonight is that I was not yet eight
when the news hit and can remember my parents at dinner—
maybe glazed ham, probably hand-whipped potatoes,

iced tea sweeter than candy, as it was high summer—
shaking their heads in passing and saying it was a shame,
but the boy should have been smarter and known never

to step out of his place, especially that far South. Did I
even guess, did I ask how a word or stray note could give birth
to murder? He was fourteen, and on our flickering new TV,

sober anchormen from Atlanta registered their shock,
while we ate our fine dinner and listened to details
from the trial in Sumner, though later everyone learned

the crime occurred in Sunflower County, and snoopy
reporters from up north had also discovered that missing
witnesses—Too Tight Collins among them—could

finger the husband Roy Bryant and his step-brother
named Milam as the men in the truck who asked, "Where
the boy done the talking?" and dragged Emmett Till

into the darkness. His mother Mamie, without whom
it would have all passed in the usual secrecy, requested
an open-casket funeral, so the mourners all saw the body

maimed beyond recognition—his uncle had known
the boy only by a signet ring—and *Jet* magazine
then showed photos, working up the general rage

and indignation, so the trial was speedy, five days
with a white jury, which acquitted, the foreman
reporting that the state had not adequately established

the identity of the victim, and I don't know how
my father the cop or his petite wife the Den Mother
took it all, though in their eighties they have no love

for any race darker than a tanned Caucasian. I need
a revelation to lift me from the misery of remembering,
as I get the stigma of such personal history twisted

into the itch of that wasp sting. Milam later told *Life*
he and Bryant were "guilty as sin," and there is some
relief in knowing their town shunned them and drove

Bryant out of business, but what keeps haunting me—
glass empty, the insect chorus fiercer, more shrill—
is the drama played out in my mind like a scene

from some reverse *To Kill a Mockingbird*—or worse,
a courtroom fiasco from a Faulkner novel—when
the prosecutor asked Mr. Wright if he could find

in the room the intruder who snatched his nephew
out of bed that night, and the old man—a great uncle,
really—fought back his sobs and pointed at the accused,

his finger like a pistol aimed for the heart. "Dar he,"
he said, and the syllables yet echo into this raw night
like a poem that won't be silenced, like the choir

of seven-year insects, their voices riddling strange
as sleigh bells through the summer air, the horrors
of injustice still simmering, and I now wonder what

that innocence I miss might have been made of—
smoke? rhinestones? gravied potatoes followed
by yellow cake and milk? Back then we called

the insect infestation *ferros*, thinking of Hebrew
captivity in Egypt and believing they were chanting
free us, instead of the *come hither* new science

insists on, but who can dismiss the thought
that forty-nine years back their ancestors dinned
a river of sound all night extending lament

to lamentation, and I am shaken by the thought
of how easy it is for me to sit here under sharp
stars which could mark in heaven the graves

of tortured boys and inhale the dregs of expensive
whiskey the color of a fox, how convenient
to admit where no light shows my safe face

that I have been less than innocent this entire
life and never gave a second thought to this:
even the window fan cooling my bedroom

stirs the air with *blades*, and how could anyone
in a civilized nation ever be condemned for
narrowing breath to melody between the teeth,

and if this is an exercise in sham shame I am
feeling, some wish for absolution, then I have to
understand the wave of nausea crossing me,

this conviction that it is not simple irony
making the whir of voices from the pine trees
now seem to be saying *Dar he, Dar he, Dar he.*

EITHNE STRONG

However Long that Dark

(from the original Irish, 1989:
Dá Fhad an Oíche)

Today will be black night
and pain will spear each pulse—
I know it;
the dark tunnel on and on—
this I understand;
life that is as death for you—
I feel it.
I know, understand, feel,
because it was for me
a like stretch of time;
by this I am marked
so that now with utter sureness
I can urge you, beloved human,
to search out your courage;
even if the bitter stone
in your chest is, you think,
for ever
and you can take no more,
hold fast, hold fast:
that stone will melt,
the tunnel will become
a flow of discovery
and it will be again morning—
I have seen it.

Nothing Heavenly

No Elysian fields, I will just walk out
one day and up that hill that watches Shannon.
At the top I will look back feeling a huge smile.
I will not laugh, need not. I will be liking
it easy, my feet loose of the knots and pits.
At the bottom down there behind me will be
fear, finished, its toxic waste a mystery,
the concern of someone else. I will have
no conscience. I will have done my peculiar
digging, persisted, puzzled at the globe.

Causes of my fear:
    you, the brilliant young who inherit.
        On the hill I will say: You are welcome:
        I took have a heritage—of Nothing.
        I will further say: Nothing, I salute you,
        I love your lack of weight, I have been
        longing for our union.

    you, abstractionists:
        your nothing seemed different,
        showing off, pseudo.

you, materialists who represent
        sleeping in cardboard boxes
        on the streetside of locked doors,
        in alleys, under bridges;
        the reduction of my kin;
        starvation amid plenty.

    our incomprehensible destructiveness

And then having enumerated, I shall remember
my Nothing, shall consider that annihilation
could be various: perhaps on that hilltop
that watches Shannon, the annihilated causes
of my fear and I will easily commingle, smile
our big big smile at the enigma, tell one another
freedom begins only where finishes fear.

Spatial Nosing

Who'll tell the story? you said.
An open issue that but—

Ah love, my love, what are you doing now?
Does the polygamous tendency persist?
I dare say there, wherever it is—
down amid the roots, the laval essences,
out in the measureless voids—it is
a fairly general condition, lightly taken
as breating. Polyandrous too. That's how
it should have been.

Too bad the way we were conditioned.
How heavily we took all that stuff,
the dark edicts Thou shalt not do this
not this nor ... I'd say it was they
that caused me mealy joints, aluminium hips,
early dentures, fogged eyes since ten.
Bionic woman my grandson calls me.
He is right.

And you, my darling? I suppose your
heaviest afflictions was the pursuit
of cure: it meant panting after it in
all those women, ending up with milky Flo;
the scrutiny of menus whereon were choices
with eclectic names like Whither Appetite?
Vindication of Eros, Reverent Quest,
Why Prostitution? Psyche in Trousers.

I am curious to know how you're doing now
if without pressure of pursuit and search.
Do they blaze a bonfire of inhibitions?
Polygamy for all, polyandry too? Is it very
dull sans tensions? What for incentive?
I'll be nosing spatially one of these days,
under and over and out—five years plus
or so I'd say: you'll fill me in?

all from Spatial Nosing: New & Selected Poems (1993)

BREDA SULLIVAN

Bone

I dust the blackboard now and think of bone
strong bone disintegrating into dust
white powder on the cold grey flags of stone.

My mother broke her hip, I heard her groan
the ambulance arrived and no one fussed
I dust the blackboard now and think of bone.

At the clinic for the screening of the bone
I check in, wait my turn, I think of rust
and powder on the cold grey flags of stone.

Back forth, back forth, back forth the scanner zone
I lie, stare ceiling-wards, I do not trust
I dust the blackboard now and think of bone.

The gene that wrecked her hip betrays my bone
already the destruction is like lust
white powder on the cold grey flags of stone.

I walk, drink milk, eat yogurt and I moan
my bone a honeycomb, this is not just.
I dust the blackboard now and think of bone
white powder on the cold grey flags of stone.

from After the Ball (1998)

Journey

Track steep, stones
sharp and loose.

On a bench
outside his log cabin

a white-bearded man
smokes a clay pipe.

I leave the track,
approach him and ask:

Is this the way
to the summit?

Is it the summit
that's important?

No I reply
it's the journey.

He goes inside,
returns with a paper bag:

a cheese sandwich
to sustain me.

from Sculpture in Black Ice (2004)

Retired

I love the morning

he rises first,
quietly. I sleep on,

unaware. My alarm
clock the clink of delph.
Reluctant to leave

my well of dreams
slowly I waken.
Before I rearrange
the pillows, sit up

he is back
beneath the duvet.
Together we sip tea,
eat brown bread
I baked

the day before,
hear the news
and weather;
morning a chink
between curtains.
I know out there:

traffic lights turn red,
pedestrians strain
for the green man,
children spill
from school buses
and someone else opens
the classroom door.

RICHARD TILLINGHAST

A Quiet Pint in Kinvara

Salt-stung, rain-cleared air, deepened as always
By a smudge of turf smoke. Overhead the white glide
Of seagulls, and in the convent beeches above the road,
Hoarse croak of rooks, throaty chatter of jackdaws.
High tide pounds stone wall.
I shut my door behind me and head downhill,

Gait steadied by the broad-shouldered gravity
Of houses from the eighteenth or nineteenth century—
Limestone, threee storeys, their slate roofs rain-slick,
Aglow with creeper and the green brilliance of mosses.
No force off the Atlantic
Could threaten their angles or budge their masses.

They rise hurriedly from the strong cellar
And hold a fleshy hand, palm outward, against the sea,
Saying "Land starts here. Go peddle your salt airs elsewhere."
From farms down lanes the meat and milk of pasture,
Root crops and loads of hay,
By hoof or wagon, come down to Kinvara quay.

And so do I—to drink in the presence
Of these presences, these ideas given substance,
Solid as your father's signature
On a letter you unfold sometimes from a quiet drawer,
Yet semi-detached, half free,
Like the road that follows the sea down from Galway,

Curving like a decorated S
Drizzled through a monk's quill plucked from the goose,
Spelling *Sanctus* onto vellum newly missed by the herd,
In a cell where the soul's damp candle flared—
Roofless now to the weather's
Inundations, while ravens walk the cloisters.

Gloria of martyrdoom, kingship's crimson
Are shattered now, buried in mire. The mizzling sky
Darkens unmitigated over thatch collapsed into famine,
Tracks leading nowhere. Absences occupy
The four kingdoms. A wide-eyed
Angel stares uncomprehendingly skyward,

Stone angel of the Island, baptised by rain,
Outlasting Viking longboat, Norman strongbow,
Face battered by a rifle butt. Tough-minded as a bloody saint.
But wherre was I off to, mind like a darkened window
This dampened afternoon?
To the pub of course. It's time for that quiet pint,

Brewed blacker than ruination, sound
As fresh-hewn timber, strong as a stonecutter's hand.
Make it stout like the roof overhead, to take off the chill
That blows through emptied fields. Let me drink my fill
And more, of that architecture—
Then ease home tight and respectable to dinner.

A Quiet Pint in Kinvara (1991)

The Emigrant

Two places only
there were:
here and America.
The four corners of the farm,
and gone-beyond-the-sea.

With a twopenny nail
he etched into the iron
shank of his spade
the word 'Destiny',
drove it with his boot smartly into the turf
and left it standing.

Abroad commenced
at the town line.
The New World blinded him
on the Navan road
and again the first time he tried to speak English
and again the first time he saw an orange.

Anaesthetized by reels and barrels of porter
and eight renditions of 'The Parting Glass',
he fell asleep to the groan of oars
and awoke to a diesel thrust
and sleet over mountainous seas.

from Today in the Café Trieste (1997)

Snowflakes & a Jazz Waltz

You have things to do, but the snow doesn't care.
As contemplation leads you
from window to window, the snow
accompanies you.
Whenever you glance up from the page, there it is—
layered, dense, constant.

It amplifies the volume of space
and gives you a way of telling time.

Eradication of emptiness, a specific against ennui,
it works, like truth, on a slant.

Its lightness
responds to gravity
by drift and evasion.
As you drive around town
it slackens and intensifies—
a sideways sizzle of dashes and dots.

While you circle the block, visualizing a parking place,
listening on tape to the cymbal-glide
and diminished chords of a jazz waltz
from forty years ago
when you were twenty,
a cash register rings

through the buzz and boozy hum of the Village Vanguard
that Sunday afternoon through cocktail chatter and
cigarette smoke exhaled
by people many of whom must now be dead.
Bill Evans is. Scott LaFaro is—
killed in a car crash
decades ago.

But not you. You drive
through the snow and the morning.
Snow drifts and ticks;

Bill Evans vamps,
and Scott LaFaro's fingers slap against the strings
of his standup bass
in time with the Honda's windshield wipers and
tires whirring over packed snow.

It snows while you go into the bank and buy euros
and it's snowing when you
come out again.

Snowflakes-white constellations
dissolving.
      Indelible
snowflakes
printing the book of your hours.

OLAF TYARANSEN

Back to Front
for the girl behind me

When I turn my back
to your front
as we lie at
equal distances from
each other on
restless sheets,
it is not because I
don't want to look at you
or lose my hair in yours
but because I need to feel
your warm breath on my back
fueling my soul and pushing me
to greater things, like an
Eastern wind to a
Westbound boat.

from *The Consequences of Slaughtering Butterflies* (1992)

My Entry to the Bewley's Poetry Competition

I'm sitting comfortably
by the window in Bewley's
with a mug of coffee
and the *Irish Times*.

I feel very secure
sitting here surrounded
by kitchen sounds, bored housewives
and ageing hippies.

There is an ad in
the paper—a picture
of a weak elderly African woman.
She looks near to death.
Underneath I am informed that
I can save her life
for a pound a day.

I look at my steaming
coffee cup. It cost fifty pence
(half a granny). Momentarily
I feel guilty.

I drink about
two lives worth of coffee
per day
in Bewley's.

But because Bewley's is a great café
with great coffee,
I turn the page
and raise my cup.

from *The Consequences of Slaughtering Butterflies* (1992)

Yours Truly

Truly I'll miss yours
Now that it's all yours
Its hot oily tang
And peach fragrance
Quivering moistness
Over my eager lips
My thrusting tongue tasting
What was to come.

First published in The Journal of Erotica (1995)

JOHN UNRAU

Walking Home To Mayfair, January 1928

a mile back now
Keatley's milking barn,
snuffle and slow crunch
and sighing of his cows

Friday night,
the weekly wage
safe in your mitt;
smell of the barn yielding
to taste of damp half-frozen wool,
the scarf she knit wrapped twice over your face

you have laboured since dawn
and now every tenth step or so
(the average toted as you walk)
drops you through the teasing crust
in snow up to your knees;
eleven miles still to home:
on Sunday night the same trek back again

at this moment though,
under a black poplar
creaking in a pulse of air
that sends ribbons of ice
falling through starlight,
you are not refugee
farm worker, husband,
provider to those six
waiting in your sod house,
nor scarcely a breathing man
as you see
what never will be seen again—
that ridge raised by

a fieldmouse under snow,
blue shadows trapped in rabbit tracks,
the glide of a snowy owl
through the reeds above
the Frenchman's frozen slough,
and in that stillness coyote calls
—Tallis voices raised across the drifts

yes it must have been like this
some time on those nights
so quietly passed over in two lines
of Uncle's computerized family history;
and as you plough onward again
I see all around
from Spiritwood and Mildred
Robinhood and Redfield
Mullingar and Whitkow
Hawkeye and Belbutte,
men walking wrapped in their own breath—
all our weary grandfathers
carrying our lives
triumphantly toward us through
blue-black Saskatchewan night

from Iced Water (2000)

Alderson, Alberta: "Star Of The Prairie"

(founded 1910; ghost town by mid-50s)

in the burnt grass
a gopher's skull
rotted clean
washed and blown
paper thin

crimson waves
of grasshopper wings
fan out over sage and cactus
ahead of my careful steps
until, near the level crossing
among fresh gopher mounds
rabbit droppings
a rattlesnake's skin,
I find four boulders
spaced much too evenly,
a rusted gearwheel
and finally
this thin sprawl
of shattered boards

I had read of your decay
in one of Aunt's old newspapers
and feeling desolate myself
came to touch,
make your desolation mine

but surrounded today
by this hot burrowing life,
those antelope grazing
where Railway Avenue ran,
a hawk overhead,
meadowlark on the wind,
I can't suppress
a quiet joy
as I stand within these
scarcely discernible

scoops and scratchings
in the dryland dirt
where your thousand walls once rose
from their shallow dream beds

from Iced Water (2000)

Vespers

Rachmaninoff, Op.37

The voices drifted away some time ago,
along with the bathwater.
No need though to rewind the old tape
with that sombre sweetness still
stirring across my throat and guts.

I've been stupefying myself again
on a giant disquietude,
the undirected cravings
your music lures me to;

and though it's been a privilege
to join you in this vigil,
the cold enamel against my spine
tells me it's time to snuff the candles,
down these 17 last drops of wine,
and hoist myself back up and out
into the smaller world I left behind
an hour or so ago;
though not without a parting glance
at whatever stars happen to be moving
across the open skylight overhead.

JEAN VALENTINE

Dufy Postcard

The postcard taped on your white kitchen has roses, in a white
bowl, on the blue and green shadowed table; the table is brown,
yellow. Down the wallpaper's field of pink roses, a violet shadow
turns brown, moves across the floor: now the lines go off the card,
the lines of the walls, one curved foot of the round table, the
oblong shadow; the floor ends mid-air, here:

> You sitting at your table
> looking at the postcard. Green
> day lights the windows; everyone
> still asleep. Taut lines.

> Day, with its hours, and buildings;
> people start, around you. You wait
> a minute more in the white room—
> white tent against the snowed-over path, the wind,
> its familiar voice—*one life*—

> Every day you move farther outside
> the outlines, kinder, more dangerous.
> Where will you be going.
> Who will the others be.

The Sea of Serenity

The Sea of Serenity:
my mother's body: ashes:
the appearance of land, and the appearance of water.

Books by the fireplace: gold brocade and silver:
but love, oh love. Outside the door.

Earth said, *Eat.*
Earth said, *Shame.*

Mother,
on my hands and knees,
face flat in the leaves,
I chomp after you like a horse.

Who died?
Who died?
Who died?

The Power Table

You, lying across the wide bed, vertical,
I, horizontal,

you, I, in a green field two green paths
flowered with xxxx's and xxxx's

you, I, lined inside
with pre-historic quarrels

old black cuts
in a wooden kitchen table

the table where you sit down with your older brothers
the table where things get settled once and for all

the cow's hip shaved down to the brand
her body divided into zones

Yes I am standing in the doorway
yes my softness and hardness are filled with a secret light,

but I want world-light
and this-world company.

all from The Under Voice: Selected Poems (1995)

PETER VAN DE KAMP

Milton Was Blind

> *Of man's first disobedience, and the fruit*
> *Of that forbidden tree, whose mortal taste*
> *Brought death into the world, and all our woe....*
>   John Milton, *Paradise Lost*

Of man's etcet.
lest we forget
how young you were
and where we met
the à la carte you ate
in *that happy state*
it put me in the red
for life,
in bed
that night
you said
the food was good,
I understood.

from Notes (1999)

5 May. Liberation Day

for Ida G.M. Gerhardt

Beyond me a peal of fallacy:
How that 'peasant poet' could sing
The parish is the universal thing!
There's no carillon in Tralee,
No grace notes lift up our eyes to Thee;
The mutable thud of the hour,
The Angelus from the bell tower—
Taped tones of doubtful quality
Amplify our sham mortality.

Discord, marching to a foreign tune,
Once flooded Holland's quays, and soon
Silenced our Dutch song with fear
Of the informer's ear.
But even then—a whiff of sound, a ray,
As a carillonist began to play,
The heavy bell a solemn theme,
The counterpoint a brightning gleam,
This fugue for liberty, lost bitterly,
Strove for the harmonies of love.

Clods mud, that poet plods
His sod to sullen fame—
Thuds dull the hour,
Noon now, night soon:
There's no carillon in Tralee.

from Notes (1999)

Interlude

Of all that's left
When we take leave—
spouses, children, pets, houses, furniture, cars, paintings, rugs,
books, computers, stereos, TVs, CDs, DVDs, videos, letters,
manuscripts, clothes and shoes, bank accounts, untraceable insurance
covers, unpaid bills, unknown friends, fountain pens, teddy bears
the King James, phone numbers, perfumes, and 'that smell'—
It's the specs.
Like on that footage from the concentration camps:
the half-gone flung carrions you stomach, just about, like myriad
butcher-vans unloading
        all at once;
the suit-cases? agh, allegorical,
the rings wrung, the jewelry gemmed,
writings-on-the-wall? literal, say-it-all, and yet failing, somehow, to
be poetical,
and the false teeth, false limbs? pathetic prostheses.
But the mountain of glasses, all in a tangle, bereft of objectivity?
closer to the bone than a heap of coffins, a bundle of bodies, all
the Jewish quartets playing Mozart's Dissonance from Bergen
Belsen to Dachau (that, you see, is, oddly, victory.
   Not so with glasses. They just lack,
      yes,
      objectivity).

MICHÈLE VASSAL

Don't Go Back To The Tree Of Sighs

on the trunk where we leaned
they've crucified a carrion crow
on its tears Death is weaned.
When we were twelve and very wise
little corpses we gleaned.
Laid them neat by the matchbox row
to measure for coffin's size.
In ashen earth they went to rest
prayers in the wind blurred
as did a lost kiss that still sings
barely heard, almost slurred.
Like a chick fallen from the nest
love is a muted bird
and Death now flutters on its wings
still we cling to the word.

from Sandgames (2000)

This Is Not A Poem About The Cat

He says my poems are
nostalgic, neurotic
and how can I write
epics about magic,
garlic or even politics,
(not to mention brothels)
but unlike Lear
and Baudelaire
never ever write about
The Cat
—*The liquid cat that pours itself*
into the smallest hollow
between us in the bed
the fairy cat fattened on darkness
that same cat I grovel to
while it ignores me
but looks in awe at him
and bites his chin.

I think not.

from Sandgames (2000)

Night Sky

She grew up amongst men
who flew by the stars
who read in the embered scrawl
each others stories mapped
hastily over the Sahara.
In 1936,
her uncle Bob crashed in the desert
and took for ever to die.
Age nine,
her father gave her the beaded sky.
She, too, read truths and prayers
in the flickering alphabet of fireflies.
Years later,
she found her very unreasonable love,
under a brittle November moon.
For sixteen swirling years
they drew their story in blazing arabesques
on ultramarine skies
until he stumbled upon dawn
in the arms of an astrophysicist:
and now her stars are quenched
and night is a blackboard
chalked with equations
brightness fluctuations
on which a pale quasar observer
writes : *QO957, Microlensing or seeing?*

EAMONN WALL

Winter Thoughts From Nebraska

What's solitude I ask myself

    to sit fishing
in a boat far from shore in Minnesota which
has 10000 lakes according to their licence
plates,

    to gaze across blowing sand and arroyos
in the Rocky Mountains thinking of trouble spots
in Africa where one outfit has replaced another,

    to retreat from prayer and sit with a book
in a white, damp cell while monks are baking
bread & clearing drains of mushed-up leaves
in early light when there's a faint chance of
seeing a fox move king-like across a wet field?

Solitude is what I fear the most, I reckon,
this having too much time on my own without
the great belly of the refrigerator gurgling,
the radio finally given-in to kitchen grease and
grime saying "I can't take it no more,"

    or the
children gone south like the snow geese seen
from the look-out point at De Soto Bend
last November,

    their rooms like tundra to the north of here,
full of absence under snow.

    I'll say to my wife
when she gets home that Americans can't wait

for their children to be grown up and gone,
& that's why they're so crazy & have to spend
so much on prescriptions because they're dreaming
too much about vacations & runs to Westroads
Mall in the Dodge Caravan. Some days
this country makes me blue, I tell you straight.

　　　Then she'll throw
a book at me written by a Frenchman on account
of the fact that she's an American and the big hardback will nearly
nail me & my *MGD* & she'll say that
"The Celtic Tiger" will do for Ireland what
the Du Ponts did for the USA back around the time
of the robber barons.

　　　Just mark my words & I will
& I'll say I'm thinking about all the lakes in Minnesota,
that's where we should go sometime in our old car
when the weather picks up. We've been to the Rocky
Mountains enough times.

　　　OK, you'll say and leave to
watch a sitcom on TV, your favourite the late-lamented
Seinfeld

　　　& I'm thinking someday I'll be as wise as my father.

I know what solitude is I tell myself, eyes roving jauntily
across a page to keep pace with breathing upstairs in
warm beds this wild winter's night,

　　　wondering if that footfall
from a car is hers come to press the doorbell and sit among
the pots and pans & tell a story about the latest crisis facing
the state of Nebraska as water boils on the red hot element
on our old electric cooker. Shine on, Street Lights, shine on.

from The Crosses (2000)

Outside the Tall Blue Building: Federal Plaza

Outside the tall blue building
a rusted metal structure
will soon be towed away because
federal employees do not like to look at it.
"An eyesore," they told *The New York Times*
and I don't want to judge a native piece of art
but I know some man laboured long and hard at it and
thought his work complete when it was taken away from him.
"Garbage," they shout well-oiled in opinion
their boss *The Great Communicator,*
his father a drunk in Illinois and his son
has a bar called after him in Tipperary.
How will they take this structure away?
You can't strip metal limb from limb
apportioning moments spent by a river in another place
to section ten, line four, please print or type:
once I stared at your uncovered breasts,
often they dried me in huge towels to have me clean
for Sunday mass, or a rough hand rubbed my head
for some old thing I had once been able to do.
Turn the page and answer No to everything concerning
communism, culture groups, and political parties.
A woman without English pleads in Spanish
is turned from the screen by an officer of the State:
"Gawd, these dumb aliens," he whispers.
He is right. We know we are.
So what will they do with this rusted sculpture?
Will knives saw it up and clerks number it
in knacker's sections? I don't know but
when I came downtown to Federal Plaza it was this
eyesore which told me where I was.

from Dyckman—200th Street (1994)

Ballagh

I.M. Simon Kehoe

This montage finds you sitting on buttercups and grass
On your memory card's faint photo.

Over your shoulder, two banks of sea sand. Between them,
One deep arroyo the spine-thin particles are falling away from.

Overhead, the sun seeks to find its space through low clouds
To bring the sea, over your other shoulder, into quadrille coastal time.

You do not reckon the bounty lost to water; these lone &
Level strands are stretching far away.

You touched the grass when you rested, counted rusted gates
On the journey, quietly pressed your words on the paved streets.

As the sun traced a path, you climbed the old & graded hills.
You heard each measure crafted on this, our slow, brief watch.

Born to a village between Oulart and Enniscorthy, the route
You took to town was your way forward. And the way itself.

from A Tour of Your Country (forthcoming)

EMILY WALL

Angle of Disorientation: Moving to Alaska One Week After Getting Married

Hemlock, spruce, some cedar, maybe,
construct the land, craze in all directions.
From the state ferry, one tree hoops, bent against the sky,
some thing turning oddly out of shape like a withered
arm tucked inside a shirt sleeve, wrist pressed
knowingly against the heart. I run my fingers
through the tree, roots to treetops and get
tangled again and again, that tree depending
on the ones beside, under, above for its own shape.
And I think, twisted over the ferry rail,
(my mother receding into phone calls and brief letters),
that I could be lost, that I could be saved.

Calling

A young man runs down the street,
clapping, calling to something I can't see—
a dog I presume, from his manner—

but it turns out, when it lifts, to be
a pigeon. This act, outside the Glory Hole,
raises a flock of questions, none of which

will be answered by me,
across the street in Heritage
drinking coffee, listening to jazz.

But I do know that desire, the craving
to touch a bird rising in flight, the ache
of those of us without pets, children,

small beings that belong to us,
and don't belong, a heartbeat and a
string of feathers we send out, we reel

back in, we touch with just these hands.

April, afternoon, thinking of my mother

Just now—look—it's raining only in the back yard
as if the spruce and hemlock were lamenting—quietly—to not
alert the front yard, stalwart flowers budding, grass greening
serenely. The street lies still. It's quiet in the sun.

But look again out back—the pines are shaking now,
trying not to, but telling us stories of jays who fell from branches
of deer who missed their lovers' scent in the moss.
Of careful needles that got lost in a wind storm

and now point only skyward, leaving
the rest of us, to find our own way home.

all from Freshly Rooted (2007)

GORDON WALMSLEY

Symposion

A moon washing the night sky white.
Yet because the moon is near the trees, and down
to a quarter, stars are as clear as a finished thought
clear as a pentagram, as a square, or triangle
and more than lines, or a level plane

Clarity. The night moon flooding a curving.
Something so secret as not to be spoken.

A sculptor of words
reckoned conversation as highest—
greater than love, greater even than light.
It is hard to imagine
conversation could be greater
than the light that touches me
though speaking with you
can open
a night

Solutions
no one man can find them.
We live in a time of
many rules.
Parliaments sit perplexed
dreaming up laws.
What was Caesar's
runs through Caesar's
fingers

finds its way into sucking caverns
splitting slopes of the red volcanoes

While the spirit of Me. Me.
Magnetic Me.
is taking, taking.
We have a task
no less
than turning rivers around
that we may emerge from under the weight of lines
electrical
heavily fallen

A web is often hard to lift.

Yet we stand
the night clearly round us
men and women
on earth

We can speak to each other.

from Terebinthos (1999)

What Is Found

Waiting
you learn to hear her silent voicings

Going
you learn to sing what she intones

Knowing
you sense her leaves ecstatic stirrings

Saying
time of autumn, time of stones

Guessing
I try to know the smallest shiftings

Worlds
most likely fallen, though they glow

Trying
the time of waiting can be trying

Glimpses
Worlds arising can be known

Tell me
lord of light and also thunder

Regents
stars and whirlings through all nights

Crowning
nature's plenitude of ashes

Chaste penumbra
shading light

Moon
you rose on through the silver ashes

Merging
fully splendrous with the sea

Thrashing
waves unbraided roaring landward

Hollows
deep resounding (inmost lee)

from Terebinthos (1999)

Poetic Sequence from Touchstones

Bring
what you can
to the silvery sea
in a silence most immense
with some few sounds
a stone's crunch
from the wren and the hobble duck
and a sun arcing down
into blood of a luminous island
rain on the water
pulls the gulls inland
and if you climb the hill to the west
you will find them resting on leeward slopes
so when it rains you are mostly alone
with the hobbling duck and the wren
you bring what you can
to a rage dissolved
to a whisper's sheen
whitening in silver
and what is above
is as it is below
the hermetic truth
split down the middle
and laid on its side
it still works, the old invocation
in the unseen world
and the world we now know

and whether you watch stilled memories
in a river s-ing south
or stand by a sea
where the gulls have flown
to rest on an unseen hill
you bring yourself naked
to the sea's reflecting
though this time
there are two young
doves

lifting away from the kelp
to the forest within
they seem to bless
the man who listens
across the darkness
in the echoing below
he is well within the silence of the sea
with some few sounds
he would know

GARY J. WHITEHEAD

Flying Kites
for Michael

All afternoon we fight the pull of string,
resist the snap of twine, the losing flight.
We roam through a wide blue, shepherding
clouds, our necks aching from the persistent
upward tilt. Far off, the flap of small sails
full of wind. When my brother unravels slack
his kite dives after mine, a dogfight to sate
that other wrestling need waiting inside us
like the glint in a stray mongrel's eyes.
Swerving, our kites peck at one another,
in their tangle give up their separate shapes,
and fall at last like one broken bird, which
all our lives we walk toward, reeling, reeling,
till the mending and the next good breeze.

from The Velocity of Dust (2004)

Bats

Come dark they drop
out of the barn's slotted roof
like a flock of birds trapped in black gloves,

a loveless, ravenous
brood of clenched leather
winging eager mouths into the bowl of sky.

Their hunger is a flower
to which they fling a song
we cannot hear because we cannot hear,

and this song,
when it comes back to them
comes back to them with the news

of what is in between
and what will feed,
and they read this news and carry off

the pollen of night
—all that knowledge—
like the black, black butterflies we make of them.

from The Velocity of Dust (2004)

Conch

Between rolling sheets of low-tide foam
    I find it—this prize I've tried for
        all week.

No crab claw, as first I thought, but a bone-
    white tube, like paper curled,
        and when I pull

it's as though the sand pulls back. I pluck it,
    a giant tooth from the mouth
        of the beach,

tip it like an urn and a drab grout weeps
    from the orange spout.
        Now it's a trumpet

clogged with a flat black foot, rough as fine-grit,
    and gray meat which when I touch it
        puckers, vaguely erotic.

I know she'll love it, will smile when I take it
    from behind my back, this living
        offering.

I know I will have to kill it, too. Already
    I'm imagining the *clickclickclick*,
        the blue tongues,

the pot and the water and the silent scream
    that is part of the taking
        requisite to giving.

Don't we each wrench the wild out of the other,
    if only to hold up to the light
        our own base origins?

When I pry out the animal it will drop in the sink

the potential music. Later, we'll soak it in a bucket
of bleach, scrub it clean for the bookcase
or the mantelpiece.

Tomorrow I'll wade in the surf searching
for another. To make a pair.
One for each of us.

SABINE WICHERT

Mixed Fates

An aproned woman was holding court
at the newsagent as I paid for
my papers: I live with five men,
she said, and one of them married,
four are my sons, the fifth is my
husband—and everyone laughed.

I live with no man, I thought,
and all of them married; is that
as good a joke, I wondered.

When I got home I wanted to write
that long overdue letter to you
explaining that the lawnmower
no longer works, a cow now and then
does the cutting; nettles grow through
the windows of my bedroom, the cats
come only rarely to be fed;
the rusty Poison Laid sign on Murray's
gate is now guarding his sheep;
they've filled the holes in the road,
shaved the trees off the hill, but I've
pinched mine for Christmas just in time.

I must read the papers now, so
forgive me, if I just send this
postcard again. Yours always.

from Sharing Darwin (1999)

While Reading Sartre

We love our friends badly—
it's all
we can do
between the first tooth
and the last.

Love
excluded by other
and self,
lost in words,
rarely rescued.

It was easier
and more difficult
before
the link between
act
and reflection.

Now one
is one,
just,
yet still
the other
and oneself.

If love
is what
remains
there might
still be
a future,

while there is
choice
and decision
and a few
friends
poorly loved.

from Tin Drum Country (1995)

'A Strip of Pavement Over an Abyss'
(V. Woolf)

Step aside and you fall—
schoolgirls conforming in rebellion
with whatever latest fashion
adults disapprove.

A north-easterly gale is blowing, straight from
the Pole it seems, whipping clouds over a milky-
blue sky, bending the branches of trees, troubling
the house-martins with its permanent uplift.

Flitting like small birds from day to night:
the schizophrenia of getting it right:
as you grow up there is little choice but
to consume what the market offers.

At night you defy the fashion,
eat, drink, put your feet up; guilty
with hangover in the morning, or the
added weight you promise virtue.

Consume therefore you are: glamorous
clothes which may not fit and gorgeous mouth-
watering food-advertisements
compete for your life.

The abyss is never quite defined
and the pavement stays narrow:
they tell you not to look down, but
up and ahead, not to bother your head.

Once you do, vertigo
sets in, difficult to
resist the pull, not to
stumble, not to fall.

ANN ZELL

Round trip

On sober Sunday mornings our kitchen
was a glue-sniffer's paradise. Name your poison,
choose your pair; liquorice, divinity, burnt-
caramel essences reeled in the air, as each
old-enough child polished somebody's shoes.

Our father administered the final high shine
while my brothers queued for the bathroom mirror
attempting quiffs and sleekness, defeated
by inherited tufts that sprang up after the comb
like uncut stalks of wheat behind a harrow.

The spirit of god burned like a fire among
Sunday-school girls intoxicated with solemnity.
We girded up our loins, fresh courage took,
and desanctified hymns—adding 'under the covers'
under our breath at appropriate moments.

What we didn't know about sex would have
filled a family bible. We were drug-innocent.
Grass was a green luxury mowed on Saturdays,
bitter strong tea was for upset stomachs.
Coke came in a bottle, taboo, like coffee.

Substance abuse: fortified by butter, eggs,
cheese, cream, and red meat almost every day
the boys went forth on sacred tours of duty
to unenlightened foreign places, preaching
words of wisdom. I took to forbidden

booze and cigarettes. Bartenders yawned
as I wept in my 3.2 beer, asking myself
what my mother would say if she could see me now.
'Whatever made you choose Belfast?' I evade.
The drink's stouter, religion is much the same.

from Weathering (1998)

The last occupant of my house

The sting of ammonia kept off buyers.
Maureen and her cats were only minding it,
they could be out in a week. It was cheap
and close to work. I said no hurry.
Nobody said she'd been minding it for years.

She had a house of her own—her birth house
across the street. She left me a bureau,
a wardrobe so big it couldn't be shifted
and the loan of her aspidistra
until it was well enough to travel.

Visiting, she gave me the street's life
over tea, but I couldn't stand the way
her hands lingered along the walls, trying
to fit my house back around her like
an old coat—the only one that kept her warm.

When I returned the aspidistra, she
made room for it in the cramped back parlour
where she camped with the cats, caretaking
a three-storey museum of family furniture,
no style on speaking terms with the rest.

She went downhill fast. On good days, she'd
lean in her doorway bombarding my house
with looks of love. I gave my conscience
into the keeping of a neighbour, who'd
known her all her life and took hot soup.

After she died—keeper of histories,
champion camogie player—the street changed.
Starter families. More old ones going.
I tell myself, move, before no other house
will fit you. The house settles, whispers No.

from Weathering (1998)

What they had to say about it

For Barney

There used to be a well right there before they made that road.
People came from all around.

I asked them if they'd keep the capstone
just to show how strong the men were then—
four men carried it right across the beach,
a great big slab of rock they pried out with crowbars—
but they broke it up to fill in the road.

When the Council said they had to mark it,
because it's on the maps, it's part of the environment,
that fool of a builder John with no pride in his work

dug it out, dumped cement down it,
put up those old crooked walls
and a great ugly slab of cement on top
with bits of board and sacking sticking out.

It looks like a kennel for a dog you wouldn't have in the house,
and that lovely water poisoned.

Ah, well, what's done is done.
What can you do?

Contributors' Notes

NADYA AISENBERG published three poetry collections: *Before We Were Strangers*, *Leaving Eden* (which won the Bruce P. Rossley Award in 1995) and *Measures*, (Salmon, 2001) She published two books on the subject of feminism, *Women of Academe: Outsiders in the Sacred Grove* (co-authored with Mona Harrington) and *Ordinary Heroines: Transforming the Male Myth*. She also published *A Common Spring: Crime Novel and Classic* and *We Animals: Poems of Our World* (Sierra Club Books). Nadya was former Adjunct Associate Professor of Women's Studies at Brandeis University. She was also a teacher of English at Tufts University, Wellesley College, and the University of Massachusetts, Boston. In the 1980s, she co-founded Rowan Tree Press, and she co-founded the Cambridge Alliance of Independent Scholars and was on the Board of Directors of the Writers' Room of Boston. She was a frequent contributor to literary journals such as *Ploughshares, Angi, Poetry* and *The Southern Review*. She was the author of the monograph, *I Fall Upwards: Images of Women and Aging in Contemporary Women's Poetry*, published by the National Policy and Resource Center on Women and Aging, Heller Graduate School, Brandeis University, Autumn 1997. She died in 1999.

NUALA ARCHER's poetry collections are *Whale on the Line* (which won the Patrick Kavanagh Award in 1981); *Two Women, Two Shores*, with Medbh McGuckian, jointly published by New Poets Series, Baltimore & Salmon Publishing, Galway, Ireland, in 1989; *Pan/ama*, a chapbook, published by Red Dust, New York, 1992 and *The Hour of Pan/ama* published by Salmon, 1992. As editor of *The Midland Review* at Oklahoma State University she produced a ground-breaking issue (Vol. 3 Winter 1986) on contemporary Irish women's writing. More recently she edited *University Over the Abyss*, collected accounts of the lectures and lecturers at the Theresienstadt concentration camp from 1942-44. Multilingual, she has written, directed, and performed for the public around the world in English, Spanish, and Hebrew. She teaches creative writing at Cleveland State University, Ohio.

LELAND BARDWELL was born in India of Irish parents in 1928 and was brought to Ireland at the age of two. She is a poet, novelist, playwright and short-story writer. Her collections of poetry are *The Mad Cyclist* (Dublin, New Writers' Press, 1970); *The Fly and the Bedbug* (Dublin, Beaver Row Press, 1984); *Dostoevsky's Grave, New and Selected Poems* (Dublin, The Dedalus Press, 1991); *The White Beach, New & Selected Poems 1960-1988* (Salmon Publishing, 1998); and *The Noise of Masonry Settling* (Dublin, Dedalus Press, 2006). Her novels are *Girl on a Bicycle* (Dublin, Co-Op Books, 1977); *That London Winter* (Co-Op Books, 1981); *The House* (Kerry, Brandon, 1984); *There We Have Been* (Dublin, Attic Press, 1989); and *Mother to a Stranger* (Belfast, The Blackstaff Press, 2002). A volume of short stories, *Different Kinds of Love* (Attic

Press, 1994) has been translated into German as Zeit vertreibt Liebe. Her plays include *Thursday*, and *Open Ended Prescription*. She has also broadcast radio plays, including *The Revenge of Constance*, and *Just Another Killing*. Her musical, *Edith Piaf*, toured Ireland. She is a member of Aosdána, and lives in Co Sligo.

MARCK L. BEGGS earned his Ph.D. from the University of Denver, his M.F.A. from Warren Wilson College, and currently teaches at Henderson State University. Mostly, though, he lives a simple life in a cabin by a pond in Arkansas, sort of like Thoreau with technology. When he is not writing, teaching, or singing his quasi-folk songs with his group, *dog gods*, he can sometimes be found watching the weeds proliferate in his garden as he daydreams of fresh tomatoes, cucumbers, and squash. Needless to say, he cites Whitman as a major influence. He is the author of *Libido Café* (Salmon, 2004) and *Godworm*, as well as the editor of the *Arkansas Literary Forum* (www.hsu.edu/alf).

MICHAEL S. BEGNAL (b. 1966) was formerly the editor of the Galway, Ireland-based literary magazine, *The Burning Bush*. His latest collection is *Ancestor Worship*, published by Salmon in 2007. His first collection, *The Lakes of Coma*, appeared in 2003 from Six Gallery Press (U.S.A.), followed in 2005 by *Mercury, the Dime*, a long poem in chapbook form. He has appeared in the anthologies *Breaking the Skin: New Irish Poetry* (Black Mountain Press) and, in Irish, *Go Nuige Seo* (Coiscéim). Begnal has appeared in numerous literary journals and was for a time a freelance journalist for the Irish-language newspaper, *Lá*. A dual Irish/American citizen, he has divided his writing career between these two countries.

MARVIN BELL has been called "an insider who thinks like an outsider." He served forty years on the faculty of the Iowa Writers' Workshop and teaches now for the brief-residency MFA program based in Oregon at Pacific University. He has collaborated with composers, musicians, and dancers and is both famous and infamous as the creator of what are known as the "Dead Man" and "Dead Man Resurrected" poems. The most recent of his nineteen collections of poetry and essays are *Rampant* (2004) and *Mars Being Red* (2007). He and his wife, Dorothy, live in Iowa City, Iowa, and Port Townsend, Washington.

EVA BOURKE is a poet and translator. She has published five collections of poetry, the most recent being *Travels with Gandolpho* (Dedalus Press, 2000) and *The Latitude of Naples* (Dedalus Press, 2005). She has published two anthologies of Irish poetry in German translation in Germany, *Hundsrose*, and *Mit Gruener Tinte/With Green Ink*, and a translated collection of the German poet Elisabeth Borchers into English entitled *Winter on White Paper* in 2002. At the moment she is working on a book of German poets in English translation. She is a member of Aosdána.

RAY BRADBURY has published more than 600 short stories over a period of sixty years. He has written short stories, novels, screenplays, plays, and poetry. His best known books are *The Martian Chronicles, The Illustrated Man, Something Wicked This Way Comes*, and in its 50th anniversary year, *Fahrenheit 451*. He wrote the screenplay for *Moby Dick* for John Huston in 1953. In 2005 a film was released, based on his short story, *A Sound of Thunder*. Other films based on his stories will be forthcoming, though as of now nothing is in production. These include a new version of *The Martian Chronicles*, produced by Universal, and *Fahrenheit 451*, written and directed by Frank Darabont. He has published several new books in the past several years, including *From the Dust Returned, One More For The Road, Let's All Kill Constance, The Cat's Pajamas*, and a book of essays, *Bradbury Speaks*, as well as a huge volume of short stories, *Bradbury Stories*. His poetry collection, *I Live by the Invisible*, was published by Salmon in 2002. He has just finished work on a new novel, *Farewell Summer*, which is the sequel to *Dandelion Wine*. 2007 saw the release of a double offering from Bradbury, *Somewhere a Band is Playing* and *Leviathan '99*. In 2001 The National Book Award was given to Bradbury for his contribution to American literature. In 2004 he was awarded the National Medal of Arts by President Bush and the National Endowment for the Arts. His contributions to architecture include creating the American Experience at the United States Pavilion at the New York World's Fair, creating the metaphors within Spaceship Earth at Disney's Epcot in Florida, and providing the blueprint for the Glendale Galleria in California. His concepts for a new mall at the corner of Hollywood and Highland has caused the Assyrian Pavilion to be built, utilizing the fabulous set of *Intolerance*, which was directed by D.W. Griffith. He lives in Los Angeles with his two beloved cats, Halli and Ditzy.

RORY BRENNAN grew up in Dublin and attended Trinity College. He worked in RTE and was Director of Poetry Ireland for a decade. He has lived in Morocco and Sweden and he spends part of every year in Greece. His collections are: *The Sea on Fire, The Walking Wounded* and *The Old in Rapallo*. His work has won the Patrick Kavanagh Award. He is a lecturer in Communications in Dublin City University.

HEATHER BRETT was born in Canada and raised in Northern Ireland. She has lived in the south of Ireland since 1984, mainly in Cavan. An artist and writer, she has been Writer-in-Residence for Cavan, Drogheda, Roslea, the Midlands Collaborative of Longford, Westmeath, Offaly and Portlaois. She is founder and editor of Windows Publications since 1992 (www.windowspublications.com). She is dedicated to the promotion of new voices in literature with emphasis on young writers. Since its conception, along with Noel Monahan, Windows has published six broadsheets, seven Introduction Series, two anthologies, and over forty issues of a monthly literary journal. Over the 15 years Windows has provided workshops, student competitions and hosted nearly 200 launches and events. Heather Brett has also edited twelve anthologies of young people's work for Cavan, Drogheda, Roslea and the Midlands. In 2005 she brought out *The Caught Bouquet* book and CD which combined music specifically written for literature alongside visual responses from artists. She has won the Brendan Behan prize for her first book *Abigail Brown* and was Bluechrome Poet of the year in 2005. *Green Monkey Travelling* (Bluechrome, 2005) is her latest collection.

PATRICIA BURKE BROGAN is a poet, playwright & painter. *Above the Waves Calligraphy*, her first collection of poems and etchings, and the script of her stage play, *Eclipsed*, were published by Salmon in 1994. *Eclipsed* has won many awards including a Fringe First at Edinburgh Theatre Festival 1992 and the USA Moss Hart Award 1994. To date there have been fifty-three productions of the play on three continents. *Eclipsed* has been excerpted in documentaries and other collected works including *The Field Day Anthology of Irish Writing*, Volumes 4 and 5, *Irish Women Playwrights of the Twentieth Century*, *Ireland's Women: Writings Past and Present*, and *Motherhood in Ireland*. Patricia received an Arts Council Bursary in Literature in 1993 and a European Script Writers' Fund in 1994. Her second published play, *Stained Glass at Samhain*, appeared from Salmon in 2003. She received an Arts Council Bursary in Drama in 2005. Her etchings have won awards at Barcelona and at International Biennale 1982. Her second collection of poetry, *Décollage*, is forthcoming from Salmon Poetry.

SIMMONS B. BUNTIN is the founding editor of Terrain.org: A Journal of the Built & Natural Environments. With a master's degree in urban and regional planning, he is a web program manager for the University of Arizona. His first book of poetry, *Riverfall*, was published in May 2005 by Salmon Poetry. He has work forthcoming in *Isotope, Pilgrimage, Weber Studies, South Dakota Review*, and *Orion*, and is a recipient of a Colorado Artist's Fellowship for Poetry and an Academy of American Poets Prize.

SAM BURNSIDE was born in Co Antrim and now lives and works in the North West. He is the author of a number of publications which have attracted prizes including an Allingham Poetry Prize, the University of Ulster's McCrea Award for Literature and a Bass Ireland Arts Award as well as the Sunday Tribune/Hennessy Literary Award for poetry and two Arts Council awards. His poetry collection, *Walking the Marches*, was published by Salmon in 1990. He established the Verbal Arts Centre on Derry's historic city walls and directed this for eleven years; in 2004 he bought and restored a derelict cottage in the Sperrin Mountains. He is currently writing a novel.

CATHERINE BYRON grew up in Belfast, raised daughters and goats in the west of Scotland, and now lives in the English Midlands. Her first collection of poetry *Settlements* (1985) was hailed as 'a classic of Irish exile'. Her sixth collection, *The*

Getting of Vellum, was published by Salmon in 2000 and was inspired by her ongoing creative collaboration with Dublin-based artist and calligrapher Denis Brown. She is also the author of *Out of Step: Pursuing Seamus Heaney to Purgatory* (1992). She teaches writing and medieval Literature at The Nottingham Trent University.

LOUISE C. CALLAGHAN was born in 1948 and grew up in County Dublin. Her poetry collections, *The Puzzle-Heart* and *Remember the Birds* were published by Salmon in 1999 & 2005 respectively. She compiled and edited *Forgotten Light: An Anthology of Memory Poems* (A & A Farmar, 2003). Her poetry, which is widely anthologised in Ireland and England, is included in the *Field Day Anthology: Vols IV & V*. A play, *Find The Lady*, based loosely on the life of Kate O'Brien, was signaled by the Abbey Theatre Company.

SEAMUS CASHMAN comes from Conna in County Cork and studied at Maynooth and University College Cork before spending some years teaching (and learning) in southern Tanzania in East Africa. He founded Wolfhound Press, the leading Irish literary and cultural publishing house, in Dublin in 1974, and was publisher there until 2001. He has had two well received poetry collections published, *Carnival* (Monarchline, 1988) and *Clowns & Acrobats* (Wolfhound Press, 2000). *That Morning Will Come: New & Selected Poems* was published by Salmon Poetry in 2007. He compiled and edited two significant and highly lauded poetry anthologies for children: the now classic historical collection, *The Wolfhound Book of Irish Poems for Young People* (co-edited with Bridie Quinn, 1975; still in print as *Irish Poems for Young People*) and in 2004, he commissioned and edited the award winning *Something Beginning with P: new poems from Irish poets* for the O'Brien Press. He has undertaken a number of writing workshop residencies with Poetry Ireland in their Development Education projects, including facilitating a children's scriptwriting project on the subject of child labour at Zion Primary School in 2005 and, with poet and school principal Tom Conaty, co-directed the resulting film, *Stitched*. In addition to his own writing and poetry, he currently works with publishers and writers as a consultant and advisor. He lives in Portmarnock, County Dublin.

DAVID CAVANAGH'S collections include *The Middleman* (Salmon, 2003) and several chapbooks, among them *Ethic = Visceral* (Wood Thrush Books, Vermont) and *Pythia*, a dramatic poem also produced on audio-cassette (Radio Théatre de la Cathédrale, Montreal). His poems have appeared in Irish, Canadian, American, and British journals, including *Poetry Ireland Review, The Shop, Southword, The Antigonish Review, The Fiddlehead, Grain, The Malahat Review, The Dalhousie Review, Green Mountains Review, Agenda*, and others. He also performs regularly with other poets and musicians in a jazzy/poetic entanglement called Pojazz. A native of Montreal with Irish ancestry and dual Canadian/American citizenship, he lives a somewhat baffled existence in Burlington, Vermont, and works as an associate dean at Johnson State College.

JERAH CHADWICK has lived on the Aleutian island of Unalaska for 26 years, where he first went to raise goats and write and has, for the past 20 years, taught for and administered the University of Alaska regional extension program. He has published chapbooks with State Street (NY) and Seal (WA) presses, received various fellowships and awards, and served as the Alaska State Writer Laureate from 2004 to 2006. Salmon published his first full length collection, *Story Hunger*, in 1999. His new manuscript in progress is *Village Beneath the Pavement*.

PATRICK CHAPMAN was born in 1968 and lives in Dublin. His poetry collections are *Jazztown* (Raven Arts Press, 1991), *The New Pornography* (Salmon, 1996), and *Breaking Hearts and Traffic Lights* (Salmon, 2007). His book of stories is *The Wow Signal* (Bluechrome, 2007). He wrote the award-winning film, *Burning The Bed* (2003), which stars Gina McKee and Aidan Gillen. In 2003, his short story, 'A Ghost' won first prize in the Cinescape Genre Literary Competition. With Philip Casey, he founded the Irish Literary Revival website. His bestselling audio play, *Doctor Who: Fear of the Daleks*, stars Wendy Padbury as Zoe and Nicholas Briggs as the Daleks.

ROZ COWMAN was born in Cork in 1942. Her collection, *The Goose Herd* (Salmon) was published in 1989. She received the Arlen House/Maxwell House award in 1982, and the Patrick Kavanagh Award for Poetry in 1985. She lives in Cork where she lectures in Adult Education.

VICKI CROWLEY is a full time visual artist working from her studio in Barna, Co. Galway. She has exhibited widely in Ireland and abroad and her works hang in many private collections and some public collections all over the world. She has received many church commissions for paintings, silk hangings and stained glass window designs. Her colourful work is inspired by her Mediterranean origins and her travels worldwide. She was born in Malta where she trained in Architectural drawing. Her collection of poetry, *Oasis in a Sea of Dust* (Salmon, 1992), was also illustrated by her. She is currently completing a solo painting exhibition depicting some of her travels from Tonga to Tibet.

MARY COLL is a poet, writer and broadcaster living in Limerick City, her work includes contributions to Sunday Miscellany, Morning Glory and the Tubridy Show on RTE Radio One, and The Quiet Quarter and Artzone on Lyric FM. She also works as a freelance theatre and visual arts critic for a number of national newspapers. Her first collection *All things Considered* was published by Salmon in 2002.

THEODORE DEPPE is the author of *Cape Clear: New & Selected Poems* (Salmon, 2002), *The Wanderer King* (Alice James Books, 1996), and *Children of the Air* (Alice James, 1990). He directs Stonecoast in Ireland, an option that enables graduate students from the Stonecoast MFA program in Maine to study in Ireland. He has won a Pushcart Prize and received two fellowships from the National Endowment for the Arts in the U.S. He has been writer in residence at the James Merrill House (1998-1999) and Philips Academy (2003-2006). As a registered nurse, he worked with abused children for many years. One of the great joys of his life was a six-month walk that circled Ireland. Dual-citizens of the U.S. and Ireland, he and his wife poet Annie Deppe presently live in Donegal.

MARY DORCEY, an award winning short story writer, poet and novelist, was born in County Dublin, Ireland. In 1990 she won the Rooney Prize for Literature for her short story collection *A Noise from the Woodshed*. Her best selling novel *Biography of Desire* (Poolbeg) was published in September of 1997 to critical acclaim. In 1990 she published a novella, 'Scarlet O'Hara', contained in the anthology *In and Out of Time* (Onlywomen Press, London). She has published four volumes of poetry: *Kindling* (Only Women Press, 1982), *Moving into the Space Cleared by Our Mothers* (Salmon, 1991), *The River That Carries Me* (Salmon, 1995), and *Like Joy In Season, Like Sorrow* (Salmon, 2001). Mary's work is taught on Irish Studies and Women's Studies courses in universities internationally. Her stories and poems have been anthologized in more than one hundred collections; performed on radio and television (R.T.E. and Channel 4.) and dramatized for stage productions in Ireland, Britain and Australia in *In the Pink* (The Raving Beauties) and *Sunny Side Plucked*. She is a Research Associate at Trinity College Dublin and writer in residence at the Centre for Gender and Women's Studies, TCD, where she gives seminars in contemporary English literature and leads a creative writing workshop. Her latest publication is a short story 'Another Glorious Day' in *The Faber Book of Best New Irish Short Stories (2006/2007)* edited by David Marcus.

CAROL ANN DUFFY was born in Glasgow in 1955. She grew up in Stafford and attended the University of Liverpool. She has written for both children and adults, and her poetry has received many awards, including the first prize in the 1983 National Poetry Competition; the Scottish Arts Council Book Awards of Merit for *Standing Female Nude* and *The Other Country*; a Somerset Maugham Award in 1988; the Dylan Thomas Award in 1989; a Cholmondeley Award in 1992; the Forward Poetry Prize and the Whitbread Poetry Award in 1993; the Signal Prize for Children's Verse, as well as the Lannan Award and the E. M. Forster Prize in America. Carol Ann's mother is Irish and her grandparents came from Carlow and Hackestown. *The Salmon Carol Ann Duffy* was published by Salmon in 2000 and contains poetry chosen specially for Salmon Poetry by Carol Ann from four of her earlier volumes and as well as some previously uncollected work. Her most recent collection, *Rapture*, which won the T.S. Eliot Prize, was published by Picador in 2006.

MICHAEL EGAN was born in Baltimore, Maryland, USA, in 1939. After earning an M.A. from the Writing Seminars of the Johns Hopkins University, he went on to publish several poetry collections, including *The Oldest Gesture* (New Poets Series), *The Tall Schooner* (SoHo Press), and *We Came Out Again to See the Stars* (Salmon Poetry). In the last decade of his life, he focused his energies on an epic poem, *Leviathan*, the first section of which is included here. He died in 1992.

MÍCHEÁL FANNING practises as a medical doctor in County Kerry. He has published three books with Salmon: *Verbum et Verbum* (1997), *The Separation of Grey Clouds* (2002), and *Homage* (2006). He has also published three chapbooks and two translations. His books in the Irish language are published by Coiscéim under his Irish name—Mícheál Ó Fionnáin. For the past number of years he has directed Féile na Bealtaine, an arts and politics festival, held annually in West Kerry.

GABRIEL FITZMAURICE was born, in 1952, in the village of Moyvane, Co. Kerry where he still lives. He has been teaching in the local primary school, where he is now principal teacher, since 1975. He is author of more than forty books, including collections of poetry in English and Irish as well as several collections of verse for children. He has translated extensively from the Irish and has edited a number of anthologies of poetry in English and Irish. He has published two volumes of essays and collections of songs and ballads. A cassette of his poems, *The Space Between: New and Selected Poems 1984-1992*, is also available. He frequently broadcasts on radio and television on education and the arts.

MÉLANIE FRANCÈS was born in Paris on October 18th, 1972, with Canadian and French origins and grew up in France. As a young girl, she lived for four years in New Delhi, India, where she learned English and started a lifelong love story with the language. As a college student, she discovered her gift for writing and developed an interest in the arts and American literature. She later moved to Montreal in Canada to pursue her graduate studies at Concordia University and obtained an M.A. Degree in English and Creative Writing. In 2001, she published her first chapbook of poetry, *The World is in your Head*, with Ginninderra Press in Australia. Her debut poetry collection, *Anatomy of a Love Affair (My Life in the Movies),* was published by Salmon Poetry in 2007. She lives in Montreal where she works in communications and public relations and is currently working on her first novel about the immigrant experience and the birth of the movies at the beginning of the century in the USA.

PHILIP FRIED has published three books of poetry: *Mutual Trespasses* (Ion, 1988), *Quantam Genesis* (Zohar, 1997), and *Big Men Speaking To Little Men* (Salmon, 2006). His poetry, reviews, and essays have appeared in numerous magazines, including

Partisan Review, Paris Review, Massachusetts Review, and *Beloit Poetry Journal*. He is the founder and editor of *The Manhattan Review* (themanhattanreview.com), an international poetry journal that will be celebrating its 28th anniversary in 2008.

ERLING FRIIS-BAASTAD was born in Norway in 1950. Though raised in Virginia, he has spent most of his adult life in Canada's Yukon Territory, where he serves as an editor for the Yukon News. His books include: *Wood Spoken: New and Selected Poems* (Northbound Press/Harbour Publishing, 2004) and *The Exile House* (Salmon, 2001). He was co-editor of *Writing North: An Anthology of Contemporary Yukon Writers* (Beluga Books, 1992).

PAUL GENEGA is the author of four full-length collections (two from Salmon) and four chapbooks. His poems have appeared in scores of journals and anthologies and were included in the 2002 monograph on the artist Aaron Fink, *Out of the Ordinary*. His earlier collaboration with Fink, *Perhaps*, is now in the permanent collections of the National Gallery of Art, Washington, D.C. and the Boston Museum of Fine Arts, among others. Paul teaches at Bloomfield College in New Jersey, where he coordinates the creative writing program.

MICHAEL GORMAN was born in Sligo and educated at Summerhill College and University College Galway. His poetry collections include *Postcards from Galway*, *Waiting for the Sky to Fall* and *Up She Flew* (Salmon, 1991). One of his poems, The People I Grew Up With Were Afraid, was chosen by Pauline McLynn for inclusion in the anthology, *Voices and Poetry of Ireland*. He teaches poetry on the MA in Writing at NUI Galway and convenes the International Writers' Summer School there also.

MARK GRANIER's first collection, *Airborne*, was published by Salmon Poetry in 2001. His second collection, *The Sky Road* (also Salmon Poetry), followed in 2007. His poems have been published widely in newspapers and periodicals in Ireland and the UK, including *The Irish Times*, *New Irish Writing*, *Poetry Ireland Review*, *The Spectator*, *The New Statesman* and *The TLS*, and have also been broadcast on Lyric FM. He was awarded an Arts Council Bursary in 2002 and the Vincent Buckley Poetry Prize in 2004.

FRANK GOLDEN was born in Dublin and has been living in the Burren, Co. Clare, for well over a decade. His poetry collection, *The Interior Act*, was published by Salmon Poetry in 1999. A new collection, *In Daily Accord: A Haiku Sequence*, is forthcoming from Salmon. His other books include *In Partial Settlement*, *On Route to Leameneh*, and his novel *The Two Women of Aganatz*. In recent years he has worked on TV and film projects and is currently writing a new novel. He has received awards from the Arts Council and the Irish Film Board. His poetry has been published extensively in periodicals and journals, including *Poetry Ireland, The Literary Review, New Irish Writing, Poetry Australia, The Sunday Tribune*, etc. He has also read his work throughout Ireland and abroad. Recent readings include: Belmullet Arts Festival, Glór Theatre Ennis, Ennis Arts Festival, The White House Limerick, De Valera Library, Eigse Cork, and Gallerie Pomie Limoges France.

ANGELA GREENE, poet and painter, was born in England in 1936 and lived from early childhood in Dublin. She was educated at Dominican College, Eccles Street and trained as a nurse at the Mater Hospital, Dublin. In 1988 she won the Patrick Kavanagh Award and in 1989 was short-listed for The Sunday Tribune/ Hennessy Literary Award. In 1987 she was a prizewinner in the Bloodaxe Books National Poetry Competition. Her collection of poetry, *Silence and the Blue Night*, was published by Salmon Poetry in 1993. Her poetry was also published in Britain and Ireland, read on RTE Radio and BBC Radio Ulster and was performed in Sunny Side Plucked at the Project Arts Centre, Dublin. Her deeply lived experience as woman, daughter, wife, mother, poet and painter is reflected in quiet, well-crafted and moving poems. The lateness of her arrival to contemporary Irish poetry and the quiet way she received her well deserved recognition, makes her loss, in 1997, all the more poignant.

MAURICE HARMON is an Irish academic and poet who was a Professor at University College Dublin for many years. His scholarly publications include *Sean O'Faolain. A Life* (Constable, 1994), *The Dolmen Press. A Celebration* (Lilliput, 2002), and *Selected Essays* (Irish Academic Press, 2006). He edited *No Author Better Served: The Correspondence between Samuel Beckett and Alan Schneider* (Harvard University Press, 1998). He edited *Poetry Ireland Review* (2001-2002). His poetry publications include *The Doll With Two Backs* (Salmon, 2004), *The Last Regatta* (Salmon, 2000), *A Stillness at Kiawah* (Three Spires Press, 1996) and the *Book of Precedence* (Three Spires Press, 1994). *The Colloquy of the Old Men* his translation of Acallam na Senorach, the medieval compendium of stories and poems, was published in 2001 by Academica Press.

CLARINDA HARRISS teaches poetry and editing at Towson University, where she chaired the English Department for a decade. Her most recent collection, Dirty Blue Voice, came out from Half Moon Editions in August, 2007. Previous collections include *Air Travel* (also from Half Moon Editions), *When Divas Dance* (co-authored with Chezia Thompson-Cager and Kenra Kopelke, Maisonneuve Press), *License Renewal for the Blind* (Cooper House), *The Night Parrot* (Salmon Publishing), and *The Bone Tree* (NPS, Inc.). She is the author or co-author of several academic texts and has won awards for her short fiction as well as for her poetry. Writing by prisoners or ex-prisoners is one of her main research interests.

ANNE LE MARQUAND HARTIGAN is an award winning poet, playwright, and artist. She has published five collections of poetry—*Long Tongue* (Beaver Row Press, 1982), *Return Single* (Beaver Row Press, 1986), *Now is a Moveable Feast* (Salmon, 1991), *Immortal Sins* (Salmon, 1993), and *Nourishment* (Salmon, 2005)—with a sixth, *To Keep the Light Burning*, forthcoming from Salmon. Her many awards include the Open Poetry Award from Listowel Writers' Week, The Mobil Playwriting Award for her play *The Secret Game*, and awards for her visual art. Her poetry has been translated and included in anthologies worldwide and Anne has enjoyed the experience of reading her poetry internationally. She performed her play *La Corbiere* at the Samuel Beckett Theatre, Dublin, as a solo work in 1996. Of her five full length plays, *Beds* and *La Corbiere* were premiered at the Dublin Theatre Festival. Her work has been performed in the USA, New Zealand, Lebanon, and at the Edinburgh Festival. Her wide ranging work includes radio, a silent mime, prose, and her recent humorous poetry for children.

MICHAEL HEFFERNAN was born in Detroit in 1942. He is a fifth-generation descendant of Daniel Heffernan of Tipperary (b. 1815) and Catherine Meehan of Ballyhooly, Co. Cork (b. 1827). His poems have appeared in a variety of American magazines, including *The American Poetry Review, TriQuarterly, The Southern Review, Hotel Amerika, The Gettysburg Review, Shenandoah, The Blue Moon Review, Witness, New Orleans Review, Margie, Crab Orchard Review, Octopus, The Kenyon Review, Typo, Boulevard, Third Coast*, and *Poetry*. His seventh book of poems, *The Night Breeze Off the Ocean*, appeared in 2005 from Eastern Washington University Press (Spokane). His eighth, *The Odor of Sanctity*, will be his third book from Salmon, along with *The Back Road to Arcadia* (1994) and *Another Part of the Island* (1999). He has received three fellowship grants from the National Endowment for the Arts, two grants from the Arkansas Arts Council, two Pushcart Prizes, and the Iowa Poetry Prize (for *Love's Answer*, 1994). He lives in Fayetteville, Arkansas, where he has taught poetry in the MFA program at the University of Arkansas since 1986. He and his wife, Ann, are often in Ireland.

KEVIN HIGGINS lives in Galway, Ireland, where with his wife Susan Millar DuMars he organises the Over The Edge: Open Reading series. His first collection of poems *The Boy With No Face* was published by Salmon in February 2005. Also in 2005 he was short-listed for the Hennessy Award for Poetry and awarded a Literature Bursary by the Irish Arts Council. *The Boy With No Face* was short-listed for the 2006 Strong Award for Best First Collection by an Irish poet. A second collection, *Time Gentlemen, Please* will be published by Salmon in 2008.

MICHAEL D. HIGGINS was born in Limerick in 1941 and reared on a small farm in County Clare. He studied at University College Galway, Indiana University and Manchester University. He represents Galway West as a Labour Deputy in Dáil Éireann. His poems have been published in several poetry journals including the *Sunday*

Tribune-New Irish Writing, Céide, The Salmon Journal, Poetry Ireland, Aishling and *Studies*. His poems are also included in the following anthologies: *Whoseday Book* (1999), *Or Volge L'Anno- At The Years Turning-Irish Poets Responding to Leopardi* (Dedalus, 1998), *The Great Book of Ireland* (1998), *I.P.A. Anthology, Wexford Anthology, Mothers, UNICEF, Human Rights have no Borders* (Amnesty, 1998), *Irish Poetry Now*, edited by Gabriel Fitzmaurice (Wolfhound, 1993), *Fathers and Sons* (Wolfhound Press, 1995), *On the Counterscarp—Limerick Writing 1961-1991* (Salmon, 1992). This poetry collections are: *The Betrayal* (Salmon, 1990); *The Season of Fire* (Brandon Books, 1993); and, *An Arid Season* (New Island, 2004).

RITA ANN HIGGINS was born in 1955 in Galway, Ireland, and still lives there. She published her first five collections with Salmon Publishing. Bloodaxe Books published her next three collections including, *Throw in the Vowels: New & Selected Poems* in May 2005, marking her 50th birthday. Her plays include *Face Licker Come Home* (1991), *God of the Hatch Man* (1992), *Colie Lally Doesn't Live in a Bucket* (1993) and *Down All the Roundabouts* (1999). She has edited *Out the Clara Road: The Offaly Anthology*, and *Word and Image: a collection of poems from Sunderland Women's Centre and Washington Bridge Centre*. She also edited *FIZZ: Poetry of resistance and challenge*, an anthology written by young people. She was Galway County's Writer-in-Residence in 1987, Writer in Residence at the National University of Ireland, Galway, in 1994-95, and Writer in Residence for Offaly County Council in 1998-99. In October 2000 she was Green Honors Professor at Texas Christian University. Her many awards include a Peadar O'Donnell Award in 1989 and several Arts Council bursaries. *Sunny Side Plucked* was a Poetry Book Society Recommendation. She is a member of Aosdána and a judge of the IMPAC fiction prize in 2005.

JOHN HILDEBIDLE lives and works in Cambridge, MA. He teaches English, American, and Irish literature at MIT, Boston, MA. He has published one book of fiction—*Stubbornness: A Field Guide*, which was winner of the John Gardner Short Fiction Prize sponsored by SUNY-Binghamton Press—and three collections of poetry: *The Old Chore* (Alice James Books. Winner of a Book Award from the San Francisco State University Poetry Center); *One Sleep, One Waking* (Enright House); and *Defining Absence* (Salmon, 1999). A fourth collection, *Signs, Translations*, is forthcoming.

BEN HOWARD is the author of six books, most recently *Dark Pool* (Salmon, 2004) and the verse novella *Midcentury* (Salmon, 1997). For the past three decades he has contributed poems, essays, and reviews to national and international literary journals, including *Poetry, Shenandoah, Poetry Ireland Review*, and *Sewanee Review*. He has received numerous awards, including the Theodore Christian Hoepfner Award from the Southern Humanities Review and a Fellowship in Creative Writing from the National Endowment for the Arts. His poems have appeared in numerous anthologies, most recently *The Book of Irish-American Poetry, 180 More: Extraordinary Poems for Every Day*, and *The POETRY Anthology: 1912-2002*. He is Professor of English Emeritus at Alfred University in upstate New York.

RON HOUCHIN lives on the banks of the Ohio River across from his hometown of Huntington, West Virginia. He has had two books published by Salmon Publishing, *Death and the River* (1997) and *Moveable Darkness* (2002) and a third book, *Among Wordless Things* (2004), by Wind Publications of Nicholasville, Kentucky. He has read his work in a wide variety of venues from Bewley's International Café, Dublin, and Sheridan's Wine Bar, Galway to the Ypsilan Theatre, Prague and The James Wright Poetry Festival, Martins' Ferry, Ohio. His work has appeared in *The Southwest Review, The Southern Poetry Review, Poetry Ireland, The Stinging Fly, The New Orleans Review, The Potomac Review, Poetry Northwest, Poetry East, Puerto del Sol, Sycamore, Sow's Ear*, and many others. He was awarded the Appalachian Book-of-the-Year for 2005, a National Society of Arts and Letters Prize, an Ohio Arts Council Fellowship, The Vesle Fenstermaker Poetry Prize from Indiana Review, a Writers' Digest Award. His work has been nominated for Pushcart and Paterson Prizes. New poems will appear in *Poetry Ireland Review, The Stinging Fly, Redactions, Now & Then, Cooweescoowee, Kestrel, Pine Mountain Sand & Gravel, Dualities: Nine Poets, Nine Images*.

GERALD HULL comes from a 'mixed generation' Irish-American family in London and has lived in Ireland for over twenty years, settling in Fivemiletown in Tyrone. He holds a Ph.D from the University of Wales and in recent years has been associated with the Pushkin Prize, Oliver Goldsmith and William Carleton International Summer Schools. He has acted as editor for *The Spark Review* in Fermanagh and as Northern Correspondent for *Windows* and *First Edition*. Gerry has read throughout Ireland and gained bursaries from Poetry Ireland and the Tyrone Guthrie Centre. He is widely published and, fitting for one whose poetry is fixated on the border counties, was guest editor for the acclaimed South-West edition of *The Honest Ulsterman* (HU). His first full collection, *Falling into Monaghan*, was published by Salmon in 1999.

THOMAS KRAMPF's collections of poetry are *Poems to My Wife and Other Women* (Salmon Poetry, 2007), *Taking Time Out: Poems in Remembrance of Madness* (Salmon Poetry, 2004); *Shadow Poems* (Ischua Books, 1997); *Satori West* (Ischua Books, 1987), and *Subway Prayer and Other Poems of the Inner City* (Morning Star Press, 1976). He has read in universities and on the media and in 2001 he was poet-in-residence at the Linenhall Arts Centre in Castlebar, Ireland. He was a principal in the 2004 Spring Writers' Festival at Alfred University, New York and, in the same year, the noted French author Raymond Bozier translated his long "Subway Prayer" poem with excerpts published in a French literary review. In 2006, he participated in the

445

"Printemps des Poetes" (Springtime of the Poets) literary festival in La Rochelle, France, with poets from France and Iran. For many years he specialized in teaching poetry and creative writing to learning disabled adults and children. He also volunteered in drug rehabilitation centres and prisons. He currently lives in Hinsdale, New York with his wife, Françoise. They have three daughters and grandchildren.

JOHN KAVANAGH is a poet and playwright with two poetry collections from Salmon—*Etchings* and *Half-Day Warriors* with a third in preparation. He has had plays performed in Ireland and the US and his audio biography and anthology on the life and poems of W.B. Yeats from Naxos won the Spoken Word Award in the UK in 2002. He is also a winner of the poetry prize at Listowel. He lives in Sligo and works at the Institute of Technology, Sligo.

ANNE KENNEDY, poet, writer, photographer and broadcaster, came from Orcas Island, off the coast of Washington State, to live in Galway, Ireland in 1977. Her first book *Buck Mountain Poems*, published by Salmon in 1989, is based on her Orcas experiences. *The Dog Kubla Dreams My Life*, also from Salmon, was published in 1994. A keen documentor of history, in 1993 she contributed an oral history project to the Duke Ellington archive in the Smithsonian Museum of American History. Anne Kennedy died on 29th September 1998.

FRED JOHNSTON was born in Belfast in 1951. He is founder of the Cúirt festival of literature and founder/manager of the Western Writers' Centre - Ionad Scríbhneoiri Chaitlín Maude, Galway. He has published eight collections of poems, including *Song at the Edge of the World* (Salmon, 1988) and *True North* (Salmon, 1997). His published prose includes *Keeping The Night Watch*, a collection of stories, and three novels. A novel set in the Paris legal world, *The Neon Rose*, is forthcoming from Bluechrome in the UK, and a new collection of poems is due from Cinnamon, UK. In 2002 he received a Prix de l'Ambassade to work on translations of the poet Michel Martin; since then, he has published translations of a number of contemporary French poets. He has given papers on contemporary Irish literature and politics at the University of Poitiers, The John Hewitt School, and while writer-in-residence to the Princess Grace Irish Library at Monaco in 2004. He is currently working with a Breton-based translator on collating a number of Breton prose pieces and translating them into English for publication. A traditional musician since his early teens, his latest solo CD is *Local Papers*. He has lived in Galway since 1976.

JESSIE LENDENNIE's prose poem *Daughter* was first published in 1988, followed in 1990 by *The Salmon Guide to Poetry Publishing* and in 1992 by *The Salmon Guide to Creative Writing in Ireland*. Her poetry has been anthologised in *Irish Poetry Now: Other Voices, Unveiling Treasures: The Attic Guide To The Published Works of Irish Women Literary Writers* and

The White Page / An Bhileog Bhán: Twentieth-Century Irish Women Poets, among others. She was nominated for a Bank of Ireland Arts Award for service to the arts in Ireland. She has conducted workshops and given readings all over Ireland and the United States for many years. She is the co-founder and Managing Director of Salmon Poetry.

JAMES LIDDY was born in the Pembroke Nursing Home in Dublin, a distinction he curiously shares with the author of a critical work on him, Brian Arkins. His parents hailed from Limerick and New York. He has lived in Wexford, Dublin and the U.S.A. While a U.C.D. student he took his camera to the unveiling of a centenary plaque on Oscar Wilde's house opposite the church where his parents were married and he was baptised. Books of his have been published by the Dolmen Press, the hit and run press, Wolfhound Press, the Malton Press, White Rabbit Press, Creighton University Press (*The Collected Poems*), Arlen House and Salmon Publishing. Salmon brought out his autobiography *The Doctor's House* in 2004. *Honeysuckle, Honeyjuice*—a Festshcrift celebrating James' life and writing, edited by Michael Begnal—was recently published by Arlen House. He teaches in the Creative Writing Program at the University of Wisconsin-Milwaukee.

DAVE LORDAN was born in Derby, England, in 1975. He grew up in Clonakilty in West Cork. He took an M.A. in English Literature at University College Cork in 1998 and an M.Phil. in Creative writing at Trinity College Dublin in 2001. In 2004 he was awarded an Arts Council bursary. In 2005 he won the Patrick Kavanagh Award for poetry. His debut collection, *The Boy in the Ring*, was published by Salmon in 2007. His work has been published widely and he is a regular and popular performer of his own work. He is an experienced creative writing teacher and workshop leader.

CATHERINE PHIL MacCARTHY was born in Co. Limerick, Ireland in 1954 and educated at University College Cork, Trinity College Dublin, and Central School of Speech and Drama, London. Her books include *How High the Moon* (Poetry Ireland, 1991), *This Hour of the Tide* (Salmon, 1994), *the blue globe* (Blackstaff Press, 1998), *Suntrap* (Blackstaff Press, 200)7 and a first novel, *One Room an Everywhere*, Blackstaff Press 2003. She has won prizes and awards including bursaries in poetry from the Arts Council, An Comhairle Ealaion, in 1994 and 1998. She was writer-in-residence for the City of Dublin, (1994) and University College Dublin (2002) and works regularly at the Irish Writers Centre.

JOAN McBREEN is from Sligo and now lives in Tuam, County Galway. Her poetry collections are *The Wind Beyond the Wall* (Story Line Press, Oregon, USA, 1990, 1991); *A Walled Garden in Moylough* (Story Line Press and Salmon Publishing, County Clare, 1995), and *Winter in the Eye: New and Selected Poems* (Salmon, 2003). Awarded an MA degree from University College, Dublin in 1997, she compiled and edited *The White Page / An Bhileog Bhan: Twentieth Century Irish Women Poets* (Salmon

Publishing 1999, 2000, 2001,2007) She has been widely published and anthologised both in Ireland and abroad, in particular in the USA. She gives readings and workshops internationally and her poetry has been translated into several languages, including Italian and French. *The Long Light on the Land: Selected Poems By Joan McBreen with Traditional Irish Airs and Classical Music* was launched by Professor Bernard O'Donoghue, Wadham College, Oxford, at the 45th Yeats International Summer School, Sligo, on August 5th 2004. *Sheltering on Heather Island*, a new collection of poetry, is due out in 2008.

JERI McCORMICK, a U.S. poet (Wisconsin), has recently retired from teaching writing in the Elderhostel program and in local senior centers. She has co-authored two texts, most recently *Writers Have No Age: Creative Writing for Older Adults* (Haworth Press, 2005). Her book of poems, *When It Came Time*, was published by Salmon in 1998. Her poems have appeared in *Kalliope, Appalachian Journal, Byline, Rosebud, Cumberland Poetry Review, Poetry Ireland Review* and other journals, plus several anthologies. Her awards include a Wisconsin Arts Board Fellowship, a Wisconsin Library Association Outstanding Achievement Award, Second Place at the Boyle Arts Festival Poetry Competition, and Second Place in the 2001 Davoren Hanna Poetry Competition, Dublin. She has benefited from many extended stays in Ireland, where she participated in the Rathmines Writer's Group (Dublin) and worked on writing at the Tyrone Guthrie Centre in Annaghmakerrig.

STEPHANIE McKENZIE has published one collection of poetry, *Cutting My Mother's Hair* (Salmon Poetry, 2006). She is an Assistant Professor in the Department of English at Sir Wilfred Grenfell College (Memorial University of Newfoundland) and the author of *Before the Country: Native Renaissance, Canadian Mythology* (forthcoming, University of Toronto Press). McKenzie is the founder of Scop Productions Inc., a west coast Newfoundland publishing and production house (which co-published *The Backyards of Heaven* and *However Blow the Winds*). She is also presently editing (with Randall Maggs and John Ennis) *The Echoing Years: Poetry from Ireland and Canada* and, with Martin Ware, co-edited *An Island in the Sky: Selected Poetry of Al Pittman* (St. John's, Breakwater Books).

ETHNA McKIERNAN was born in New York in 1951 and raised there, in Dublin, and in Minnesota, where she lives now with her two college-age sons. Her second book, *The One Who Swears You Can't Start Over*, was published by Salmon in 2002, and her first book, *Caravan*, was co-published by Dedalus and Midwest Villages and Voices in 1989. She is a former recipient of a Minnesota State Arts Board Literature Fellowship and she earned her MFA from Warren Wilson College in 2004. Her poetry has recently appeared in *The Notre Dame Anthology of Irish American Poetry*, and in *To Sing Along the Way: An Historical Anthology of Minnesota Women's Poetry*.

TED McNULTY, an Irish American poet, was raised in New York City by parents from counties Cavan and Clare. A onetime news reporter and university lecturer, he began writing poetry in his 50s and won the Hennessy/Sunday Tribune Prize as New Irish Writer in 1991. He published two collections of poetry with Salmon: Rough Landings (1992) & On the Block (1995). With the poet, Sheila O'Hagan, he conducted workshops for prisoners in Wormwood Scrubs Prison, London, and for inner city youth in Dublin and London. He lived in Dublin for many years prior to his untimely death in 1998.

MÁIGHRÉAD MEDBH was born in Newcastle West, County Limerick. Since the publication of her first collection, *The Making of a Pagan* (Blackstaff Press), in 1990, she has become widely known as a performance poet. The voice in Máighréad's poetry is consciously channelled via the body, whose senses and rhythms are, respectively, the originators and interpreters of concepts. She has performed at many venues in Ireland, Great Britain and the United States, and also on the broadcast media. Máighréad's work has been included in a wide range of anthologies. Her other full collections are: *Tenant* (Salmon, 1999) and *Divas* (Arlen House, June 2003). A CD featuring her more popular pieces was produced in 2002, and is available from Odin Poetries (Ireland). At the moment, Máighréad is also writing for children, and a text set to music is to be broadcast by Lyric FM later in 2006. A new poetry collection is presently with a publisher.

JOHN MENAGHAN has published two poetry collections, both with Salmon Poetry: *All the Money in the World* (1999) and *She Alone* (2006). He is the winner of an Academy of American Poets Prize and other awards, and has published poems and articles in Irish, American, and Canadian journals. He teaches literature and creative writing at Loyola Marymount University in Los Angeles, where he also serves as Director of both the Irish Studies & Summer in Ireland programs and runs the annual LMU Irish Cultural Festival. His one-act play *A Rumor of Rain* was performed at the Empty Stage Theater in Los Angeles and given staged readings at the ATHE theater conference in San Francisco, by the Women in Theatre group in Los Angeles, and as part of the New Works Festival at Loyola Marymount University. Two other one-acts, *What?* and *Break of Day*, have been given staged readings at Barnsdall Park in Hollywood, the latter directed by the author himself. He is currently working on two full-length plays, one set in Berkeley, California and the other in Belfast, Northern Ireland and a sequence of short plays on the theme of leaving and being left behind. His third volume of poetry is forthcoming from Salmon Poetry in Autumn 2009.

ÁINE MILLER is from Cork City. She was educated at St. Aloysius' School, University College, Cork, and at University of Dublin, Trinity College where she took the M.Phil (Creative Writing) in 1998. Her first collection *Goldfish in a Baby Bath* (Salmon, 1994) won the Patrick Kavanagh Award. Her second collection was *Touchwood* (Salmon, 2000). Her work is featured in many anthologies including *Dancing with Kitty Stobling* (The Lilliput

Press, 2004), *Volume* (Crawford Municipal Art Gallery, Cork, 1997), *Out to Lunch* (Bank of Ireland Arts Centre, 2002), *Jumping Off Shadows* (Cork University Press, 1995), *Stream and Gliding Sun* (Wicklow County Council, 1998) and *The Field Day Anthology of Irish Writing V* (2002). She lives in Dublin where she teaches for the V.E.C. and other bodies.

PATRICIA MONAGHAN is an award-winning poet whose work has been set to music and is performed around the world, most recently by folk composer Michael Smith, whose setting of Patricia's "Songs of a Kerry Madwoman" will be released shortly with vocals by Jamie O'Reilly. Her most recent books of poetry are *Homefront* (Word Tech Press), a sequence of poems about the effect of war on families; an expanded edition of the award-winning *Seasons of the Witch* with double CD of music; and *Dancing with Chaos* (Salmon Poetry), which explores scientific theories of chaos in personal terms. Patricia holds a PhD in literature and environment from the Union Institute and an MFA in creative writing from the University of Alaska. In her position as a member of the interdisciplinary faculty at DePaul University, Patricia teaches classes in mythology, environmental studies, and arts. She is a Senior Fellow of the Black Earth Institute, dedicated to connecting arts, spirituality, environment and politics.

NOEL MONAHAN is a widely published writer at home and abroad and he has won several national literary awards for his work including: The SeaCat National Poetry Award, 2001, The Hiberno-English Poetry Award, 2004, The P.J.O'Connor RTE Radio Drama Award, 2001, for his play, *Broken Cups*, The A.S.T.I. (Association of Secondary Teachers Ireland)Award for his contribution to literature at home and abroad, The William Allingham Poetry Award and The Kilkenny Prize for Poetry. He has published four poetry collections with Salmon Poetry: *Opposite Walls* (1991), *Snowfire* (1995), *Curse of The Birds* (2000) and *The Funeral Game* (2004). His poetry has been translated into Italian, Romanian, French and Russian. Noel is a founder member and co editor of Windows Publications. His plays include: *Half A Vegetable, Talking Within, Where Borders Begin*, and *To Walk On The Wind*. Noel Monahan was born in Granard, Co. Longford and now lives in Cavan.

ALAN JUDE MOORE was born in Dublin in 1973. He graduated from Trinity College Dublin with degree in political science. His poetry has been widely published in Ireland, Europe and the USA by publications such as *Poetry Ireland Review, The Stinging Fly, The Burning Bush, Kestrel, The Black Mountain Review, Poetry Salzburg Review* and in translation by Italian annual *Pelagos*. His fiction has been short-listed for the Hennessy Literary Award and published in various journals. His first collection of poetry, *Black State Cars*, was published by Salmon Poetry in 2004. A selection of poems from Black State Cars was published earlier this year in translation by Russian literary journal, *Novaya Junost*. Alan currently lives in Dublin.

TOM MORGAN was born in Belfast in 1943. His collections are *The Rat-Diviner* (Dublin, Beaver Row Press, 1987); *Nan of the Falls Rd Curfew* (Beaver Row Press, 1990), which was nominated for the Irish Times/Aer Lingus Awards; *In Queen Mary's Gardens* (Salmon Publishing,1991); and *Ballintrillick in the Light of Ben Whiskin* (Lagan Press, 2006). He has collaborated with artists Patric Coogan, Brendan Ellis and Catherine McWilliams in joint poetry-painting exhibitions in Sligo, Belfast, Galway, Dublin and New York, and has worked with composer Frank Lyons for the Visconic Arts Festival in Belfast. He lives in Belfast and Ballintrillick, Co Sligo.

JUDE NUTTER was born North Yorkshire, England, and grew up in Hohne, in northern Germany. She holds a BA in Printmaking and an MFA in Poetry. Jude Nutter moved to the US in the late 80's and spent ten years homesteading on Wrangell Island in Alaska. Her poems have appeared in numerous national and international journals, including: *Alaska Quarterly Review, Another Chicago Magazine, Atlanta Review, Chautauqua Literary Journal, Indiana Review, JAMA: Journal of the American Medical Association, Marlboro Review, MARGIE, Missouri Review, Nimrod International Journal, Notre Dame Review, Stand* (UK) and *Words and Images*. Her poems have been nominated four times for a Pushcart Prize, and she is the recipient of several awards and grants including two Minnesota State Arts Grants, the Robinson Jeffers Tor House Prize, the Listowel Prize (Ireland), the Larry Levis Prize, the International War Poetry Award and The Marjorie J. Wilson Award for Excellence in Poetry. Her first book-length collection, *Pictures of the Afterlife* (Salmon Poetry), was published in 2002. In 2004 she spent two months in Antarctica as a participant in the National Science Foundation's Writers and Artists Program. *The Curator of Silence* (University of Notre Dame Press), her second collection won the Ernest Sandeen Prize from the University of Notre Dame and was awarded the 2007 Minnesota Book Award in Poetry. A third collection, *I Wish I Had A Heart Like Yours, Walt Whitman* is forthcoming.

JEAN O'BRIEN, a Dubliner, has had two collections of poetry published, *The Shadow Keeper* (Salmon, 1997) and her more recent *Dangerous Dresses* (Bradshaw Books, 2005). She also had two Chapbooks published: *Working the Flow* and *Reach* both with Lapwing in Belfast. In 2005 Jean worked as the writer-in-residence for County Laois. Her work is widely published both in Ireland, the UK and the USA., most recently in *Cyphers, The Stinging Fly, The Cork Literary Review* and *Agenda* (UK). She has a poem in the 2008 Oxfam Calendar. Her works has been broadcast on RTE1, Lyric Fm and various local radio stations. She hold an M.Phil degree in creative writing from Trinity College Dublin and teaches creative writing in places as diverse as prisons, schools, travellers centres, and for Dublin City Council and various County Councils around the country. She currently teaches in the Irish Writers Centre in Dublin.

CLAIRR O'CONNOR, poet, playwright, and fiction writer, was born in Croom, Co Limerick and raised in Limerick and Listowel, Co Kerry. She was educated at St. Mary's, Limerick and NUI Cork and Maynooth. She taught English in secondary schools for over three decades. Widely represented in anthologies such as: *Midland Review* (U.S.A. ed. Nuala Archer 1986), *Pillars of the House* (Ed. A.A. Kelly 1987) *Mad and Bad Fairies* (Attic 1987), *On the Counterscarp: Limerick Writing 1961-1991* (Eds: A O Brien, C O Driscoll, J Slade, M Whelan.) *Wildish Things* (Ed. Ailbhe Smyth 1989) *Ireland's Women: Writings Past and Present* (Eds. Katie Donovan, Norman Jeffares, Brendan Kennelly, 1994), *Irish Poetry: Other Voices* (Ed. Gabriel FitzMaurice, 1993), *Kerry Through its Writers* (Ed. Gabriel Fitzmaurice 1993), *Virgins and Hyacinths* (Ed. Caroline Walsh 1993), *The Limerick Compendium* (Ed. Jim Kemmy 1997), *Jumping the Bus Queue* (Ed. Mary Rose Callaghan 2000), *The White Page/An Bhilleog Bhan: Twentieth Century Irish Women Poets* (Ed. Joan McBreen, 1999), *The Kerry Anthology* (Ed. Gabriel Fitzmaurice 2000). She is also represented in the *Field Day Anthology: Irish Women's Writings and Traditions*, 2002. Her poetry collection, *When You Need Them,* was published by Salmon in 1989. Medbh McGuckian said of it, "Each bright and fluid poem attains 'the white of pearls' by soothing the raw, rough, reasonless edges in woman's experience". Her second collection, *Breast*, was published by Astrolabe in 2004.

HUGH O' DONNELL was born in Dublin. He has been writing for 25 years. His first collection, *Roman Pines at Berkeley*, was published by Salmon Publishing in 1990. He has had poems published in the U.K., Australia, U.S.A. and in many Irish journals and has been successful in various literary competitions. His poems have been read on RTÉ as a winner in the national competition to mark 75 years of broadcasting and as a winner in Rattlebag's sponsored Slam 2004. In the mid 1990's, he co-edited with Isabelle Cartwright, four issues of the literary magazine, *Cobweb*, from NUI Maynooth. Most recently, he won the Scriobh (Sligo) poetry competition (2005) and had a poem selected by Sinead Morrissey for Oxfambooks Calendar, Poems for 2006.

MARY O'DONNELL was born in Monaghan and educated at St. Louis Convent and later at Maynooth University where she obtained a degree in German and Philosophy, with further postgraduate German studies. She has published five collections of poetry, three of these with Salmon. Her first two collections were nominated for an Irish Times Literature Award. *The Place of Miracles* (new and selected poems), was published by New Island Books in 2006 and will be followed by a new short story collection from that publisher in 2008. Her first novel *The Light-Makers* was named the Sunday Tribune's Best New Irish Novel in 1992. Since then she has published the novels *Virgin and the Boy* and the critically acclaimed novel, *The Elysium Testament* (Trident Press, 1999). She is a member of Aosdána and lives near Straffan, Co. Kildare.

MARY O'DONOGHUE was born in 1975 and grew up in Co. Clare. Her first poetry collection *Tulle* was published by Salmon Poetry in 2001, and her second, *Among These Winters*, appeared from Dedalus Press in 2007. Her poems have appeared widely in Irish and international periodicals and anthologies, including *The New Irish Poets* (Bloodaxe, 2004). She has also collaborated with Louis de Paor on translations of his poetry. Her short stories have been published in *The Dublin Review*, *The Recorder*, *AGNI* and elsewhere. She lives in Boston.

CIARAN O'DRISCOLL was born in Callan, Co. Kilkenny in 1943, and presently lives in Limerick, where he lectures in the School of Art and Design at the Limerick Institute of Technology, and is a committee member of Cuisle Limerick City International Poetry Festival. He has written five collections of poetry, including *Gog and Magog*, his first collection, published by Salmon in 1987, and re-issued on the internet by the Irish Literary Revival in 2006. His New and Selected Poems, *Moving On, Still There*, was published by Dedalus in 2001. In the same year, Liverpool University Press published his childhood memoir, *A Runner Among Falling Leaves*. He has won a number of awards for his work, including a Bursary in Literature from the Arts Council/An Chomhairle Ealaíon, as well as the Patrick and Katherine Kavanagh Fellowship in Poetry. He has read from his work and lectured on art and literature at various venues in Europe and America. His poetry has been translated into several languages, and this year an Italian translation of his fourth collection of poems, *The Old Women of Magione*, based on a year he spent in Italy, was published by Volumnia Editrice (Perugia). Also in 2006, a chapbook of 21 new poems, *Surreal Man*, is being published by Pighog Press (UK).

SHEILA O'HAGAN began writing poetry in 1984 while studying at Birkbeck College, London University. In 1988 she won the Goldsmith Award for Poetry, and in 1990 returned to live in Dublin. Since then she has three times been awarded prizes at Writers' Week in Listowel. In 1991 she won the Patrick Kavanagh Award for a First Manuscript of Poetry and in 1992 the Hennessy/Sunday Tribune Award for New Irish Poet of the year. She has been widely published in Ireland, the UK, America, Canada and Australia. Her collections of poetry, The Peacock's Eye (1992) and The Troubled House (1995) were both published by Salmon.

MARY O'MALLEY was born in Connemara and educated at University College, Galway. Her collections of poetry are *A Consideration of Silk* (Salmon, 1990), *Where the Rocks Float* (Salmon, 1993), *The Knife in the Wave* (Salmon, 1997), *Asylum Road* (Salmon, 2001), *The Boning Hall* (Carcanet, 2002), and *A Perfect V* (Carcanet, 2006). She is currently working on her seventh collection. She teaches on the MA in Writing at NUI Galway. She has just completed Residency at Sea. She travels and lectures widely in Europe and the U.S. She has written for both radio and television and is a frequent broadcaster. She is a member of Aosdána.

TOM O' MALLEY was born 1942 in County Mayo. He has taught in secondary schools in Belfast and County Meath. His collection of poems *Roots and Instincts* won the Patrick Kavanagh award in 1984 and a version was published in 1985 by Beaver Row Press, entitled *By Lough Mask*. He was awarded the Meath County Council/Tyrone Guthrie Centre Regional Bursary Award 1998/9. His poetry has appeared in many journals and anthologies (most recently *Dancing with Kitty Stobling* by The Lilliput Press 2004). Others include *Poetry Ireland Review, New Irish Writing, The Irish Times, Lichen and Quarry* (Canada) and *The Café Review* (USA). His collection, *Journey Backward*, was published by Salmon Poetry in 1998.

BARBARA PARKINSON was born and grew up in Galway and was educated in Galway's R.T.C. where she studied Science. She was one of the first women to fish salmon for a season off the Connemara coast. She was nominated for a Hennessy Award in 1992, and awarded second place in The Patrick Kavanagh Awards in 1993. She was shortlisted for the Open American Poetry Competition in 1994. Her radio play *Choices* was nominated for the P.J. O'Connor Awards in 1992. Barbara's desire to 'deal with a thing while it is still nothing' has led her to writing screenplays in more recent years.

GWYN PARRY's third collection of poetry, *Crossings*, was published by Salmon in 1998. His work has been widely published in magazines and journals including, among many others, *Poetry Wales, Poetry Ireland, The Anglo-Welsh Review, Planet Magazine*, and *Acorn*. His poetry has also been broadcast on BBC Radio 3 and is included in *Burning the Bracken* (Seren Books), an anthology of Welsh writing. An interest in music led him to songwriting and he performed with the band Dtour from its inception in 1997 to 2000. Gwyn, who plays harmonica, regulary performs in North Wales and Ireland, most recently with The Martin Daws Quintet.

PAUL PERRY was born in Dublin in 1972. He has won the Hennessy New Irish Writer of the Year Award and The Listowel Prize for Poetry and has been a James Michener Fellow of Creative Writing at The University of Miami, and a Cambor Fellow of Poetry at The University of Houston. His work has appeared in numerous publications, including Poetry Ireland Review, Cyphers, TLS, Granta and The Best American Poetry 2000. He has been a Writer in Residence for Co. Longford, the University of Ulster, and Rathlin Island. His first book *The Drowning of the Saints* was published by Salmon in 2003 to critical acclaim. *The Orchid Keeper* appeared from the Dedalus Press in 2006.

ADRIENNE RICH is one of America's most distinguished poets. She was born in Baltimore in 1929. Over the last forty years she has published more than sixteen volumes of poetry and four books of nonfiction prose. Salmon's *Adrienne Rich Selected*

Poems 1950-1995 came out in 1996. Rich's work has achieved international recognition and has been translated into German, Spanish, Swedish, Dutch, Hebrew, Greek, Italian, and Japanese. She has received numerous awards, fellowships, and prizes, including the Ruth Lilly Poetry Prize, the Lenore Marshall/Nation Prize for Poetry, the Fund for Human Dignity Award of the National Gay Task Force, the Lambda Book Award, the Los Angeles Times Book Prize for Poetry, the National Book Award, the Poet's Prize, the MacArthur Fellowship, and, most recently, the Dorothea Tanning Prize of the Academy of American Poets and the Lannan Foundation Lifetime Achievement Award (2000). Since 1984 she has lived in California.

MARK ROPER'S collections include *The Hen Ark* (Peterloo/Salmon 1990), which won the 1992 Aldeburgh Prize for best first collection; *Catching The Light* (Peterloo/Lagan 1997); a chapbook, *The Home Fire* (Abbey Press 1998) and *Whereabouts* (Peterloo/Abbey Press 2005). He was Editor of Poetry Ireland for 1999. A *New & Selected Poems* is forthcoming from Dedalus Press.

TOM SEXTON was a founding editor of *Alaska Quarterly Review* and its poetry editor for over a decade. He was appointed Alaska's poet laureate in 1994 and served in that position until 2000. *Autumn in the Alaska Range*, his third collection of poetry, was published by Salmon in 2000. His latest collection, *A Clock With No Hands*, was published by Adastra Press in 2007. His work has appeared in *The Hudson Review, The Paris Review, Poetry* and other journals. He has lived in Alaska for over forty years and now spends every other winter with his wife, Sharyn, in Eastport, Maine.

JANET SHEPPERSON was born in Edinburgh in 1954. She was educated at Aberdeen University. She has worked as a trainee journalist, community services volunteer, administrative assistant and primary teacher. She has lived in Belfast since 1978. Her publications include: *Trio 5* (Blackstaff, 1987, with Martin Mooney and Dennis Greig); *A Ring With A Black Stone* (Lapwing, 1989); *Madonna of the Spaces* (Lapwing, 1993); *The Aphrodite Stone* (Salmon, 1995); and, *Eve Complains to God* (Lagan Press, 2004). Her poems are widely anthologized and her translations of Carmen Firan's Romanian poems appear in *Sorescu's Choice, Young Romanian Poets* (Bloodaxe, 2001). Her short stories have been published in many periodicals, with two shortlisted for Hennessy Awards. She has facilitated workshops for W.E.A., Queen's University School of Lifelong Learning, the former Maze Prison, N.I. Arts Council's "Writers in Schools" scheme, Poetry in Motion, Creative Youth Partnerships, and many others.

JAMES SIMMONS (1933-2001) was born in Derry and educated at Campbell College and Leeds University. He taught at Amando Bello University in Nigeria and The University of Ulster. He founded *The Honest Ulsterman* in 1968 and in 1990, with his wife the poet Janice Fitzpatrick Simmons, founded The Poets' House. James

Simmons published thirteen books of poems, including *The Company of Children* (Salmon, 1999) and Mainstream (Salmon, 1995), four plays, four albums of his own songs and a critical biography on Sean O'Casey. He won the Gregory and Cholmondeley Awards for his poetry.

JANICE FITZPATRICK SIMMONS has published widely in journals in the USA, Ireland and the UK. She has three books of poems; *The Bowsprit* (Lagan Press, 2005), *Starting At Purgatory* (Salmon, 1999), and *Settler* (Salmon, 1995); a pamphlet *Leaving American* with Lapwing in 1992. A new book is due out in 2008. Janice with her husband James Simmons founded The Poets' House and is now Head of Creative Writing, The Poets' House Centre, Waterford Institute of Technology.

ROBIN SKELTON, born in Yorkshire, England in 1925 and emigrated to Victoria, British Columbia in 1963, was a distinguished poet, author and literary critic. He founded the department of creative writing at the University of Victoria and worked there as a professor until his death in August, 1997. He was prolific, both as a creator of literature and as a critic. He edited works on John Millington Synge, anthologies of promising new writers, and poetic collections. He wrote or edited over one hundred books and chapbooks during his professional life, and was a founding editor for *The Malahat Review*, an internationally-published Canadian literary quarterly. His poetry collection *Samhain* was published by Salmon in 1994.

KNUTE SKINNER was born in St. Louis, Missouri, and has had a home in Ireland since 1964. He has taught at the University of Iowa and at Western Washington University, where he was a Professor of English. Retired from teaching, he lives in Killaspuglonane, County Clare with his spouse, Edna Faye Kiel. His most recent publication is *Fifty Years: 1957-2007* (Salmon, 2007), which collects fifty years of published work, beginning with poems which first saw serial publication in 1957 and continuing through thirteen books.

JO SLADE lives and works in Limerick. She is the author of four books of poetry — *In Fields I Hear Them Sing* (Salmon, 1989); *The Vigilant One* (Salmon, 1994) which was nominated for an Irish Times/Aer Lingus Literature Prize; *Certain Octobers* (Editions Eireanna, Quimper France 1997) which received a publication grant from the Centre du Livre, Paris; and her most recent collection, *City of Bridges* (Salmon, 2006). She was Writer-in-Residence at The Centre Culturel Irlandais, Paris, in Winter 2007.

R.T. SMITH was born in Washington, D.C., and has lived in Georgia, North Carolina, Alabama and Virginia. He has taught at Appalachian State University, Auburn University, where he served as Alumni Writer-in-Residence and co-editor of Southern Humanities Review, and Washington and Lee University. His collections *The Cardinal Heart* and *Trespasser* were nominees for the Pulitzer Prize in Poetry, and he has received grants in literature from the National Endowment for the Arts and Arts International. In 1998 he was Artist-in-Residence at the National Historical Park at Harpers Ferry, WV. He has been a resident at the Tyrone Guthrie Centre, the Wurlitzer Foundation and the Millay Colony and has spent extensive time in Ireland, notably Galway. Mr. Smith, whose collection of stories is entitled *Faith*, currently resides in Rockbridge County, Virginia, where he edits. *Split the Lark: Selected Poems* was published by Salmon in 1999. His latest collection, *Outlaw Style*, will appear from the University of Arkansas Press in late 2007.

EITHNE STRONG was born in Co. Limerick in 1923 and died in Monkstown, Co. Dublin, in August 1999. In 1942, she joined the Irish language movement in Dublin and published her first poetry in Irish in An Glór and Comhar. She married the poet and psychoanalyst Rupert Strong in 1943 and, nine children later, she entered Trinity College, in 1969, as a mature student. She worked in publishing, freelance journalism, teaching and as a facilitator in creative writing courses. Eithne wrote poetry and short stories in both English and Irish throughout her life. Her poetry included *Songs of Living* (1961), *Sarah, in Passing* (1974), *Flesh: The Greatest Sin* (1982), and two collections with Salmon, *Let Live* (1990) and *Spatial Nosing: New & Selected Poems* (1993). Her work was also widely anthologised in Ireland and overseas, she frequently gave readings at home and abroad. Her poetry was translated into French, Italian and German. A frequent broadcaster in Irish and English, she was granted many travel bursaries and was a member of Aosdána. She published a collection of short stories, *Patterns* (Poolbeg Press, 1991) and two novels. She continued in the eighth decade of her life to write poetry and prose in Irish and in English. The Rupert and Eithne Strong Award, established in memory of the lives and work of Rupert and Eithne Strong by the Strong family, annually awards a prize to the author of the best debut collection of poetry in Irish or English.

BREDA SULLIVAN was born in 1945 in Athlone, Co. Offaly. She received her education in St. Peter's Primary and Secondary Schools, Athlone and in Mary Immaculate Training College, Limerick where she qualified as a Primary School Teacher in 1965. That same year she arrived in Streete, Co. Westmeath to her first teaching post in St. Fintan's N.S. where she taught until her retirement. She lives with her husband Basil. Since her daughter and three sons became adults, her current playmates and time thieves are her three grandchildren. Twenty years ago curiosity and an interest in writing brought her to a meeting of Granard Writers' Group. Encouraged by the group she began to write poetry. Soon, it was being published and winning awards. To date she holds over twenty awards for poetry including the National Women's Poetry Competition, Boyle Arts Festival, Hopkins, Clogh, and KISS. Her work is included in *The Field Day Anthology of Irish Writing, Volume IV*. Her three collections *A Smell of Camphor* (1992), *After the Ball* (1998), *Sculpture in Black Ice* (2004) were published by Salmon. 'Bone' was a finalist in the Frogmore Poetry Competition 1995 and was published in the Frogmore Papers. 'Retired' was a finalist in the Fish Inaugural Poetry Competition and was published in *The Fish Anthology 2006*.

RICHARD TILLINGHAST is an American poet living between Kilkenny and Clonmel on the slopes of Sliabh na mBan. He is the author of eight books of poetry-most recently *Six Mile Mountain* (Story Line Press, 2000). In 1997 Salmon published a new and selected poems in this country under the title *Today in the Café Trieste*, as well as an earlier chapbook, *A Quiet Pint in Kinvara*, in 1991. His poems have appeared in periodicals such as *American Poetry Review, The New Yorker, Paris Review, Poetry, New Left Review, Poetry Ireland Review, Irish Pages, PN Review, Poetry Review, Poetry London*, and elsewhere. In the field of criticism and travel writing he has published in *The Irish Times, The Washington Post, The Wall Street Journal* and *The New York Times*. Two books of his literary essays have appeared: *Robert Lowell's Life & Work: Damaged Grandeur* (1995), and *Poetry and What Is Real* (2004). He has taught at Berkeley, Harvard, San Quentin Prison, the Poets' House, and Trinity College, Dublin.

OLAF PAUL TYARANSEN was born in Dublin in 1971, but spent his formative years in Galway. His first and only poetry collection, *The Consequences of Slaughtering Butterflies*, was published by Salmon in 1992. He has since authored an autobiography, *The Story of O*, and two bestselling collections of journalism—*Sex Lines* and *The Palace of Wisdom*. He is currently a columnist with the Evening Herald and is also Hot Press magazine's 'Writer-At-Large'.

JOHN UNRAU was born in 1941 in Saskatoon, Saskatchewan in a Mennonite family. He was a Rhodes Scholar at Oxford in 1962 and received his MA and D.Phil from Oxford in 1969 with a thesis on John Ruskin's architectural writings and drawings. His first poetry collection, *Iced Water*, was published by Salmon in 2000. He has also published two books on Ruskin, *Looking at Architecture with Ruskin* (1978) and *Ruskin and St. Mark's* (1984), both with Thames & Hudson, London. *The Balancings of the Clouds: Paintings of Mary Klassen*, was published by Windflower Publications, Winnipeg, in 1991. He has recently retired from Atkinson College, York University, Toronto, Canada and now lives near Minden, Ontario.

JEAN VALENTINE was born in Chicago, earned her B.A. from Radcliffe College, and has lived most of her life in New York City. She won the Yale Younger Poets Award for her first book, *Dream Barker*, in 1965. She has published eight books, including *The UnderVoice* (Salmon, 1995). Her most recent collection, *Door in the Mountain: New and Collected Poems 1965 - 2003*, is the winner of the 2004 National Book Award for Poetry. She has received a Guggenheim Fellowship and awards from the NEA, The Bunting Institute, The Rockefeller Foundation, The New York Council for the Arts, and The New York Foundation for the Arts, as well as the Maurice English Prize, the Teasdale Poetry Prize, and The Poetry Society of America's Shelley Memorial Prize in 2000. She has taught at Sarah Lawrence College, the Graduate Writing Program of New York University, Columbia University, and the 92nd Street Y in Manhattan.

PETER VAN DE KAMP was born in 1956, in Bethlehem (a lying-in hospital in The Hague, which was demolished soon after). He taught English and Anglo-Irish Literature and Language Acquisition at Leiden and UCD, whence he received his Ph.D. and where he was a Newman Scholar. Currently he teaches at the Institute of Technology Tralee. In Kerry he founded K.I.S.S., a Summer School of living Irish Authors. He has published sixteen books-biographies, anthologies, literary criticism, translations of poetry. He enjoys collaborating: with Jacques Chuto (et al.) on the *Collected Works of James Clarence Mangan*, with Peter Costello on a biography of Flann O'Brien, and, recently, with A. Norman Jeffares on four anthologies of Irish Literature (appropriately titled *Irish Literature*). His first book of poems, *Notes*, was published by Salmon in 1999. He lives in Tralee with his wife Caroline and their bearded collie Mickey.

MICHÈLE VASSAL, originally from the Provençal Alps, spent thirty years of her life in Ireland before returning to France. She has been published in various anthlogies and magazines, in Ireland and abroad. She won the Listowel Writers' Week Poetry Prize in 1999 and, her collection *Sandgames* was published by Salmon in 2000. She lives in a tower with three cats who boss her about and sleep on the keyboard, and a slightly better behaved husband.

EAMONN WALL, a native of Enniscorthy, Co. Wexford, has lived in the US since 1982. He is the author of four collections of poetry: *Refuge at De Soto Bend* (2004), *The Crosses* (2000), *Iron Mountain Road* (1997), and *Dyckman-200th Street* (1994), all published by Salmon. *From the Sin-e Café to the Black Hills*, a collection of essays, was published by the University of Wisconsin Press in 2000 and awarded the Michael J. Durkan Prize by the American Conference for Irish Studies for excellence in scholarship. Eamonn Wall lives in St. Louis, Missouri, and teaches at the University of Missouri-St. Louis.

EMILY WALL studied poetry at Colby College and received her MFA from the University of Arizona. She currently teaches creative writing at the University of Alaska Southeast. Emily has published in a wide variety of literary journals and has won several poetry prizes. Her debut collection, *Freshly Rooted*, was published by Salmon in 2007. She and her husband and daughter live in Douglas, Alaska.

GORDON WALMSLEY was born and raised in New Orleans. He attended Princeton University and has lived in Copenhagen, Denmark, for over twenty years. He has published four books of poetry: including *Terebinthos* and *Touchstones* (both with Salmon). He edited *Fire and Ice: Poets from Scandanavia and the North* (Salmon, 2003) Following the tragedy of Hurricane Katrina, he spent time in New Orleans doing poetry readings and writing workshops

GARY J. WHITEHEAD is the author of *The Velocity of Dust* (Salmon, 2004) and three chapbooks of poetry. A second full-length collection, *Measuring Cubits while the Thunder Claps*, is forthcoming in 2008 from David Robert Books. Among other awards, Gary has received a New York Foundation for the Arts Individual Artist Grant in Poetry, a Pearl Hogrefe Fellowship in Creative Writing at Iowa State University, and a Princeton University Distinguished Secondary School Teaching Award. He has held writing residencies at Blue Mountain Center, Mesa Refuge, and the Heinrich Boll cottage.

SABINE WICHERT was born in Graudenz, West Prussia (now Grudziadz, Poland) and grew up and was educated in West Germany. She has been teaching history at Queen's University, Belfast since 1971 and has a special interest in the visual arts. She was a member of the Arts Council of Northern Ireland from the mid-1980s to 1994 and a member of the Board of Annaghmakerrig appointed by both Arts Councils in Ireland for ten years. She has published two collections with Salmon: *Tin Drum Country* (1995) and *Sharing Darwin* (1999). Her third poetry collection, *Taganrog*, was published in 2004 in Belfast by Lagan Press Poetry. In 2006 her poems appeared in two anthologies: *Magnetic North*, (Lagan Press), edited by John Brown, and *The Blackbird's Nest: An Anthology of Poetry from Queen's University Belfast*, edited by Frank Ormsby (Blackstaff Press). She was a member of the Board of Annaghmakerrig for ten years, and a Trustee for the Ormeau Baths Gallery.

ANN ZELL was born and raised in Idaho, USA, and after time spent in New York and London, moved to Ireland in 1980, where she is settled in West Belfast. She has two collections, *Weathering* (Salmon, 1998) and *Between Me and All Harm* (Summer Palace Press, 2006).

Bibliography

Nadya Aisenberg	*Measures* (2001)
Nuala Archer	*The Hour of Pan/amá* (1992) *From A Mobile Home* (1995)
Leland Bardwell	*The White Beach: New & Selected Poems 1960-1998* (1998)
Marck L. Beggs	*Libido Café* (2004)
Michael S. Begnal	*Ancestor Worship* (2007)
Marvin Bell	*Wednesday: Selected Poems 1966-1997* (1998)
Pat Boran	*Strange Bedfellows* (1991) — Short Stories *The Portable Creative Writing Workshop* (1999 & 2000)
Eva Bourke	*Gonella* (1985) *Litany for the Pig* (1989)
Ray Bradbury	*I Live By The Invisible* (2002)
Rory Brennan	*The Old In Rapallo* (1996)
Heather Brett	*Abigail Brown* (1991)
Patricia Burke Brogan	*Eclipsed* (1994, reprinted 1997, 2001 & 2005) — Play *Above the Waves Calligraphy* (1994) *Stained Glass at Samhain* (2003) — Play
John Brown, ed.	*In The Chair: Interviews with Poets from the North of Ireland* (2002)
Simmons B. Buntin	*Riverfall* (2005)
Sam Burnside	*Walking the Marches* (1990)
Catherine Byron	*The Getting of Vellum* (2000) [Published simultaneously in England by Blackwater Press, Leicester]
Louise C. Callaghan	*The Puzzle-Heart* (1999) *Remember the Birds* (2005)
Moya Cannon	*Oar* (1990)

Seamus Cashman	*That Morning Will Come: New & Selected Poems* (2007)
David Cavanagh	*The Middleman* (2003)
Jerah Chadwick	*Story Hunger* (1999)
Patrick Chapman	*The New Pornography* (1996) *Breaking Hearts & Traffic Lights* (2007)
Mary Coll	*All Things Considered* (2002)
Roz Cowman	*The Goose Herd* (1989)
Vicki Crowley	*Oasis in a Sea of Dust* (1992)
Theodore Deppe	*Cape Clear: New & Selected Poems* (2002)
Gerard Donovan	*Columbus Rides Again* (1992) *Kings and Bicycles* (1995) *The LightHouse* (2000)
Mary Dorcey	*The River That Carries Me* (1995) *Moving into a Space Cleared by Our Mothers* (1991, reprinted 1994 & 1995) *Like Joy In Season, Like Sorrow* (2001)
Theo Dorgan	*The Ordinary House of Love* (1992) *Rosa Mundi* (1995)
Carol Ann Duffy	*The Salmon Carol Ann Duffy: Poems Selected* *and New 1985-1999* (2000)
Michael Egan	*We Came Out Again To See The Stars* (1986)
Joseph Enzweiler	*A Curb in Eden* (1999)
Mícheál Fanning	*Verbum et Verbum* (1997) *The Separation of Grey Clouds* (2002) *Homage* (2006)
Gabriel Fitzmaurice	*Kerry On My Mind: Of Poets, Pedagogues & Place* (1999) — Essays Twenty One Sonnets (2007)
Mélanie Francès	*Anatomy Of A Love Affair: My Life in the Movies* (2007)
Philip Fried	*Big Men Speaking to Little Men* (2006)
Erling Friis-Baastad	*The Exile House* (2001)

Paul Genega	*Striking Water* (1989) *That Fall: New & Selected Poems* (2001)
Frank Golden	*The Interior Act* (1999)
Michael Gorman	*Up She Flew* (1991)
Mark Granier	*Airborne* (2001) *The Sky Road* (2007)
Robert Greacen	*Robert Greacen: Selected & New Poems* (2006) [Edited by Jack W. Weaver]
Angela Greene	*Silence and the Blue Night* (1993)
Maurice Harmon	*The Last Regatta* (2000) *The Doll With Two Backs and Other Poems* (2004)
Clarinda Harriss	*The Night Parrot* (1988)
Anne Le Marquand Hartigan	*Now is a Moveable Feast* (1991) *Immortal Sins* (1993) *Clearing the Space: A Why of Writing* (1996) — Essay *Nourishment* (2005)
Michael Heffernan	*The Back Road to Arcadia* (1994) *Another Part of the Island* (1999)
Kevin Higgins	*The Boy With No Face* (2005)
Michael D. Higgins	*The Betrayal* (1990)
Rita Ann Higgins	*Goddess on the Mervue Bus* (1986) *Goddess & Witch* (1990) *Face Licker Come Home* (1991) — Play *Philomena's Revenge* (1992) *Higher Purchase* (1996) *Witch in the Bushes* (1998)
John Hildebidle	*Defining Absence* (1999)
Ron Houchin	*Death and the River* (1997) *Moveable Darkness* (2002)
Ben Howard	*Midcentury* (1997) *Dark Pool* (2004)
Gerald Hull	*Falling into Monaghan* (1999)

Fred Johnston	*Song at the Edge of the World* (1988)
	True North (1997)
John Kavanagh	*Etchings* (1991)
	Half-Day Warriors (1999)
Anne Kennedy	*Buck Mountain Poems* (1989)
	The Dog Kubla Dreams My Life (1994)
Thomas Krampf	*Taking Time Out: Poems in Remembrance of Madness* (2004)
	Poems to My Wife and Other Women (2007)
Jessie Lendennie	*Daughter* (1988)
	The Salmon Guide to Poetry Publishing in Ireland (1989)
	The Salmon Guide to Creative Writing in Ireland (1992)
	(with Paddy Hickson)
	Daughter and Other Poems (2001)
James Liddy	*Gold Set Dancing* (2000)
	The Doctor's House (2004)
Dave Lordan	*The Boy in the Ring* (2007)
Catherine Phil MacCarthy	*This Hour of the Tide* (1994)
Joan McBreen	*A Walled Garden in Moylough* (1995)
	The White Page / An Bhileog Bhán: Twentieth Century Irish Women Poets (1999. Reprinted 2000, 2001, 2007)
	Winter in the Eye: New & Selected Poems (2003)
Linda McCarriston	*Little River: New & Selected Poems* (2000)
Jeri McCormick	*When It Came Time* (1998)
Medbh Mc Guckian and Nuala Archer	*Two Women, Two Shores* (1989)
	[Co-publication with New Poets Series, Baltimore, MD.]
Stephanie McKenzie	*Cutting My Mother's Hair* (2006)
Ethna McKiernan	*The One Who Swears You Can't Start Over* (2002)
Ted McNulty	*Rough Landings* (1992)
	On the Block (1995)
Máighréad Medbh	*Tenant* (1999)
John Menaghan	*All the Money in the World* (1999)
	She Alone (2006)

Áine Miller	*Goldfish in a Baby Bath* (1994) *Touchwood* (2000)
John Millett	*The World Faces Johnny Tripod* (1992) [Co-publication with South Head Press & Story Line Press]
Patricia Monaghan	*Dancing with Chaos* (2002)
Noel Monahan	*Opposite Walls* (1991) *Snowfire* (1995) *Curse of The Birds* (2000) *The Funeral Game* (2004)
Alan Jude Moore	*Black State Cars* (2004)
Tom Morgan	*In Queen Mary's Gardens* (1991)
Jude Nutter	*A Prayer for Robert Lee* (2001) *Pictures of the Afterlife* (2002)
Jean O'Brien	*The Shadow Keeper* (1997)
Anthony O'Brien, Ciaran O'Driscoll, Jo Slade, & Mark Whelan, editors	*On the Counterscarp: Limerick Writing 1961-1991* [Co-publication with FourFront Poets] — Anthology
Clairr O'Connor	*When You Need Them* (1989)
Hugh O'Donnell	*Roman Pines at Berkeley* (1990)
Mary O'Donnell	*Reading the Sunflowers in September* (1990) *Spiderwoman's Third Avenue Rhapsody* (1993) *Unlegendary Heroes* (1998)
John O'Donohue	*Echoes of Memory* (1994. Published in a new edition in 1997)
Mary O'Donoghue	*Tulle* (2001)
Peadar O'Donnell	*Monkeys in the Superstructure* (1986) — Essay
Ciaran O'Driscoll	*Gog and Magog* (1987)
Desmond O'Grady	*Tipperary* (1991)
Sheila O'Hagan	*The Peacock's Eye* (1992) *The Troubled House* (1995)

Mary O'Malley	*A Consideration of Silk* (1990)
	Where the Rocks Float (1993)
	The Knife in the Wave (1997)
	Asylum Road (2001)
Tom O'Malley	*Journey Backward* (1998)
Barbara Parkinson	*No Change for the Jugglers and Other Poems* (1995)
Gwyn Parry	*Crossings* (1998)
Angela Patten	*Still Listening* (1999)
	Reliquaries (2007)
Paul Perry	*The Drowning of the Saints* (2003)
Joyce Pye	*Ireland's Musical Instrument Makers* (1990) — Non-fiction
Adrienne Rich	*Adrienne Rich Selected Poems 1950-1995* (1996)
Mark Roper	*The Hen Ark* (1990)
	[Co-publication with Peterloo Poets, England.]
'The Salmon'	A literary journal, published three times yearly, which incorporated poetry, prose and the work of graphic artists and photographers (1981-1992).
Tom Sexton	*Autumn in the Alaska Range* (2000)
Janet Shepperson	*The Aphrodite Stone* (1995)
James Simmons	*Mainstream* (1995)
	The Company of Children (1999)
Janice Fitzpatrick Simmons	*Settler* (1995)
	Starting at Purgatory (1999)
Robin Skelton	*Samhain and Other Poems* (1994)
Knute Skinner	*Learning to Spell Zucchini* (1988)
	The Bears & Other Poems (1991)
	What Trudy Knows and Other Poems (1994)
	The Cold Irish Earth: New & Selected Poems of Ireland 1965-1995 (1996)
	Stretches (2002)
	Fifty Years: 1957-2007 (2007)

Jo Slade	*In Fields I Hear Them Sing* (1989)
	The Vigilant One (1994)
	City of Bridges (2005)
Laura Lundgren Smith	*Sending Down the Sparrows* (2001) — Play
	Digging up the Boys (2007) — Play
R.T. Smith	*Split the Lark: Selected Poems* (1999)
Eithne Strong	*Let Live* (1990)
	Spatial Nosing: New & Selected Poems (1993)
Breda Sullivan	*A Smell of Camphor* (1992)
	After the Ball (1998)
	Sculpture in Black Ice (2004)
Richard Tillinghast	*A Quiet Pint in Kinvara* (1991)
	[Co-publication with Tir Eolas, illustrated by Anne Korff]
	Today in the Café Trieste (1997 & 1999)
Olaf Tyaransen	*The Consequences of Slaughtering Butterflies* (1992)
John Unrau	*Iced Water* (2000)
Jean Valentine	*The Under Voice: Selected Poems* (1995)
Peter van de Kamp	*Notes* (1999)
Michèle Vassal	*Sandgames* (2000)
Eamonn Wall	*Dyckman—200th Street* (1994)
	Iron Mountain Road (1997)
	The Crosses (2000)
	Refuge at DeSoto Bend (2004)
Emily Wall	*Freshly Rooted* (2007)
Gordon Walmsley	*Terebinthos* (1999)
	Fire & Ice: Nine Poets from Scandinavia and the North (2003)
	(editor) — Anthology
Gary J. Whitehead	*The Velocity of Dust* (2004)
Sabine Wichert	*Tin Drum Country* (1995)
	Sharing Darwin (1999)
Ann Zell	*Weathering* (1998)